The Next Australian City

The Suburban Evolution

Edited by Guy Gibson and Ross Elliott

THE SUBURBAN EVOLUTION

THE NEXT AUSTRALIAN CITY

EDITED BY
GUY GIBSON & ROSS ELLIOTT

connorcourt
PUBLISHING

About Suburban Futures

Suburban Futures is a not-for-profit collaboration of individuals and organisations established to highlight the critical role that Australia's suburbs and regions play in the economy, vibrancy and liveability of the nation.

Our advocacy is built on an evidence-based platform of commissioned research, global insights and shared public policy and market intelligence.

We welcome corporate members and supporters...please subscribe to get involved in our activities and events.

Visit www.suburbanfutures.com.au for more information.

OUR MISSION:

To promote a better understanding of the important role of the suburban economy in the life of our cities, through shared insights, information and analysis.

OUR VISION:

Progressive cities where quality social and economic infrastructure is equitably distributed across both suburban and inner urban locations.

OUR GOAL:

Equitable quality of life for suburban residents by facilitating greater employment, leisure and retail choices closer to where people live.

Table of Contents

Preface

Conversations around the suburban nature of Australian cities are often tinged with notes of derision or even occasional ridicule by professionals who, for whatever reason, believe the suburban preference of many residents and businesses is somehow inferior to their vision of a centralised urban utopia. This prejudice has lasted as long as many Australians have voted with their feet (and mortgages) for suburbia – when that choice is available. This has shaped our cities - in particular since the post World War II era – into large sprawling metropolises with high density commercial cores and dispersed middle and outer suburbs with occasional centres, most of which are serviced by a "hub and spoke" transit model.

A new suburbanism is once again reshaping how our cities operate, and once again this can be at odds with the preferred or "authorised" version of urbanism extolled by many professions. Its origins predated the upheaval brought on by COVID lock downs and their lasting impacts. It reflects a new economic model where the "9 to 5" commute is less and less a reflection of life for the average Australian city dweller, who is increasingly working in suburban located health or education industries or – if in previously city-based occupations – who is now preferring their suburban home as a workplace over their glamourous but distant city office tower.

This collection of essays aims to explore the many legitimate versions of analysis and explanation of the forces that have shaped Australian cities in the past, and where this is leading us in the future. To do so, we have drawn on international as well as local expertise, and have assembled a never-before-seen collection of highly respected authors from diverse backgrounds, all turning their attention to a similar topic.

Suburban Futures is a not-for-profit membership organisation dedicated to promoting a better understanding of the important role of the suburban economy in the life of our cities, through shared insights, information and analysis. Our interest is in promoting a better understanding of the social, workplace, technological, economic and other factors that will potentially reshape our urban futures –

with more opportunities to work closer to where people live and access to more affordable housing and workplace options among many possible benefits. We hope this book contributes to that mission.

The book is structured into three main parts: Part one looks at the role of suburbs and includes contributions from the USA and Canada as well as Australia, to set the context. Part two addresses contemporary suburban development in Australia, with a chapter on each Australian State and Territory to explain the main trends and issues regarding suburban development in each jurisdiction. Part three looks at (sub)urban futures and the continuing evolution of suburbs, including their renewal.

We hope that the book finds a wide readership and that the varied views included will encourage more informed and non-prejudiced discussions about desirable futures for Australian cities and suburbs.

Guy Gibson and Ross Elliott, 2024

Part One:
The Role of Suburbs

1

The Evolution of Suburban Planning
in Australia

Robert Freestone

Introduction

Australian cities were suburban almost from birth.[1] By the turn of the twentieth century the pronounced "movement towards the suburbs" had caught international attention.[2] As the need for forward planning became slowly more appreciated from this time, the fate of suburban design was increasingly tied up with the emergence of broader metropolitan planning. "Suburban planning" is neither new nor an oxymoron but has progressed in fits and starts, being most decisively expressed in site and community plans rather than wider strategic strategies. But it is an important and distinctive narrative in appreciating the evolution of planning for Australian cities and towns, and has never been more important.

Colonial Era

The conceptualisation of Australia as a suburban nation is a cultural construct as much as a spatial or functional reality, and glosses over a diversity of forms and morphologies.[3] There were no grand plans. Suburban life developed organically and opportunistically with the ubiquity of the humble freestanding cottage as the dominant British dwelling chosen to claim and colonise a "wide brown land." With intensification of development in the bigger coastal cities, cleavages along class lines became more evident. Denser working-class row and terrace housing contrasted with the more substantial villas of the elite, the latter claiming the best terrain and soon assuming a spacious and leafy character to establish the benchmark for the suburban idyll.

Colonial town planning was rudimentary and arguably most evident in country towns. Framed within a broader imperial annexation of unceded Indigenous lands, the 1829 regulations by Governor Ralph Darling for eastern Australia codified contemporary thinking to establish the essential character of gridiron towns of large allotments and wide streets. The town-suburban-country templates adapted from the inspired plan for Adelaide with its privileging of public open space did likewise under "systematic colonisation" in South Australia. In the cities, it was largely a case of every citizen for themselves. An overall but unrealised plan for the development of Sydney's lower north shore by Darling's Surveyor-General Thomas Mitchell was more the exception than the rule. Many arterial roads often followed Aboriginal pathways. Colonial governments sought to standardise minimum design standards but the driving force in town and country was piecemeal speculative development bequeathing a legacy of network and social infrastructure issues to later generations.

Stirrings Toward Town Planning

By the late nineteenth century the increasing scale of urbanisation exposed the various dysfunctionalities of limited foresight: in the allocation of land use, environmental deterioration, inattention to civic design, and growing transportation needs. The early centres of settlement were in transition to central business districts ringed by higher density housing with extensive low density suburban tracts beyond fracturing the close nexus between home and work. Two statements that highlighted the need for a more integrated approach to suburban land development were by the Melbourne surveyor-engineer John Keily and Sydney architect John Sulman. In 1889 Keily argued that expansion "should not be left to the chance addition of house to house, and of street to street" and that a "pre-existing design" with suburbs limited in size was needed with each to have a "centre of unity".[4] A year later Sulman who advocated radial "spiders-web" street layouts similarly contended that suburbs should not be allowed to sprawl with a "belt of reserved land" as parkland framing all new accretions.[5]

Both visions offered a more synoptic gaze as to the desired size, shape and structure of metropolitan form but made little impact in this more holistic sense. However authorities did pay more attention to allotment sizes, the width of streets and lanes, and provision of open spaces. Highlighting the possibilities for how more informed guidelines might be creatively assembled were the so-called "model suburbs" which coincided with the land boom of the late 1880s. Ambition outstripped reality, but these estates sought to inject more design excellence with respectable villas, boulevard-type streets, nature strips, tree planting and parks. Kensington in Sydney was the subject of a design competition with the winning entry co-authored by Walter Liberty Vernon promising not only a pleasant assemblage of crescents, parks and squares but completion of all water and sewerage works in advance of occupation. Hopetoun on the present-day site of Roxburgh Park in Melbourne and designed by Phillip Treeby was a composite of morphological typologies inspired variously by utopian cities, romantic garden suburbs, and Melbourne's own elite mid-Victorian precinct of St Vincent Place.

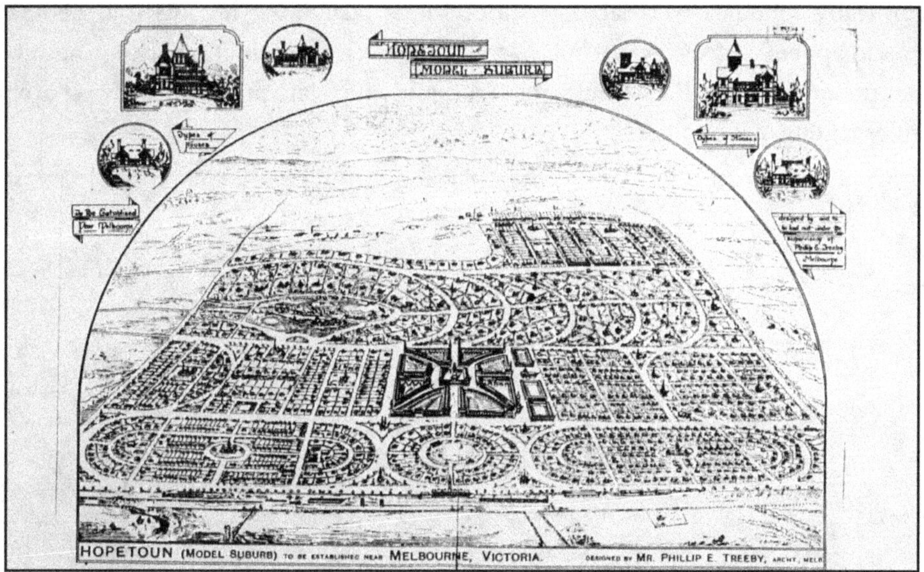

Figure 1.1: Proposed Hopetoun Model Suburb in Melbourne, 1889

(*Building and Engineering Journal*, August 1889)

The Garden Suburb Movement

The rise of a formal town planning movement nationally in the 1910s heightened concern with living conditions. The major foci were cleaning up the slums and developing new house-and-garden suburbs on the city fringes. Influenced by the British garden city movement and American community planning of the day, a package of recurring principles crystallised, many enduring to the present day: density controls, stricter building standards, walkable tree-lined streets, local community amenities, open spaces and pocket parks.[6] Local adaptations of Raymond Unwin's famous demonstration of "nothing gained by overcrowding" compared the limitations of "chessboard" plans to the garden city approach.

The lead was often taken by State Governments to develop demonstration projects as inspirational beacons to councils and private developers, for example Dacey Garden Suburb in Sydney, Colonel Light Gardens in Adelaide, and Garden City in Melbourne. The private sector responded and making their mark were "town planning surveyors" like Hope and Klem in Perth and Saxil Tuxen in Melbourne. Walter Burley and Marion Mahony Griffin were in demand into the early interwar period. In the late 1920s they initiated their own project with the Greater Sydney Development Association at Castlecrag which introduced a distinctive conservationist ethic. Many schemes were at best subdivisions fashioning layouts into geometric shapes to appeal to prospective purchasers. However, the actual practice of suburban development remained a spatially-scattered and stop-start process involving a chain of independent stakeholders.

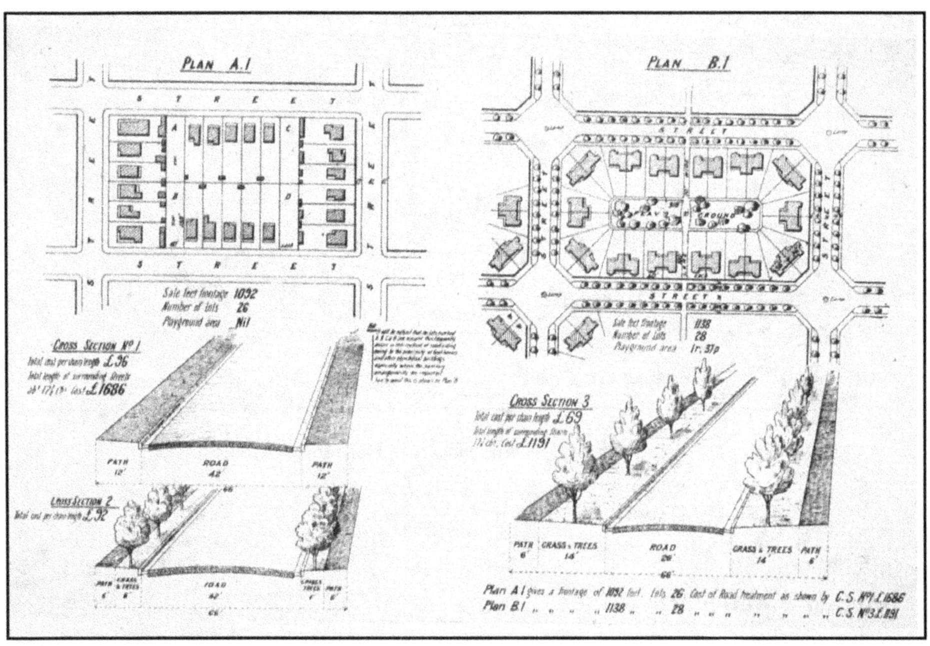

Figure 1.2: Demonstrating the value-add from garden suburb planning

(Official Volume of proceedings of the First Australian Town Planning and Housing Conference and Exhibition, 1917)

Limited Forward Planning

Beyond the refinement of new estate plans, attention to a more coordinated meshing of street networks, and awareness of public health and social issues, there was limited attention to overall spatial form. The first comprehensive inquiry into urban conditions was the Royal Commission for the Improvement of the City of

Sydney and its Suburbs in 1908-09. The main target was the economic needs of the port, secondary industry and commerce in the inner city as well as metropolitan transportation. The analysis conveys the reality of a spreading city but falls short of delivering an integrated spatial vision. Instead, the recommendation is made to follow the British lead with town planning legislation to enable local authorities to prepare statutory planning schemes for the "suburb salubrious". Suburban planning rested on the simplistic solution that "workmen should be encouraged to live in separate houses in the suburbs".[7]

Some guidance was available. The federal capital competition of 1911-12 produced new conceptions of the scale of urban planning, prominently in the winning Griffin plan for a "city and environs" of 75,000 population. Sulman in his 1921 textbook canvassed alternative regional footprints: concentric rings, corridors and wedges, and, developing his nineteenth century ideas, planetary or satellite suburbs. In Canberra he not only replanned some of Griffin's inner suburbs to eliminate bothersome interior parks but also sought to apply his ideas of closely knit but physically distinct suburban centres.

The idea of the park belt as a synthesis of British garden city and American parkway thinking drew attention as a means to rein in diffuse suburban development. Perth Town Clerk William Bold had commended this idea in 1914 following a world tour of planning developments. As an influential leader of the local planning movement Bold was a key player in the west. He commissioned and forged ahead with the Hope and Klem 1925 master plan for the city's Endowment Lands stretching westward to the Indian Ocean with two new suburban townships separated by open country to prevent "straggling settlement". The same idea was picked up in Adelaide by Charles Reade in 1919 to counter "the haphazard development of suburban areas". William Earle similarly recommended an agricultural belt for Brisbane as early as 1928.

Figure 1.3: Housing as an integral issue for the early town planning movement

(Second Australian Town Planning Conference and Exhibition, Volume of Proceedings, 1918)

The two most substantive planning reports produced between the wars, and perhaps the climax of the early planning movement, were the reports of the Melbourne (1930) and Perth (1931) Metropolitan Town Planning Commissions. Yet they did not seriously engage with suburban planning beyond a tidying up of the status quo. The

Melbourne plan was the more detailed, providing a fully worked-out zoning scheme in the cartographic image of the contemporaneous Regional Plan of New York and its Environs. It was attentive to land use allocation, different types of residential district, progressive site planning, local transport needs, open space and provision of local services particularly at major road intersections and along tram corridors. But advance planning to an outer line set only by its jurisdictional reach meant just a densification of the existing built-up area rather than the reshaping and extension that would be hallmarks of the post-war plans to come.

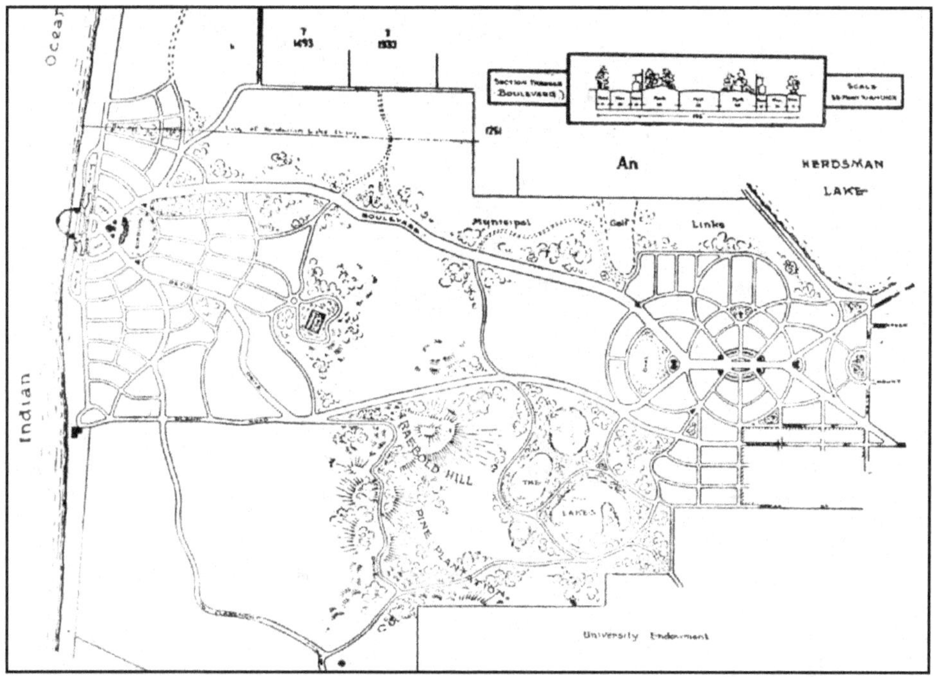

Figure 1.4: Master plan for suburban sector expansion for Perth in the 1920s

(*Perth City Council, Lord Mayor's Report, 1926-1927*, reproduced in Robert Freestone, *Model Communities*, Nelson, 1989)

The Greenbelt City

The Great Depression of the 1930s dampened the pace of suburban development and accordingly checked enthusiasm for more adventurous conceptions. However, this was a decade of major developments abroad – the maturing of the British garden cities and calls for a national new towns program; green girdles and satellite communities; the greenbelt cities of the US Resettlement Administration; the functional metropolitan ideal of CIAM; recognition of the demands of the motor vehicle; and the mainstreaming of the neighbourhood unit as the building block of planned suburbia.

In Australia by the mid-late 1940s at the height of a national drive toward postwar reconstruction led by the Commonwealth Government, many planning ideas then "in the air" solidified into a conventional wisdom of the "greenbelt city" to direct long term urban growth and avoid suburban sprawl and scatteration.[8] Many concepts which now drive liveable and healthy community planning become evident at this time, particularly around the themes of walkable communities self-contained for everyday life and grouped around higher order suburban town centres.

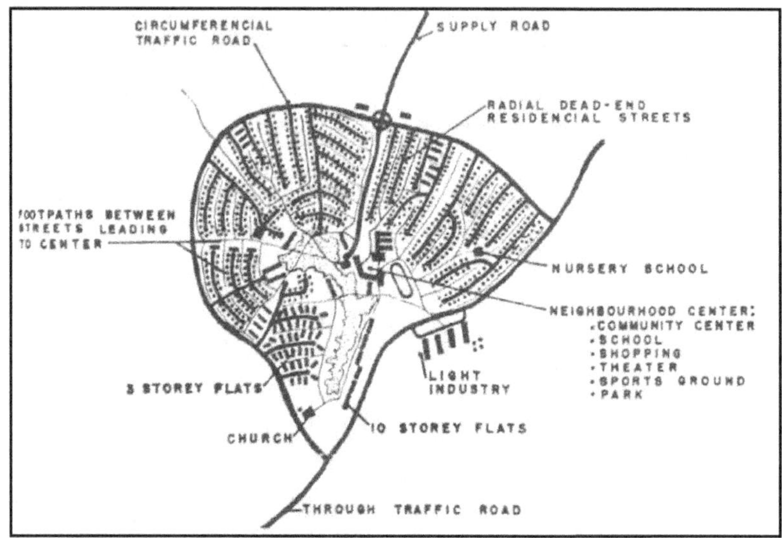

Figure 1.5: An ideal Radburnised postwar community plan by Harry Seidler
(*The Voice,* February 1953, reproduced in Robert Freestone, *Model Communities,* Nelson, 1989)

The Cream Brick Frontier

The first generation of postwar metropolitan strategies were all geared to suburban growth but at a more gentlemanly pace than what transpired under a vigorous national immigration program. The ambitious Sydney plan (1948), unadopted Brisbane template (1949), conservative Melbourne scheme (1954), and the pragmatic Perth strategy (1955) shared many common aspirations of traditional town and country planning. But all were overtaken into the 1960s by sustained development pressures through a long economic boom underpinned by accelerated population growth. "The opportunity for decentralisation of population and industry was lost" as "housing needs overshadowed all else". Hence, the "broader aspects of planning which could have been achieved so painlessly ... were often overlooked" with the accent on greenfield suburban development[9] or the so-called "cream brick frontier".[10]

Intellectual and design critiques like Robin Boyd's *The Australian Ugliness* (1960) counterpunched with accounts and evidence of subtopian sprawl, soulless suburbs, streetscapes of mediocrity, long commutes, social inequality, and isolated women. Many of these ills were blamed on "a style of monolithic middle-class planning".[11] Also becoming evident was increasing attention to government requirements for infrastructure and for this to be significantly privately funded.

Adelaide's second-generation plan (1962) introduced corridor-orientated planning that proved more resilient to sustained growth but in the process rescripted Australia's first postwar satellite town of Elizabeth modelled on Britain's first new town Stevenage as a planned metropolitan "district". Canberra's Y-Plan (1970) took this approach further and formulated an almost scientific hierarchical system of road, centre and community unit planning which was thoroughly implementable in a unique Australian city where land remained in public ownership and the planners enjoyed unprecedented powers. It brought together a melange of influences including Ebenezer Howard's garden city, Clarence Stein's regional city, Walter Christaller's central places, and Humphrey Carver's city in the suburbs. Hugh Stretton, a leading urban commentator of compassion and reason, backed the National Capital Development Commission's production-line greenfield planning as humane and efficient. He quoted a Canberra planner: "We plan for three bedrooms, a Holden and a motor mower".[12]

A Canberra resistance movement contested the technocratic ideology and modernist homogeneity but it proved an influential model in various forms in every capital city. Even when the Commonwealth experimented with new regional growth centres in the 1970s in places like Albury-Wodonga and Bathurst-Orange, the importation into new fringe housing estates of a Canberra style of suburbanism was evident.

Paradigm Shift

Through the 1970s into the 1980s metropolitan planning remained substantially suburban planning. There was nevertheless a penchant for experimentation with townhouses, cluster housing and eco-suburbs breaking up the more traditional template laid down by what has been dubbed "Holdenist suburbia" with all the vulnerabilities of dependence on depleting fossil fuels.[13] A more sustained pushback ramped up with the urban consolidation agenda, fuelled by anti-sprawl rhetoric, a public fiscal crisis, demographic and lifestyle changes, and peak oil. Metropolitan strategies assumed a new hybridity as they sought a balance between greenfield and brownfield, productivity and sustainability, low and higher density development.

By the early 2000s the recurrent themes for planning at metropolitan scale were containment, consolidation and centres.[14] This convergence in strategic planning has been criticised in the light of shortcomings in implementation and the costs imposed on developers and the community.[15] Other themes were intertwined: new urbanism, master planned communities and sustainability.

New Urbanism

The 1980s saw an uplift of interest in the design standards of planned residential developments, breaking from conventional postwar models, and somewhat remarkably led by the Australian Government under Prime Minister Bob Hawke. The first edition of the Australian Model Code for Residential Design (AMCORD) in 1989 delivered an influential toolkit of suburban design principles to deliver more economically rational and environmentally sustainable housing solutions. This segued into the Green Street Joint Venture in the 1990s promoting a multi-stakeholder commitment to more responsive performance-based planning in the interests of housing choice and affordability.

From the mid-1990s an Australian chapter of the new urbanist movement conflated a number of progressive planning campaigns globally such as Smart Growth, Transit-Oriented Development, Urban Villages and Placemaking into an holistic agenda standing for sustainability, reduced car dependency, mixed-use town centres, permeable street grids, the public realm and vernacular urban design. Wendy Morris addressed the Australian Council for New Urbanism Conference in 2005 on some of the distinctive attributes of Australian vis a vis American projects including more focus on systemic improvement than on "gem" projects and greater responsiveness to and leverage from stronger planning systems and culture.[16] Variously impacting processes, codes, strategies and implementation mechanisms, a 2006 survey also identified nearly 90 Australian new urbanist greenfield and infill projects.[17] The branding power of new urbanism has weakened as it has mainstreamed and other issues like climate change and catchphrases like "20 minute neighbourhoods" have become more prominent.

Master Planned Communities

Large-scale master planned suburban estates, many flavoured by new urbanist precepts, establish a continuity with earlier garden suburbs and pioneering community developments commenced in the 1960s by companies such as AV Jennings and

Hooker-Rex. They are "ready-made" neighbourhoods featuring house-and-land packages, with community and commercial facilities, an accent on quality open space, environmental amenity and sustainability, overall design character, and heritage elements and latterly Indigenous values. Targeted mainly at families, they aim at building active and resilient collaborative social networks. Some are gated but high securitisation has not had the same take-up seen in other countries. Others are more self-selecting, such as niched lifestyle developments for particular sub-markets such as seniors living. Their scale is expanding with locations more distant from central cities. In that respect they are not just about suburban place-making but decisively shaping the structure and character of urban regions. A showpiece development is Springfield in south-east Queensland an hour from the Brisbane CBD. While not self-contained, this is a new town-scaled development which has successfully attracted substantial external investment in health, education and transport infrastructure.[18]

Figure 1.6: Harrington Park, Greater Sydney, c2005: Promoting the features of the master planned community (photograph by the author)

Sustainability

Post-Brundtland 1987 sustainability has been a major aspiration and requirement of suburban planning. Peter Newman and Jeffrey Kenworthy's landmark critique of automobile dependence had international as well as national reverberations. An early statement outlined a three-pronged response based on urban villages, traffic calming and light rail.[19] This has upscaled to a multi-pronged city agenda with outer suburbs integrally linked to the inner city and transit systems extended into poorly served suburbs with cross-suburban and orbital linkages plus strategic new urban nodes connected to them.[20] These are major infrastructural moves that sit alongside a palette of initiatives for greening suburbs such as conservation of the natural environment, addressing energy consumption and the urban heat island effect, promoting walkability, and enhancing food production within the community. Showcase "Green Star" planned suburbs such as Ginninderry in Canberra now integrate sustainability planning, lifestyle and management into everyday long-term commitments for the community, developers and government.

Figure 1.7: Ginninderry, Canberra, 2022 – The planned sustainable suburb (photograph by the author)

Suburban Renewal

Since the 1990s suburban planning as greenfield planning has been joined by new waves of regeneration. This commenced with the makeover of obsolescent postwar public housing estates often also suffering social problems. Associated with this was replanning to convert Radburn site plans considered progressive in the 1950s and 1960s in separating pedestrians from cars but creating stigmatised "back-to-front" estates with a surfeit of amorphous open space. In high amenity and accessible suburbs, sizeable tracts of rezoned older detached housing have been acquired for higher density development, with a trend to resident-led aggregation selling. First generation post-World War Two suburbia in middle ring and outer suburbia is now an urban renewal target through more sustainable redevelopment of not only housing stock but other land uses such as town centres and retail complexes.

Residential renewal proceeds down two pathways: spontaneous and incremental "knock down and rebuild" governed only by conventional site-specific planning regulations rather than any strategic overlay or, secondly, more comprehensive precinct replanning. The latter approach to "greening the greyfields" seeks to leverage partnerships between the public, private and community stakeholders to maximise the collective environmental and social dividend.[21]

Conclusion

Australia is a suburban nation on a "suburban planet".[22] Suburbia now presents a more challenging environment than it ever did. As Jago Dodson comments, "the contemporary social, cultural and political complexity, the interwoven contradictions and combinations of opportunity and vulnerability, the environmental costs and the infrastructure needs of Australian suburbia now come together as a 'problem' in national life."[23] Urban policy is in many respects now suburban policy. After a stuttering early rehearsal to a recognisable suburban planning from the late twentieth century, the requirement for productively moving onwards seems clearer if daunting. It demands the right sort of collaborative, democratic, transparent, market responsive, innovative, and socially value-adding sustainable planning intertwined with an equally informed approach from the cultures of property development, architecture, landscape and urban design.

Endnotes

1   R. Freestone, B. Randolph, and S. Pinnegar (2018) "Suburbanization in Australia". In B. Hanlon and T.J. Vicino, eds. *Routledge Companion to the Suburbs,* New York: Routledge, 72-86.

2   A.F. Weber (1899) *The Growth of Cities in the Nineteenth Century: A study in statistics,* New York: Columbia University/Macmillan, 36.

3   G. Davison (1995) "Australia: The First Suburban Nation" *Urban History,* 22, 40-74.

4   J. Keily (1891) "Study on unity of design in planning new towns and new suburbs", *Victorian Institute of Surveyors, Transactions and Proceedings,* 3, 88-104.

5   J. Sulman (1921) *Introduction to the Study of Town Planning in Australia.* Sydney: Government Printer, Appendix A.

6   R. Freestone (1989) *Model Communities: The Garden City Movement in Australia.* Melbourne:

Thomas Nelson.

7   Report of the Royal Commission for the Improvement of the City of Sydney and its Suburbs (1909) *NSW Parliamentary Papers,* Vol 5, Sydney: Government Printer, p. xxviii.

8   F.K. Maher (1947) "The Greenbelt City", *Twentieth Century,* 1(3), 18-24.

9   G. Rudduck and R. Grounds (1955) "The Application of the Social Sciences to Town Planning in Australia" *International Social Science Bulletin,* 7, 221.

10   G. Davison, T. Dingle and S. O'Hanlon, eds.(1995) *The Cream Brick Frontier: Histories of Australian Suburbia.* Monash Publications in History No 19.

11   R. Bunker (1989) "A reappraisal of Australian suburbia" *Journal of Australian Studies,* 25, 82.

12   H. Stretton (1970) *Ideas for Australian Cities,* Melbourne: Georgian House, 73.

13   J. Dodson and N. Sipe (2008) *Shocking the Suburbs: Oil vulnerability in the Australian city.* Sydney: UNSW Press.

14   C. Forster (2006) *Australian Cities: Continuity and Change.* Melbourne: Oxford University Press.

15   R. Elliott (2017) "Australia's Misplaced War on the Suburban Dream", in A. Berger and J. Kotkin, eds. *Infinite Suburbia,* Princeton: Princeton Architectural Press, 104-113.

16   W. Morris (2005) "Australian New Urbanism in Practice". https://fdocuments.in/document/australian-new-urbanism-in-morrispdfaustralian-new-urbanism-in-practice-an-introduction.html?page=1

17   *Australian New Urbanism: A Guide to Projects,* 2nd ed, 2006.

18   M. King and D. Fagan (2018) *Greater Springfield: Australia's Newest City.* Brisbane: University of Queensland Press.

19   P. Newman, J. Kenworthy and L. Robinson (1992) *Winning Back the Cities.* Sydney: Australian Consumers Association.

20   P. Newman and J. Kenworthy (2015) *The end of automobile dependence.* Washington, DC: Island Press.

21   P.W. Newton, P.W.G. Newman, S. Glackin and G. Thompson (2022) *Greening the Greyfields: New models for regenerating the middle suburbs of low density cities,* Singapore: Palgrave Macmillan.

22   R. Keil (2017) *Suburban Planet: Making the world urban from the outside in.* Cambridge: Polity.

23   J. Dodson (2016) "Suburbia in Australian Urban Policy", *Built Environment,* 42(1), 26.

2

Everywhere and Nowhere:
The Contradictions of Australian Suburbia

Paul Burton

In this contribution I want to revisit the historical origins of the suburban form and lifestyle, how it came to Australia and to reflect critically on how the idea of suburbia continues to play such an important part in dominant imaginaries of the Australian good life. While many claim that suburbia remains the most important part of any imagined next Australian city, I have argued for some time that its analytical value has been stretched to breaking point in its reference to almost anywhere beyond the centre of cities and its descriptive accuracy is now weak as the ideal suburban lifestyle disappears on the ground (Burton, 2015). If suburbia is to be a positive part of the next Australian city, much work needs to be done in delivering as well as simply imagining its virtues.

Back to the Future

Let us cast our minds back to England in the middle of the 18th century, when the thoughts of some were turning to the imagined opportunities offered by the Great Southern Land for economic exploitation and as a place for dumping unwanted criminals and political agitators. At this time a new class was emerging in England and starting to think about how and where it should live. Described vividly a century later by Marx and Engels, the wealth of this modern *bourgeoisie* was created in cities and its vanguard members were city dwellers rather than members of the landed gentry who owned large estates in the countryside. But these rapidly growing and

27

changing English cities were not ideal places in which to live a *bourgeois* good life. Increasingly dirty, noisy, unhealthy and violent, they were also places that housed another emergent and fast-growing class – the urban proletariat – that was also becoming aware of its own existence and power. In short, English cities and especially London were increasingly unattractive places for the *nouveau riche* to live and display their wealth through their property, not least because it was impossible to avoid living cheek by jowl with this new and potentially revolutionary urban working class.

Across the channel, Moliere had already satirised the pretensions of these *bourgeois gentilhommes* but they were to come to a rather different solution to that of their English counterparts. In Paris they chose to make the inner urban spaces of Paris more clearly their own and push their revolting poor to the fringes of the city, to the places now known as *banlieues*. In England, however, the emerging *bourgeoisie* took the opposite approach and looked to the edges of their cities for the chance to combine the best of both worlds – the vitality and economic opportunities of the city with the healthy air and relative tranquillity of the countryside – while distancing themselves from their own urban poor and chose to colonise this urban fringe space that allowed ready access to both.

Slowly and through trial and error, this new place and way of life took shape and form as what we now recognise as embryonic suburbia. For the urban historian Robert Fishman, this *bourgeois* utopia was "...perhaps the most radical rethinking of the relation between residence and the city in the history of domestic architecture" and a "cultural creation, a conscious choice" that reflected a devotion to leisure, neighbourliness, prosperity and family life that persists to this day (1987:3). But these self-made men had not become successful simply by espousing fine principles and values, they were successful businessmen and entrepreneurs and the new landscapes they began creating could also be highly profitable as relatively cheap farmland was transformed through processes of suburban development. Over the centuries this underlying economic imperative and profit motive has continued to sit alongside the social and cultural virtues of a suburban lifestyle advocated by its supporters. In short, this emerging suburban landscape became a place in which to enjoy the use value of property while at the same time bolstering its exchange value through restrictions and limitations on how it could be used. Robert Fogelsong's perceptive account of the early years of suburban development in the USA in his book, *Bourgeois Nightmares*, shows how developers came to embrace and employ a range of restrictions on the rights of individual property owners to maintain the collective property values of the wider suburb. These early forms of development control planning serve as a useful reminder that trying to balance private property rights with a broader public interest is an enduring challenge for capitalist urban development and not a feature of state planning that can simply be eradicated, as some contemporary commentators seem to think.

Of course, the detailed form of suburban development has changed over time and varies from country to country, but some fundamental features have persisted. Fishman's definition remains valuable: for him suburbia refers to places "...large enough and homogenous enough to form a distinctive low density environment defined by the primacy of the single family house set in the greenery of an open, parklike setting" (1987: 5).

This was the new landscape emerged around London just as the British state began looking for new places to export its convicted felons and political troublemakers after the Revolutionary War of the late 18th century stopped their carriage to North America. It would be presumptuous to suggest that images of prospective suburban landscapes were front of mind among members of the First Fleet, but the Great Southern Land did prove to be fertile ground for these emerging suburban ideas as the colony was established. As Bill Garner observes in his splendid book on Australian camping, *Born in a Tent*, in order to impress or at least appease his masters in the Admiralty, Arthur Phillip concluded that moving out of tents and into "solid English buildings" was a priority. It might have been a priority, but it was difficult to realise in practice, not least because the materials needed to construct solid English buildings were not readily available and almost a century passed before Arthur and Robert Bunning began selling timber and other building materials in Perth, laying the foundations, literally as well as metaphorically, for another pillar of contemporary Australian suburban life.

So, we might speculate that not only was the "convict stain" a source of shame to many Australians, but that the obligation to live in tents during the formative years of the colony and some subsequent boom periods accounts, to some extent, for our devotion to the respectability of that epitome of the solid English building, the detached (and later, semi-detached) suburban cottage or bungalow.

The heyday of Australian suburbanisation

Graeme Davison has famously observed that modern Australia was born urban, but quickly became suburban: a place where the potential of suburban life was fully realised (Davison, 2013: 830). During the first half of the twentieth century, perhaps the heyday of the Australian suburb, the modest detached cottage on a reasonably sized block of land did indeed make the dream of home ownership accessible to millions of Australians, as the "cream brick frontier" described by Davison advanced rapidly. While it might have taken a while for infrastructure such as reticulated water and sewerage to come to some of these suburbs, they allowed many aspiring homeowners, including those on modest incomes and new migrants, to take their first step on the housing ladder and, significantly, to have room to expand their housing footprint in the future, even if it meant taking some of their beloved backyard.

More recently, however, the promises of suburbia set out in the sales brochures of developers are less evident on the ground and in the realities of suburban life. One of the most significant features of contemporary suburban developments is the fact that in a somewhat vain attempt to maintain the affordability of old, typical lot sizes have shrunk, but house footprints have not shrunk at the same rate. My late colleague, Tony Hall demonstrated vividly that in the last two decades we have seen the effective disappearance of the suburban backyard – just one of several ways in which the suburban dream has been eroded in reality.

There is a compelling view that designing anything within substantial constraints brings out the best in the designer, while having *carte blanche* and unlimited resources so often seems to encourage ordinariness and the unremarkable, or even a unique form of "Australian ugliness" as Robin Boyd observed. We see this in so many contemporary suburban developments, even those that boast of being "master planned". It is easier to bring in some more earth movers to flatten the landscape and offer preformed blocks on which to commission a very ordinary dwelling from the pattern book of a master builder, than it is to work with and reflect the landscape. Even the constraint of increasingly small blocks of land has yet to provoke much more than a scaled-down version of the McMansion. While there might be an occasional row of town houses, and maybe a smattering of duplexes, there is precious little evidence of master planned suburban developments attempting to bring significant diversity to the built form or offering much variety through well-designed small lot housing.[1] The detached single or two-storey dwelling continues to rule...and to sell.

Defenders of the faith

Because of this historical and enduring commitment to suburban detachment in Australia, criticism of its form, culture or sustainability is often met with outrage. Defenders of the faith in suburbia come from across the spectrum – from the scholarly to the populist with a good measure from self-serving spruikers or *suburbanistas*. Some invoke the continuing market demand for freehold ownership of detached dwellings. But if the only way to avoid the inconveniences of strata title living and the tyranny of the body corporate, or to achieve a semblance of ontological security in the face of capricious landlords and their agents is to buy at all costs, then this is simply one of the rational choices so beloved by neoliberals.

Furthermore, it is almost impossible to discuss Australian suburbanism in a rigorous manner without acknowledging the significance of class. And of course, this is especially difficult in a country that prides (or perhaps deludes) itself on being a classless society. While Marxists, Weberians and believers in the post-political might still be at loggerheads over their conceptions and definitions of class, its rejection in Australia seems principally to be that the many subtle cultural gradations of the British class system are absent here, alongside a stubborn commitment to the notion that hard work and aspiration will see you right and that structural inequities are only a product of the fevered imaginations of left-wing academics. The transformation of the bourgeois utopias described by Fishman to the apparent landscape of choice for virtually all Australians – except for the minority of latte-sipping metrosexual elites who choose inner city apartment living – is one of the reasons that criticism of Australian suburbanism remains so fraught.[2]

However, if we look a little more closely the *suburbanistas* who enthusiastically support everything to do with suburbia as a place and suburbanism as a lifestyle have a few other items on their agenda. Some simply don't like planning and its interference with property and development rights and have latched onto suburbia as "anywhere but the inner city". Some make superficially plausible arguments in favour of substantial reallocation of public investment away from mass transit infrastructure (they really do not like metros or light rail) designed to get people into and out of the CBD where the benefits of agglomeration stubbornly persist and towards peripheral road upgrades. More recently some have jumped also onto the autonomous vehicle bandwagon as the solution to suburban congestion. Others claim that detached living, preferably owner-occupied, is self-evidently an essential feature of human nature as shown by the fact that when presented with the opportunity to embrace it, most people do, even if they have grown up in different built forms and landscapes. Thus. the popularity of suburban Sunnybank in Brisbane among migrants from China is presented as *prima facie* evidence of this validity of this assumption, rather than an interesting but somewhat exceptional case of an ethnic enclave.

When comparing the attractions or downsides of different built forms we all too often take a static rather than dynamic view and think about it only as it applies to contemporary circumstances and to our lives now. Historically and in most countries the first step on the ladder of homeownership is a very modest one – mine was small Victorian terraced house on the "wrong" side of the river in Bristol. For many it will be a modest apartment, or even a block of land on which to put up a temporary structure, perhaps a shed, a tent or a caravan, or a building that can be added to over time. And at the other end of the lifecycle, many who have spent much of their middle years in suburban or peri-urban settings choose to downsize and move closer to the amenities and facilities that have become more important to them, whether they are health or cultural services.

Suburbia is no longer the only answer

So, what is the problem with contemporary suburbanisation and why am I not convinced it is the key to imagining and planning the next Australian city? In short because it takes a lot of land in a very important part of our metropolitan regions and uses it to create a built environment that can never offer a very sustainable lifestyle. While many, like the late Patrick Troy, have argued that detached dwellings consume less energy in their construction and running costs than higher rise apartment blocks in city centre locations, this is not uniformly accepted and can and is being addressed through the development and use of new construction materials and techniques. Furthermore, other aspects of contemporary suburban landscapes are more significant, and this is where an historical perspective is important.

The land in demand for contemporary suburban development is valuable for a number of reasons: some but certainly not all is good quality agricultural land that helps feed city dwellers even as food supply chains become increasingly global; most provides essential habitat for fauna that helps define Australia, such as koalas and other marsupials and a range of birds; and some allows us to spend time in a relatively natural environment that we know can be a great protector of our mental health and well-being. And we should not, of course, forget that in Australia the early processes of suburban expansion took place on Aboriginal land taken violently, and still without proper compensation, from their ancient occupants as historians like Henry Reynolds and academic activists like Gary Foley continue to remind us.

The problem with the contemporary suburb, including the master planned estates on the fringes of our cities, is that they seem so incapable of the improvement advocated by one of Australia's greatest urbanists, Hugh Stretton. In its unswerving commitment to detachment, increasing site coverage leaves literally no room for future expansion or even any significant modification of the original dwelling. While there is increasing talk of retrofitting suburbia (eg Beske and Dixon, 2018) to enable a more sustainable or even decarbonised lifestyle, there seems little that can be done incrementally to these contemporary master planned environments except for extensive demolition to make way for townhouses or medium rise apartment blocks. The business model of suburban development shows little or no appetite for including from the outset this kind of flexibility and adaptability by design.

The modification seen in older suburbs, and now resisted vigorously but somewhat ironically by many local residents, was possible because additional dwellings and extensions could be built on generous backyards. The landscape this produced was not always very attractive but at least it enabled change and adaptation. And even greater change could be achieved by the modest amalgamation of a few lots and the construction of low to medium-rise apartment blocks.

So, if we are to continue to encourage and build master planned "communities" way beyond the urban fringe, even if land there is relatively cheap, then we should at least pay some attention to how that population are going to get to their jobs, services and places of leisure and learning. Too often the master planned promise of self-containment and local provision never quite seems to materialise, or if it does it comes much later when the children of the pioneer settlers have had children of their own. While the classic suburbs of North America and Britain grew rapidly and often successfully because they were connected back into the cities by railways and trams, their contemporary equivalents rarely enjoy good quality public transport infrastructure and instead become places noted for the traffic congestion they inevitably generate.

A way forward?

In summary, contemporary Australian debates about how best to accommodate a growing population have become unhelpfully polarised. Too much of contemporary debate about the future of our cities is framed by a false dichotomy between the high rise and the quarter acre block, when they represent in fact the ends of a spectrum of many more opportunities. Despite the best efforts of those advocating an expansion of the "missing middle" in the overall typology of built forms, many still insist that suburbia is the only way forward. A relatively low-density landscape of detached houses, located in the peri-urban hinterlands of our major cities, where the car is still king is seen as both natural and an undeniable reflection of the housing aspirations of most Australians. Those calling for more housing diversity and greater density within the existing footprint of our cities are dismissed by some as "academics following overseas fashions" or "single purpose activists" or intellectuals who are really "city people at heart".

My concern with the notion of suburbia as the most significant feature of the next Australian city is that it has been stretched as an analytical concept to include almost anything and everywhere. While some scholars continue to resist this temptation and explore the subtleties and global varieties of suburbanisation, others appear more than happy to join a more overtly political project of supporting one particular fraction of the development sector in its contradictory calls for less state regulation through planning but more state subsidised infrastructure to bolster profitability. The recent call by Nicholas Phelps, Paul Maginn and Roger Keil for a more focused and sustained concern with *peripheries* in urban studies is interesting and certainly worthy of debate, but it appears unable to bring more precision to the analytical challenge when they open their recently published critical commentary on this topic by declaring "Periphery is everywhere". Recognising the oxymoronic nature of this statement while claiming it as an intellectual provocation, demonstrates to me the prescience of Beck's observation back in 1968 when he sang, "You're everywhere and nowhere, baby".

Meanwhile, on the peripheral ground around most Australian cities the master planned suburban estates continue to replace what were once valuable ecosystems, and underpin my second main concern. There is no denying the apparent popularity of these places which offer a first step on the ladder of homeownership to many and attractive investment opportunities to others. But the reality of life here remains to be analysed through rigorous longitudinal study. While the sales brochures promise safety and sociability amidst a smattering of eco-parklets and clusters of nationally recognisable shops, fast food outlets and service stations, there is anecdotal evidence of some serious underlying social problems among resident children, who will soon grow into resident teenagers. Despite the promises of suburban economic growth, car dependency in what remain essentially dormitory settlements is likely to present an ever-growing challenge to affordable, congestion-free living and there is increasing recognition of the damaging public health impacts of suburban heat islands.

Italo Calvino's collection of tales of invisible cities describe places imagined by Marco Polo on his travels throughout the empire of Kublai Khan. A contemporary version might describe fabulous places where happy families have room to play in their own backyards, where good neighbours become good friends and where the jobs and economic opportunities of cities are as accessible as the therapeutic benefits of the nearby bush. But these places are becoming increasingly rare in Australia, except in the sales brochures and promotional videos of developers. On the ground we are building places with almost non-existent backyards, where parents are extremely reluctant to let their kids play in the front streets which are often crowded with the cars they are unable to fit in their *bijou* garages and which are necessary for all adult family members to have to get to and from their places of work or study. And as these suburban dwellings become increasingly attractive to investor purchasers, long term community building becomes an increasing challenge among a relatively transient renter population.

While the political, cultural and economic momentum behind continued suburban development in Australia remains as strong as it does, the suggestion that it is a lifestyle or built form under serious threat from the critiques of a handful of academics and commentators or from unhelpful planners and their poorly conceived planning schemes seems fanciful. Focusing instead on the detail of how to enable established inner suburbs to modernise through high quality, well-designed infill that is affordable to first time buyers remains important. And providing well-designed and affordable homes for more people in the new peripheral suburbs, that are designed to allow growth and change in the future, while delivering sustainable lifestyles in the present would be a good start and a better use for the energies of contemporary *suburbanistas*.

So, the idea of suburbia remains attractive even though the lived experience fails increasingly to match the dream. But the resolution of this problem does not necessarily lie in abandoning the dream as unachievable. Instead, planners, architects, urban designers, engineers and developers could work together to see if it is still possible to create places that fulfill at least some elements of the suburban dream at a price that is affordable to Australians on modest incomes and delivers an acceptable rate of return to developers.

Endnotes

1   The architect/developer Amy Degenhart is an exception and has advocated for, and designed and built, small lot housing in these settings for many years.

2   As in some other areas of public debate, there appears to be a paradoxical fear that something as entrenched as the Australian suburban ideal could be undermined by a few sharp words from Germaine Greer or Elizabeth Farrelly.

References

Beske, J. and Dixon, D. (2018) *Suburban Remix: Creating the Next Generation of Urban Places,* Island Press, Washington, DC

Burton, P. (2015) "The Australian Good Life: The Fraying of a Suburban Template", *Built Environment,* vol 41, no 4, pp. 504-515

Davison, G. (2013) "The Suburban Idea and Its Enemies", *Journal of Urban History,* vol 39, no 5, 829-847

Fishman, R. (1987) *Bourgeois Utopias: The Rise and Fall of Suburbia,* Basic Books

Fogelsong, R. (2005) *Bourgeois Nightmares: Suburbia, 1870-1930,* Yale University Press, New Haven

Foley, G. (2011) "Black Power, Land Rights and Academic History", *Griffith Law Review,* vol 20, no 3, pp 608-618

Garner, B. (2013) *Born in a Tent: How camping Makes Us Australian,* NewSouth Publishing, Sydney

Hall. T. (2010) *The Life and Death of the Australian Backyard,* CSIRO Publishing

Phelps, N., Maginn, P. and Keil, R. (2022) "Centring the periphery in urban studies: Notes towards a research agenda on peripheral centralities", *Urban Studies,* available at: https://doi.org/10.1177/00420980221135418.

Reynolds, H. (2021) *Truth-Telling: History, Sovereignty and the Uluru Statement,* NewSouth Publishing, Sydney

Stretton, H. (1989) *Ideas for Australian Cities,* 3rd ed, Transit Australia Publishing, Sydney

3

Killing the Dream Worldwide

Joel Kotkin and Wendell Cox

The great aspiration of people throughout the Western world has been to find a decent, relatively spacious home of their own. Today from Sydney to San Francisco, this aspiration is rapidly fading, creating a gap between the past generation and the newer one, between aspiration and disappointment, could define our demographic, political and social future.

The problem is largely the result of massively increasing land costs, which have made housing severely unaffordable. According to OECD (in *Under Pressure: The Squeezed Middle-Class*) "the middle-class faces ever rising costs relative to incomes and that its survival is threatened." This is at least partly because "... the cost of essential parts of the middle-class lifestyle have increased faster than inflation..." Owned housing prices "have been three times faster than household median income over the last two decades." OECD concludes that "Housing has been the main driver of rising middle-class expenditure." Rising rents are also part of the problem, because of their strong relationship to house prices. For example, in the United States rents had a 0.85 correlation to house prices among the 384 metropolitan areas (2019).[1]

The French leftist economist Thomas Piketty has identified high housing costs as a driver of increasing inequality around the world.[2] Much of this greater inequality is attributable to the rise in housing wealth, according to research by Matthew Rognlie, at Northwestern University.[3] In the United States over the past decade the proportion of real estate wealth held by middle class and working owners fell substantially while that controlled by the wealthy grew from under 20 per cent to over 28 per cent.[4] In the last decade, high income households enjoyed 71 per cent of all housing gains while the shares of middle and lower income families declined precipitously.

In a Bank for International Settlements (Berne) paper, economist Gianni La Cava associated rising inequality in the United States with increased housing values in more severely regulated markets.[5] By definition, house price increases that exceed household income growth result in *greater inequality*, advantaging buyers, and disadvantaging others. In the United States, more than 85% of the difference in cost of living between metropolitan areas is attributable to differences in housing affordability.[6]

The Decline in Home Ownership

There is considerable consensus that there is now a "cost of living" crisis, led by house price increases relative to incomes, but further exacerbated by energy cost increases, rising inflation and interest rates.[7] One critical sign of this trend has been the difficulty for young people to achieve home ownership.

US Millennials were less likely in 2015 to be homeowners than baby boomers and Gen Xers. The homeownership rate among millennials ages 25 to 34 was 8 percentage points lower than baby boomers and 8.4 percentage points lower than Gen Xers when they were 25-34. By 2021 home ownership among ages 25-34 dropped from 45.4% in 2000 to 41.5 per cent, a decline of nearly 10 per cent.[8]

Even before the interest rate rise, similar trends are seen in other high-income countries, including Australia, Ireland, and the United Kingdom. Australia historically has had high rates of homeownership, but the rate among[9] those between 25 and 34 years old dropped from more than 60 per cent in 1981 to only 45 per cent in 2016. The proportion of owner-occupied housing has dropped by 10 per cent in the last 25 years. A trend toward long-term "rentership" is also seen in the United Kingdom, where only a third of millennials own a home, compared with almost two-thirds of baby boomers at the same age. At least one-third of British Millennials[10] are likely to remain renters for life.

Without a home, these millennials will face a "formidable challenge" in boosting their worth. Property remains key to financial security: homes today account for roughly two-thirds of the wealth of middle-income Americans; and home owners have a median net worth more than 40 times that of renters.[11]

Understanding the Urban Form

Historically urban areas have adjusted to higher prices by expanding outwards. Urban expansion, suggests former World Bank principal planner Alain Bertaud, has helped foster a more prosperous world[12] with a higher standard of living and lower poverty rates. Cities, he adds, "are the major engines of economic growth, and living in cities is the only hope of escaping poverty for billions of people."[13] Of course, urban areas must also have adequate personal security and be sufficiently free from disease[14] and crime.[15]

Yet as Bertaud and others suggest, the key to successful urbanisation lies in the ability and willingness to extend the urban area. The dynamics change with changes in transportation technology.

This spatial expansion of urban areas has occurred more quickly in the last two centuries, as travel times have been shortened as automobiles and transit replaced walking as the principal means of travel.

This decentralisation of the city involved far greater population growth in the "suburbs,"[16] which were on the periphery of the core LGA (core city). Spatial expansion is referred to as "suburbanisation," which historian Kenneth Jackson defined as "the systematic growth of fringe areas at a pace more rapid than that of core cities."[17] As one report put it, "human settlement has always tended to sprawl out from key urban centres."[18]

Defining Cities

Historically, the principal term denoting urbanisation has been "city." Yet, especially over the last two centuries, the term "city" has become increasingly obscure, with unprecedented population increases and transportation improvements that have made larger expanses of urbanisation practical.

The term "city" can be used to describe core local government authorities[19] (LGAs), which are legally defined general-purpose governments, urban areas (continuous urbanisation) and metropolitan areas (labor markets defined by commuting). With few exceptions, each of these has the same principal name, such as the City of Sydney (the core LGA), the Sydney urban centre (urban area) and the Sydney Greater Capital City Statistical Area (GCCSA), which is the metropolitan area (Figure 3:1).

Urban areas and metropolitan areas nearly always contain more than one core LGA, except in China, and can contain more than 1,000.[20] Travel across an urban area or a metropolitan area can include multiple LGAs, which are often indistinguishable, even at their borders. The generic terms for the urban organism are urban areas and metropolitan areas.

(1) Urban areas are the city in its physical form, the continuously built-up urban form. According to the World Bank, an urban area "refers to the de facto population contained within the contours of a contiguous territory inhabited at urban density levels *without regard to administrative boundaries.*[21] The urban area is defined by the large expanse of lights seen from a high-flying airplane contrasted with the darkness or intermittent lights in the largely rural surroundings. In urban geography, the urban area is referred to as the "physical city." All land in the urban area is by definition classified as urban.

(2) Metropolitan areas are the city as a labor market or functional area (the urban area plus economically integrated territory largely defined by commuting.). Metropolitan areas contain both rural and urban land, and usually include more rural than urban land.[22]

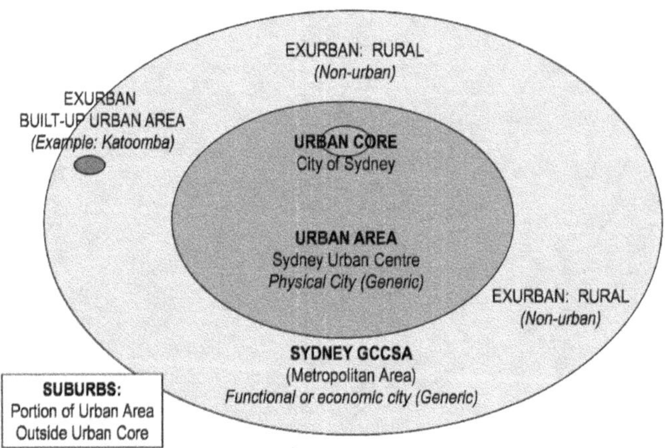

Figure 3.1: Urban Areas &Metropolitan Areas: Contrast
Example: Sydney Urban Centre and GCCSA

Transportation Defines the Urban Form

The pattern of urbanisation can be defined by the dominant transportation technologies. Before the first half of the 19th century, most travel within urban areas was by walking. Walking, because it was so slow, required high population densities and limited the size of urban areas. In a few cases, urban areas exceeded 1,000,000 population (such as Beijing, in 1800), but all of them fell back to below 1,000,000.[23]

Gradually, the second era saw the walking city supplanted by one dominated by mass transit, beginning in the first half of the 19th century; this allowed urban areas to expand materially, lowering population densities, as a result of the increased travel speed. At the same time, walking remained important as a method of mobility in the mass transit urban area. By 1900, London had reached 6.5 million, New York 4.2 million and Paris 3.4 million.

In the years that followed, the "automobile era" (the third era) further transformed the urban area, leading to the largest urban areas of from 30 million to 40 million (such as Tokyo-Yokohama, Jakarta, and Delhi) by the 2020s.[24] The automobile allowed dispersed urban origins and destinations, which led to far larger urbanised land areas.

Today we are entering the fourth era, the "virtual era," as online activities, such as remote work and shopping displace some urban travel. This era may ultimately be more accurately called the "virtual automobile" era, since a large portion of today's mobility cannot be replaced by online activities. As with the previous eras, it can be expected that walking and mass transit will continue to play a role, but the virtual era seems likely to lead to lower population densities, which for many households enables less geographical connection between home and work as well as doing daily chores.

The Global Pattern is Dispersion

The virtual shift is likely to continue the decline in urban population densities, a pattern that predated by a generation the rise of Zoom, as New York University Marron Institute of Urban Expansion's Shlomo Angel et al have shown.[25] Contrary to the claim that density represents today, as it did in past, a sign of social and economic progress, increasingly the wealthier countries an ever more decentralised city involved far greater population growth in the "suburbs."[26]

Survey of World Urban Areas: Urban Cores and Suburbs

The changes have been dramatic. This is indicated by a sample of 18 world urban areas comparing core LGA[27] and suburban populations from the mid-20th century to the present (Table 3.1). The sample includes 12 urban areas in United Nations "more developed regions" and 6 urban areas in UN less developed world regions. The examples are limited to urban areas *for which comparable urban core data is available* from about 1950[28] (just after World War II) and excludes urban areas where LGA land areas have substantially expanded by annexation or consolidation with other jurisdictions, such as Toronto, Seattle, and Rome. In most such cases these jurisdictional expansions substantially reduced core LGA population densities (Table 3.1).

The trend to the suburbs has been overwhelming both in the more developed regions and the less developed regions, though has occurred more recently in the less developed regions. This trend has resulted not only from improved transportation, but also from substantially rising incomes that have permitted more housing choices.

In 1950 the average population share in the LGAs was 60% of the urban area population; by 2021, the core LGA average had dropped to 25%, a decline of 58%.

Among the 12 urban areas in the more developed regions, the urban core LGA share of the population has dropped from 55% to 30%, a decline of 45%. The suburbs grew from 40% of the urban area population in 1950 to 70%, an increase of 56%. The suburbs had 97% of the urban area growth, on average, since 1950.

Even in less developed world the urban core LGA share of the population in six major urban areas (Buenos Aires, Kolkata, Lagos, Manila, Mexico City and Shanghai) - has fallen from 70% in 1950 to 15% in 2021, a drop of 78%. The suburban population has increased from 30% to 85%, a gain of 182%. The suburbs had 96% of the urban area growth, on average, since 1950.

Virtually all the growth of the urban areas has been in the suburbs since 1950.

Table 3.1: International Urban Area Examples: Data

	1950 Era			2021 Estimates			Growth		Region
Urban Area	1950	Core LGA	Sub-urbs	2021	Core LGA	Sub-urbs	Total %	Suburb Share	
Barcelona	1.8	71%	29%	4.7	35%	65%	162%	87%	More Developed
Chicago	4.9	74%	26%	8.6	31%	69%	75%	125%	More Developed
Copenhagen	1.2	63%	37%	1.6	49%	51%	33%	92%	More Developed
London	8.4	44%	56%	11.1	33%	67%	33%	101%	More Developed
Melbourne	1.3	7%	93%	4.6	4%	96%	248%	97%	More Developed
Milan	1.9	67%	33%	5.0	28%	72%	165%	96%	More Developed
New York	12.3	64%	36%	19.5	44%	56%	58%	92%	More Developed
Paris	6.3	44%	56%	11.0	20%	80%	76%	113%	More Developed
San Francisco	2.0	38%	62%	3.8	22%	78%	87%	98%	More Developed
Tokyo	11.3	48%	52%	39.1	24%	76%	247%	86%	More Developed
Vancouver	0.6	62%	38%	2.4	29%	71%	337%	81%	More Developed
Zurich	0.5	83%	17%	0.9	47%	53%	87%	94%	More Developed
Buenos Aires	5.2	58%	42%	16.2	19%	81%	214%	99%	Less Developed
Kolkata	4.6	64%	36%	18.7	24%	76%	306%	89%	Less Developed
Lagos	0.3	66%	34%	15.5	1%	99%	4665%	100%	Less Developed
Manila	1.5	65%	35%	24.0	8%	92%	1453%	96%	Less Developed
Mexico City	3.4	66%	34%	21.5	9%	91%	539%	102%	Less Developed
Shanghai	4.3	100%	0%	22.1	30%	70%	416%	87%	Less Developed
(Population in Millions)									
Average	4.0	60%	40%	12.8	25%	75%	511%	96%	
More Developed Regions	4.4	55%	45%	9.4	30%	70%	134%	97%	
Less Developed Regions	3.2	70%	30%	19.7	15%	85%	1265%	96%	

The Suburban Preference is Irrefutable

It seems clear that most people in urban areas prefer a suburban environment. A Statistics Canada analysis of 2021 census results indicates that more than 75% of the population in the largest metropolitan areas lives in the suburbs. More than 80% of the growth between 2016 and 2021 was in the suburbs.[29]

Much the same can be seen in United States. An analysis of the 53 US major metropolitan areas finds that more than 85% of residents live in the suburbs or exurbs and that more than 90% of the population growth since 2010 has been in the suburbs and exurbs.[30] Even in transit-rich and land-short Japan, Tokyo and Osaka are dispersing away from the urban core to suburban and exurban areas after having nearly monopolised national population growth over the previous decade.[31] Much the same can be said of Seoul, which is even denser than the Japanese megacities.[32]

Suburbanisation, with its lower population densities, is necessarily associated with lower density housing. Among nations in the UN's more developed regions (Table 3.2), single-family housing is dominant. On average 72% of housing in these nations is single-family, including 52% detached and 20% attached. The balance of 28% is in apartments (multi-family housing). Australia has 78% of its occupied housing stock in single-family.[33] Since 2010, 58% of new housing consents have been detached, after having dipped to 50% in mid-decade. In 2021 detached consents reached 65%, the highest figure since 2010.[34]

In Canada, the US and Australia, the vast majority of homes are single family.[35] This is also true in the United States[36] and is also the case even in crowded Japan.[37] In the similarly crowded United Kingdom, this is also the case.[38] Since 2010, ground oriented housing (detached, semi-detached and terraced) has represented, on average, 79% of new dwelling unit construction in the United Kingdom.[39] In the European Union, single family housing accounts for about 70% of housing, with 40% in detached housing and 30% in attached. Multi-family accounts for 30% of occupied housing.[40]

Table 3.2: Housing Types: More Developed Regions

	Detached	Attached	Apartment	Year	GDP/Capita
Australia	74%	13%	13%	2016	84%
Canada	54%	13%	33%	2016	74%
United States	67%	6%	27%	2018	100%
Japan	54%	3%	44%	2018	67%
United Kingdom	26%	53%	20%	2017	74%
European Union	40%	30%	30%	2017	71%
Average	52%	20%	28%		77%

GDP per capita in International 2020 $

The Great Betrayal

Over the past decade or even earlier in some urban areas, densification policies have been adopted, and widespread home ownership begun to erode. Indeed, an analysis of Canadian poll results by Sotheby's suggests a "disconnect" between urban planning and consumer preferences:[41] the "picture is of young urban families overwhelmingly preferring detached houses, and decidedly not the condominiums into which planners are driving them." As Sotheby's puts it, "The report dispels myths about young, urban families' housing preferences."

In many countries, government policy is denying household preferences by making housing more costly. Australia, US States, especially California, Oregon, Washington and Colorado, the United Kingdom, and New Zealand, all cite environmental concerns to impose a large regulatory noose around new developments, particularly in the periphery (usually urban growth boundaries or greenbelts). Overall, far fewer Californians can afford to buy a median-priced home today than in 2000, even though nationally the percentage of people who can afford homes has actually increased.

The price spike has been worsened as well-funded investors, expectedly attracted by windfall profits by the artificially rising prices which have been largely associated with regulatory restraints.

Shlomo Angel of the New York University Marron Institute of Urban Expansion found that most world urban areas are subject to urban containment,[42] also called compact city policy. These policies seriously restrict housing development beyond the existing urban footprint. This creates a shortage of land, which drives up prices land prices throughout the metropolitan area (housing market).[43]

"As a result, forced densification through the explicit containment of urban expansion – by greenbelts, as in Seoul, Korea or in English cities, by urban growth boundaries, as in Portland, Oregon, or by environmental restrictions as in California – has inevitably been associated with declines in housing affordability."[44]

Indeed, *all* of the major metropolitan areas (more than 1,000,000 population) with severely unaffordable housing (median multiple over 5.0) in the last pre-pandemic year of 2019 had urban containment (*Demographia International Housing Affordability Survey*).[45]

An irony is that planning literature associates higher densities with greater housing affordability.[46] Yet, in the United States, higher urban population densities are strongly associated with housing that is less affordable.[47]

Largely due to regulatory policies, Australia's once affordable metropolitan areas are among the world's most expensive. Prices for homes in Sydney are *higher relative to incomes* than Los Angeles, London, New York, Singapore, and Washington. Even Adelaide, an isolated and declining industrial hub, has higher prices, based on income, than Seattle, one of the world's most dynamic tech hubs.

The impact on prices is severe. In Sydney planning regulations, according to a recent Reserve Bank study,[48] now adds 55% to the price of a home. Australian cities once filled with family friendly neighborhoods are becoming dominated by dense apartments. According to projections from the Urban Taskforce, apartments will make up half of Sydney's dwellings mid-century, whereas only one quarter of Sydney dwellings will be family-friendly detached homes.

These policies are widely supported among planners, academicians and the media[49]; in virtually all countries the cognitive elites – congregated in expensive urban cores – vehemently oppose suburban growth. Indeed when I showed data that most Australians are continuing to move to the periphery, even in New South Wales, the moderator, Australian Broadcast commentator Ali Moore, described much of suburbia as "the wastelands". It led one conventioneer to wonder after "what country" she inhabited given that 80 per cent of all Australians live in suburbs, with more than four-fifths of families prefer living in single family homes.[50]

The Impact of the Pandemic

During the pandemic, there was a substantial increase in remote and hybrid working arrangements, which has allowed households to move to suburban and exurban areas and even beyond, without changing jobs. Remote working (both hybrid and full-time) can be characterised as the most environmentally friendly way to access employment, by eliminating the environmental costs of the physical commute.[51] Finally, future information technology improvements, especially virtual reality, could support even greater remote working. Recent research by the US government sponsored Federal Home Loan Mortgage Corporation ("Freddie Mac") indicates that "The pandemic amplified existing urban deconcentrating by threefold, from large, expensive metro areas to smaller, more affordable destinations."[52]

This exodus has the potential to improve housing affordability, as households move to less costly areas. But the planning regimes that have so substantially contributed to the severe unaffordability in metros like Vancouver, San Francisco, London, and Sydney must be left behind. Otherwise, any gains are likely to be soon lost, as demand overwhelms supply. Already, for example, the rapidly deteriorating housing affordability of Toronto is being exported to the nearby, smaller metros, as households seek the housing, they desire by moving.[53] Just between the 2016 and 2021 censuses, a net 280,000 migrants left the Toronto metro area, all but 9,000 to less expensive markets in Ontario.

The Greens and the Housing Market

Angel stresses the need for urban expansion to improve housing affordability. Both the OECD and Matthew Rognlie have urged review of land use regulations to address the cost-of-living crisis.

One oft-celebrated driver for eliminating middle-class, family-friendly housing are the so-called YIMBYs ("Yes in my backyard"). YIMBYs, notes an investigation in the leftist *In These Times,* enjoy fevered support from Wall Street and tech leadership.[54] They also have strong ties with green progressives, like the Democratic Socialists of America.[56] These groups disdain suburbia, promote dense apartment living,[55] and have little interest in expanded homeownership. Indeed some are open collectivists[57] who reject the very idea of individual ownership and would welcome the prospect of a massive expansion of public housing.[58] These investors have powerful allies both on the right and left.

The Future Battle over Ownership

In the coming decades, declining home in ownership could have profound implications. For one thing it will remove for most of the current generation – most of whom still believe in creating wealth through ownership.[59]

This may not be the future preferred by many people, most of whom[60] are out of the market due to costs, but still seek to own a home.[61] Yet the reduction in the chance of ownership is already shaping the politics of the future, particularly among young who are unable to afford ownership and face strongly rising rent. Not surprisingly, many favour socialist policies such as subsidies and rent control – like those of Bernie Sanders or France's Jean Luc Melenchon.

All this suggest a future where economic autonomy, the key to democracy, will barely exist for most families besides the most affluent. Ultimately the battle over land and property will define our future and whether we provide hope to the next generation or force them to accept a lifetime of rental serfdom and permanent subservience to the state, or big capital, or both.

The Green Agenda

Historically, opposition to suburban lifestyles was based on aesthetic, social or even economic considerations. Yet today it often centres around "green" and "sustainability" concerns. The environmental magazine *Grist* envisioned "a hero generation" that will escape the material trap of suburban living and work that engulfed their parents.[62] One magazine editor proudly declared herself a part of the GINK generation (as in "green inclinations, no kids") that she said meant not only a relatively care-free and low-cost adult life, but also "a lot of green good that comes from bringing fewer beings onto a polluted and crowded planet."[63]

This view is widely shared by some major Wall Street investors both the oligarchy and the upper echelons of the planning establishment. They favour a more "ordered" planet, but in ways that do not threaten their own power or quality of life. Those at the top of pyramid can purchase the modern equivalent of "indulgences" for their consumption by investing in forests, driving electric cars, solarising their homes, while their wealth allows them to purchase hideously expensive inner-city flats.

This meme is usually applauded in the media, such as the *Australian Financial Review*, which insists Millennials do not want to live in suburbia. This is largely specious.[64] In survey after survey, most millennials, in the United States and elsewhere, say they want a single family house.[65] Their problem simply that they can't afford them, particularly in the highly regulated regions as in California, Australia, Canada, or the UK.

This sets a stage for a future political conflict. Even in the face of policies that seek to discourage suburban growth, in most high-income countries (see above), such as Canada, Australia and the US, suburban tastes remain predominant,[66] and could become more so. In America among those under 35 who do buy homes, four-fifths[67] choose single-family detached houses. According to a recent[68] report, over 66 per cent, including those living in cities, actually prefer a house in the suburbs.

Upward Mobility or Neo-Feudalism

In the vision of many planners, green activists and some in the real estate industry, the future of housing removes middle income aspirations, creating a mass of permanent renters. This may end the dream of ownership that defines the middle class as Wall Street increasingly assumes the role of landlord.[69]

This virtual feudalisation is being driven by many forces, including foreigner investors, notably from China.[70] In the notorious words of the World Economic Forum, "You will own nothing, and love it."

On both sides of the Atlantic, large financial institutions like Britain's Lloyds Bank and BlackRock[71] have placed multi-billion dollar bets on buying homes for the rental market.[72] In the first quarter of 2021, investors accounted for roughly one out of every seven homes bought, a marked increase from previous years. The popular notion is of a "rentership" society where people remain renters for life, enjoying their video games or attending to their houseplants,[73] never knowing the pleasure of having a real garden or backyard of their own. It might assure a steady profit for the landlord class, but would destroy the dream of ownership for the average person.[74]

To save itself, the middle class needs to overturn the current housing agenda.

Our middle-class societies will not likely survive this shift. At best, even the young see home ownership not as something they can achieve on their own but only if they can tap their parents so they can enter what one writer calls "the funnel of privilege".[75] In America, like Australia a country whose mythology disdains the power of inherited wealth, millennials increasingly are counting on inheritance for their retirement at a rate three times that of the boomers. Among the youngest cohort, those 18 to 22, over 60 per cent see inheritance as their primary source for their wealth as they age.[76] These feudalistic attitudes are not the fault of the young but reflect the shortcomings of the older generation. "Young people," wrote Montesquieu in the mid-18th century, "do not degenerate; this only occurs only after grown men have become corrupt."[77] In restricting suburban development, and thus homeownership, planners, investors, and the media are removing the very conditions that created the affluence of their parents.

This represents a threat to democracy rarely discussed in the mainstream media, or in the political world. A strong land-owning middle class has been essential in democracies from ancient Athens, the Roman and Dutch Republics to contemporary Europe, North America, and Australia. Now with fewer owning land, and many without even a reasonable expectation of acquiring it, we may be entering an era portrayed as progressive, woke and multi-cultural but will be ever more feudal in its economic and social form.

Endnotes .

1   Wendell Cox (March 11, 2021), "The Cost of Moving Up to Home Ownership, www.newgeography.com.

2   Thomas Piketty, (2014). *Capital in the twenty-first century.*

3   Matthew Rognlie, "A note on Piketty and diminishing returns to capital," June 15, 2014.

4   Nicole Freidman (March 9, 2022), "U.S. Housing Wealth Skewed Even More Toward Affluent Over Past Decade, *The Wall Street Journal.*

5   Gianni La Cava, Housing Prices, "Mortgage Interest Rates and the Rising Share of Capital Income in the United States," *BIS Working Paper*, No. 572.

6   Wendell Cox (2020), *URI Standard of Living Index,* Urban Reform Institute.

7   Late 1970s. See: Harry Freedman, "Now is the winter of discontent", *The Guardian*, 10 October 2009, https://www.theguardian.com/careers/careers-blog/winter-of-discontent

8   Calculated from US Census Bureau data.

9   Leith Van Onsolen (August 7, 2018), "The Sad Death of Australian Home Ownership", macrobusiness.com.

10   BBC (April 17, 2018), Up to a third of millennials "face renting their entire life".

11   Joel Kotkin, "Americans won't live in the pod", *New Geography*, 29 September 2020, https://www.newgeography.com/content/006789-americans-wont-live-pod

12   Bertaud is referring to "labor markets," also called metropolitan areas or functional cities, which comprise the built-up urban area (the "physical city") and the principally rural areas commuting area beyond. The urban area is the large expanse of lights seen from a high-flying airplane contrasted with the darkness or intermittent lights in the rural surroundings.

13   Palaash Roy, "Catalytic Urbanscape", CEPTPORTFOLIO M2023, https://portfolio.cept.ac.in/fp/up-4000-2-up4000-3-spring-2020/catalytic-urbanscape-spring-2020-pg190646

14   Edward L. Glaeser, "Cities and Pandemics Have a Long History", *City Journal*, Spring 2020,

https://www.city-journal.org/cities-and-pandemics-have-long-history; Franz Vanderschueren, "The Evolution and Challenges of Security within Cities, *UN Chronicle,* August 2013, No.2 Vol. L, Security https://www.un.org/en/chronicle/article/evolution-and-challenges-security-within-cities

15   Franz Vanderschueren, "The Evolution and Challenges of Security within Cities, *UN Chronicle,* August 2013, No.2 Vol. L, Security https://www.un.org/en/chronicle/article/evolution-and-challenges-security-within-cities

16   By contrast, the term "suburb" is used in Australia to denote geography corresponding to a post code in urban areas, regardless of location. This chapter uses the international definition. The Oxford Reference definition is "The outer part of a city or urban area, close to the urban-rural boundary, with limited commercial land use and low-density residential development. Also known as suburbia."

17   Sam Roberts, "How a Ferry Ride Helped Make Brooklyn the Original Suburb", *New York Times,* 29 December 2014, https://www.nytimes.com/2014/12/30/nyregion/how-a-ferry-ride-helped-make-brooklyn-the-original-suburb.html

18   Historical distribution of population in Australian cities, https://www.accc.gov.au/system/files/Appendix%20C%20-%20Urban%20growth.pdf

19   The core LGAs (excepting Brisbane) of the largest Australian urban areas/metropolitan areas tend to be much smaller in population than in other urban areas of similar size.

20   The Paris metropolitan area (aire urbaine) has more than 1,700 local government authorities.

21   Italics are ours. Metadata Glossary, The World Bank, https://databank.worldbank.org/metadataglossary/world-development-indicators/series/EN.URB.MCTY#:~:text=According%20to%20the%20United%20Nations,without%20regard%20to%20administrative%20boundaries

22   For example, among Greater Capital City Statistical Areas of Australia with more than 1,000,000 residents, the core urban areas (core urban centres) accounted for only 22% of the metropolitan area (GCCSA) territory, with 78% of the land outside the urban area. This ranges from a high in the Perth urban centre of 27% to a low of 13% in the Brisbane core urban centre (Derived from 2016 census community profiles data).

23   Tertius Chandler (1987), *Four Thousand Years of Urban Growth: An Historical Census,* St. David's Press.

24   Demographia, *Demographia World Urban Areas,* 19th Annual Edition, August 2023, http://demographia.com/db-worldua.pdf

25   Shlomo Angel, Jason Parent, Daniel L. Civico, and Alejandro M. Blehttps, "The Persistent Decline in Urban Densities: Global and Historical Evidence of 'Sprawl'", 2010, Lincoln Institute of Land Policy Working Paper, www.lincolninst.edu/sites/default/files/pubfiles/1834_1085_angel_final_1.pdf

26   By contrast, the term "suburb" is used in Australia to denote geography corresponding to a post code in urban areas, regardless of location. This chapter uses the international definition. The Oxford Reference definition is "The outer part of a city or urban area, close to the urban-rural boundary, with limited commercial land use and low-density residential development. Also known as suburbia."

27   Today's core LGAs, except for London (Inner London, which was the London County Council as of 1965), Tokyo, defined as the 23 special wards constituting the core LGA until

1943, Mexico City as of 1950, Shanghai (Present districts of Yangpu, Hongkou, Zhabei, Puto, Changning, Jing'an, Luwan, Huangpu and Xuhui), and Lagos (Lagos Island LGA).

28   No single source provides fully comparable data for world urban areas or metropolitan areas. Any analysis requires consulting multiple sources, which though not completely consistent, are sufficiently comparable so to indicate general trends. This 1950 to 2021 is based on national statistical bureau sources, the United Nations, and *Demographia World Urban Areas: June 2021*, our product that relies upon the European Commission Global Human Settlement Layer (GHS2015) 250 meter grid (https://ghsl.jrc.ec.europa.eu/ghs_pop2019.php) In this report, the latest source data is adjusted to 2021 by population projection rates.

29   Wendell Cox (May 2022), "Suburbanizing Canada: The 2021 Census," Frontier Centre for Public Policy https://fcpp.org/wp-content/uploads/FB129_Suburbanizing_MA2522_F2.pdf

30   Wendell Cox (April, 2022), "All Major Metropolitan Area Growth Outside Urban Core: Latest Year", *New Geography*, 28 April 2022, https://www.newgeography.com/content/007430-all-major-metropolitan-area-growth-outside-urban-core-latest-year

31   Wendell Cox (June 2022), "Tokyo, Osaka & Nagoya Cores: Migration Losses", *New Geography*, 10 June 2022 https://www.newgeography.com/content/007476-tokyo-osaka-na-goya-cores-migration-losses

32   Wendell Cox (July 2022), "Korea: Moving to the Suburbs of Seoul", *New Geography*, 3 July 2022, https://www.newgeography.com/content/007504-korea-moving-suburbs-seoul

33   Data derived from 2016 census.

34   ABS, *Building Approvals, Australia,* December 2023, https://www.abs.gov.au/statistics/industry/building-and-construction/building-approvals-australia/latest-release

35   Derived from 2021 census.

36   Derived from American Community Survey 2016-2020.

37   Statistics Bureau, Ministry of Internal Affairs and Communications, Dwellings by Type of Dwelling, Type of Building (2008 to 2018), https://www.stat.go.jp/data/nenkan/70nenkan/zuhyou/y702103000.xlsx

38   Derived from BRE Trust, *The Housing Stock of The United Kingdom,* February 2020https://files.bregroup.com/bretrust/The-Housing-Stock-of-the-United-Kingdom_Report_BRE-Trust.pdf

39   Table 254: Housing supply: indicators of new supply, England https://assets.publishing.service.gov.uk/government/uploads/system/uploads/attachment_data/file/1084088/LiveTable254.ods

40   Derived from BRE Trust, op. cit.

41   Sotheby's International Realty, *2018 Modern Home Family Trends Report,* https://sothebysrealty.ca/insightblog/en/2018/11/01/2018-modern-family-home-ownership-trends-report/; Wendell Cox, 'Canadian Families Denied Preferred Detached Houses, Forced into Condos: Survey", *New Geography,* 9 January 2019, https://www.newgeography.com/content/006189-canadi-an-families-denied-preferred-detached-houses-forced-condos-survey

42   Shlomo Angel, Alejandro M. Blei, Jason Parent, Patrick Lamson-Hall, and Nicolas Garlar-za Sanchez, with Daniel L. Civco, Rachel Qian Lei, and Kevin Thom, *Atlas of Urban Expansion - 2016 Edition*, Lincoln Institute of Land Policy, October 2016, https://www.lincolninst.edu/publications/other/atlas-urban-expansion-2016-edition

43   No single source provides fully comparable data for world urban areas or metropolitan areas. Any analysis requires consulting multiple sources, which though not completely

consistent, are sufficiently comparable so to indicate general trends. This 1950 to 2021 is based on national statistical bureau sources, the United Nations, and Demographia World Urban Areas: June 2021, our product that relies upon the European Commission Global Human Settlement Layer (GHS2015) 250 metre grid. In this report, the latest source data is adjusted to 2021 by population projection rates.

44   Shlomo Angel, Patrick Lamson-Hall, Alejandro Blei, Sharad Shingade and Suman Kumar, "Densify and Expand: A Global Analysis of Recent Urban Growth", *Sustainability* 2021, 13, 3835, https://www.mdpi.com/2071-1050/13/7/38355

45   Demographia, *16ᵗʰ Annual Demographia International Housing Affordability Survey: 2020*, http://www.demographia.com/dhi2020.pdf

46   OECD, Rethinking Urban Sprawl, 14 June 2018, https://www.oecd.org/publications/rethinking-urban-sprawl-9789264189881-en.htm

47   Wendell Cox, "Higher Urban Densities Associated with the Worst Housing Affordability", *New Geography*, 18 October 2021, https://www.newgeography.com/content/007221-higher-urban-densities-associated-with-worst-housing-affordability

48   Ross Kendall and Peter Tulip, *The Effect of Zoning on Housing Prices*, Reserve Bank of Australia, Research Discussion Paper RDP 2018-03 https://www.rba.gov.au/publications/rdp/2018/pdf/rdp2018-03.pdf

49   Investor's Business Daily, "Don't Tell Anyone, But We Just Had Two Years of Record-Breaking Global Cooling", 16 May 2018, https://www.investors.com/politics/editorials/climate-change-global-warming-earth-cooling-media-bias/

50   Liz Allen, Anna Reimondos and Edith Gray, "Fewer Occupants, More Bedrooms: Census Shows Australians Prefer Bigger Houses", *The Conversation*, 29 June 2012, http://theconversation.com/fewer-occupants-more-bedrooms-census-shows-australians-prefer-bigger-houses-7871

51   Wendell Cox, "Record Low Congestion Levels - Seattle, LA, San Francisco: the 2021 Urban Mobility Report", *New Geography*, 9 July 2021, https://www.newgeography.com/content/007104-record-low-congestion-levels-seattle-la-san-francisco-the-2021-urban-mobility-report

52   FreddieMac, *In Pursuit of Affordable Housing: The Migration of Homebuyers within the U.S. - Before and After the Pandemic*, Research Note, 22 June 2022 https://www.freddiemac.com/research/insight/20220622-pursuit-affordable-housing-migration-homebuyers-within?twclid=2-6qlpgd-8biko7u5cp4vuysnvfh

53   Demographia, *16ᵗʰ Annual Demographia International Housing Affordability Survey: 2020*, http://www.demographia.com/dhi2020.pdf

54   Toshio Meronek, "YIMBYs Exposed: The Techies Hawking Free Market 'Solutions' to the Nation's Housing Crisis", *In These Times*, May 21 June Issue https://inthesetimes.com/features/yimbys_activists_san_francisco_housing_crisis.html

55   Antonia Stolark, "Socialism Against Sprawl", *Socialist Forum*, Winter 2019, https://socialistforum.dsausa.org/issues/winter-2019/socialism-against-sprawl/

56   Paul Bergeron, "Tech Companies Cast Their Eyes on Apartment Portfolios", *Globest*, 16 June 2022 https://www.globest.com/2022/06/16/tech-companies-cast-their-eyes-on-apartment-portfolios/?kw=Tech+Companies+Cast+Their+Eyes+on+Apartment+Portfolios

57   Victoria Fierce, "Opinion: Why Building Housing Near Mass Transit Promotes Collectivism", *East Bay Express*, 9 April 2018, https://eastbayexpress.com/opinion-why-building-housing-near-mass-transit-promotes-collectivism-2-1/

58   Robert Stilson, "The Left's Campaign for Socialized Housing", *The American Conservative*, 20 August 2021 https://www.theamericanconservative.com/urbs/the-lefts-campaign-for-socialized-housing/

59   Aleksandra Vayntraub, "More than half of Americans believe they can build generational wealth", *SWNS Digital*, 6 July 2022, https://swnsdigital.com/us/2022/07/more-than-half-of-americans-believe-they-can-build-generational-wealth/

60   Dana Anderson, "Affordability is the Number-One Factor Keeping Renters From Becoming Homeowners: Redfin Survey", *REDFIN News*, 7 April 2022, https://www.redfin.com/news/survey-renters-homebuying-affordability/

61   Samuel J. Abrams, "Op-Ed: Is the dream of owning a home losing its appeal?", *Los Angeles Times*, 7 March 2021, https://www.latimes.com/opinion/story/2021-03-07/homeownership-american-dream-survey-values

62   Claire Thompson, "Millennial medium chill: What the screwed generation can teach us about happiness", *Grist*, 30 April 2013, https://grist.org/living/millennial-medium-chill/

63   Lisa Hymas, "Say it loud - I'm childfree and I'm proud", *Grist*, 31 May 2010 https://grist.org/article/2010-03-30-gink-manifesto-say-it-loud-im-childfree-and-im-proud/

64   Katie Warren, "Millennials don't want to buy Boomers' sprawling, multi-bedroom homes", *Australian Financial Review*, 29 May 2019, https://www.afr.com/real-estate/residential/millennials-don-t-want-to-buy-boomers-sprawling-multi-bedroom-homes-20190329-p518rs

65   For example, see Julia Falcon, "Millennials want a single-family house, even if it means a long commute", *Housing Wire*, 22 November 2019, https://www.housingwire.com/articles/millennials-want-a-single-family-house-even-if-it-means-a-long-commute/

66   Wendell Cox, "Suburban Nations: Canada, Australia and the United States", New Geography, 30 December 2016, http://www.newgeography.com/content/005495-suburban-nations-canada-australia-and-united-states

67   National Association of Realtors, *2016 Profile of Home Buyers and Sellers*, 2016 https://www.nar.realtor/sites/default/files/reports/2016/2016-profile-of-home-buyers-and-sellers-10-31-2016.pdf

68   Kris Hudson, "Generation Y Prefers Suburban Home Over City Condo", *The Wall Street Journal*, 21 January 2015, http://www.wsj.com/articles/millennials-prefer-single-family-homes-in-the-suburbs-1421896797

69   Ryan Dezember, "House Money: Wall Street Is Raising More Cash Than Ever for Its Rental-Home Gambit", *The Wall Street Journal*, 9 July 2018, https://www.wsj.com/articles/house-money-wall-street-is-raising-more-cash-than-ever-for-its-rental-home-gambit-1531128600

70   Jerry Dunleavy, "China is top foreign buyer of US Housing at $6.1 billion last year", *Washington Examiner*, 21 July 2022, https://www.washingtonexaminer.com/foreign-policy/news/china-top-foreign-buyer-us-housing-6-billion-2021

71   Simon Neville, "Lloyds Bank aims to be UK's biggest private landlord by 2025", *Independent*, 19 August 2021, https://www.independent.co.uk/business/lloyds-bank-aims-to-be-uk-s-biggest-private-landlord-by-2025-b1905081.html

72   Erik Sherman, "While For Sale Demand Weakens, SFR Stays Optimistic, *Globest*, 28 June 2022 https://www.globest.com/2022/06/28/while-for-sale-demand-weakens-sfr-stays-optimistic/?kw=While%20For-Sale%20Demand%20Weakens%2C%20SFR%20Stays%20Optimistic&utm_source=email&utm_medium=enl&utm_campaign=spotlightonalert&utm_content=20220628&utm_term=rem

73   Lisa Boone, "Must Reads: They don't own homes. They don't have kids. Why millennials are plant addicts", *Los Angeles Times,* 25 July 2018, http://www.latimes.com/home/la-hm-millennials-plant-parents-20180724-story.html.

74   Ryan Dezember, op. cit

75   Gillian B. White, "Millennials Who Are Thriving Financially Have One Thing in Common", *The Atlantic,* 15 July 2015 https://www.theatlantic.com/business/archive/2015/07/millennials-with-rich-parents/398501/

76   Wojciech Kopczuk and Joseph P. Lupton, *To Leave or Not to Leave: The Distribution of Bequest Motives,* NBER Working Paper 11767, https://www.nber.org/papers/w11767.pdf

77   Joel Kotkin, "Property and Democracy in America", *New Geography,* 22 September 2019, https://www.newgeography.com/content/006419-property-and-democracy-america

4

Land Use and Transportation Dynamics in Modern Cities

Peter Gordon

Adam Smith famously asked why some nations are rich and others poor. It's still a great question. Many discussions and elaborations have since followed and there will surely be more.

The outcomes that we in the rich countries cherish, our prosperity and the possibility of flourishing, are delivered via the magic of the market. This is more than a glib cliche; it refers to the uncountable number of complex supply chains that emerge (and are continuously managed almost unnoticed) to serve us. Shoppers casually take items off shelves and have not the slightest idea how they got there. "A humble cup of coffee requires 29 firms to collaborate across 18 countries ..."[1] And that's just a cup of coffee. Even better, consumers need not worry over any of the details. We only need to know about the last mile: where do we go to make the purchase?

Under what conditions do we get this happy outcome? Here is Smith again: To "carry a state to the highest degree of opulence from the lowest barbarism, [requires nothing] but peace, easy taxes, and a *tolerable* administration of justice." (1776; italics inserted). Smith was concise. We can elaborate.

Most supply chains develop and succeed in cities. The link between cities (actually metropolitan areas which better approximate labour markets) and prosperity seems fairly clear. Cities have been called "engines of growth". Edward Glaeser went further, calling cities "our greatest invention."[2] Once beyond a size threshold, cities become the places where a variety of characters encounter other smart and perhaps congenial characters. All these characters have brains; brains are networks of chemically connected neurons and connected brains are bigger networks. Having found each other, these characters start to exchange and test ideas. They may even decide to go further and co-venture in business. Interaction is fundamental to how imaginative people develop and cultivate new thoughts, insights, and projects. What could be more essential for discovery and human flourishing?

What are some essentials? First, the city (the metropolitan area, the local market) must be big enough for specialisation to pay off. Specialisation is necessary for diversification. A diversified portfolio is usually the safest. The biggest metropolitan areas remain atop the city size distributions because they are capable of nurturing new industries to replace declining ones. The smaller places are less likely to pull off this survival trick. In Australia, the Sydney and Melbourne metropolitan areas have been the biggest for some years. Around the world, Beijing, London, Tokyo, Istanbul have stayed atop national size distributions for many years.

Metropolitan areas are many things. Economists see them as labour markets, places that somehow match specialised jobs with highly specialised workers. Many analysts, however, work with highly aggregated available data which obscure the real-world variability of skills and jobs. Not all medical doctors want a job working in all of the sub-specialties of medicine. Likewise, not all math professors are comfortable teaching any area of mathematics, etc. Not all engineers can operate in any of the many sub-fields of engineering. There are uncountable examples of the same simple idea. All workers are most comfortable (and most productive) doing what they do best. There is usually some unemployment due to labour market mismatch, when unemployed workers find they cannot easily transfer their skills.

In popular discussions, planning is presumed to be a top-down (government) activity. But this misses the point that all individuals, all households, all businesses make plans. Markets famously reconcile and coordinate the plans of an uncountable number of people and firms. Cooperation and coordination occur because all the decision makers are guided by market prices. Market-based prosperity is in great part attributable to all of this bottom-up planning. It is now true that most modern market economies are a blend of top-down and bottom-up plans. There are many views on what the best mix, the best doses of each, might be. Matt Ridley noted that "We have erred on the side of thinking that things are more top-down than they are."[3] Who are "we"? Inevitably, there are many with (or seeking) political influence who support the top-down view.

In light of real-world complexity, can labour market matching be accomplished top-down? Top-down is always risky. Information is dispersed; no one person or group has all of it. This is why we rely on markets to provide our daily bread – and much more. This is also why central planning of an economy has been abandoned almost everywhere. Where it remains, people's material lives are poor and their personal lives are precarious because a police state is required to control people who sense they are deprived and that those in control live well simply because they are on top. Yet, remarkably, many people around the world cling to the idea that urban development must be managed top-down.

Many city planners believe they can manage labour market matching via planned jobs-housing balance. They do not accept that it is better to allow enough land use flexibility to let workers and employers figure out where they can operate best. In light of the immense complexity, market-based matching is more promising. It is essential for productivity and competitiveness to be sustained. Highly specialised workers must find employers. Employers must find the specialists they need.

Spatial organisation and infrastructure must each be accommodating. Many studies have found that the thirty-minute (or less) commute is achieved by a surprisingly large number of commuters in many cities of the developed world. Where it occurs, this is auspicious because such favourable outcomes (wherever we find them) occur on networks that are badly managed. Recall from Econ 101 that unpriced resources will be used inefficiently. Urban economists have for many years urged that peak-load pricing be implemented on urban roads. Modern technologies make it inexpensive to set up and manage. Yet, serious attempts around the world are few, with possible exceptions being London, Singapore, and Stockholm.[4] Most politicians remain reluctant to try or even propose it. They worry about being seen as taking away what many people think of as "free stuff." Moreover, planners and policy makers around the world seemingly prefer to build new facilities to managing the facilities already in place. It is hard to compete with ribbon-cutting opportunities. I bring this up to make the point that it is amazing that the thirty-minute (or less) commute remains widespread.

Not only do land markets and transportation markets have to cope with the limitations imposed by politics but local history is inevitably influential. Writing about our major modern cities, analysts find it convenient to emphasize the legacies of the various transportation (and communications) modes dominant in various eras. For example, some cite the "walking city" era (pre-1880), the "streetcar city" (1880-1920), the "automobile city" (post-1920) – and perhaps eventually the "smartphone city" (post-2010)?[5] Most structures are durable and depreciate at different rates, so most cities include remnants from previous eras. In each period, opportunities and also preferences were formed and evolved in light of the possibilities perceived by businesses and residents.[6]

Yet, of all the cases of improved mobility and innovative technologies re-shaping cities, the 20th century's massive and fast-paced switch to the internal combustion engine stands out. Few technologies have impacted so many people's lives so profoundly and so quickly. In their personal as well as their business lives, many discovered new location options, new ways of communicating and operating, and even new lifestyles. As often happens, new ways were continuously imagined, tested, and refined. Many businesses were no longer tied to rail yards or ports or raw materials sites. People and businesses recognised and appreciated new freedom and footlooseness. Geographic dispersion of all sorts of activities was the unmistakable result. It is on-going and has likely accelerated in the post-COVID years. People and businesses were prompted to use the internet in new ways. Many chose to order home deliveries instead of in-person shopping. Many accepted the option of attending meetings and classes via Zoom. This revolution is probably just starting. Technological change, lifestyle changes and some institutional change (adaptation) had to move almost in-sync. All three had to change, more or less together. In the recent pandemic, they did and thereby mitigated the shock. In so doing, they fast-forwarded the world toward the cities of the future. Of the three adaptations, the third involved the rules. That leg of the three-legged stool is usually the least reliable but was seemingly forced by events.

So much for the dynamics. Progressive Era thinking still dominates the city planning and governance professions in the modern advanced countries, including Australia. City planning is presumed to be "scientific" and best left to experts and professionals. But this view practically ignores powerful social and economic evolutions. Hayek saw the problem as planners' "fatal conceit" which combines an obliviousness to real world complexity with an amazing over-estimation of their (the "experts'") capabilities. It includes a misunderstanding of emergent orders, especially as they are seen in modern cities. Jacobs said it best: "[t]heir intricate order – a manifestation of the freedom of countless numbers of people to make and carry out countless plans – is in many ways a wonder".[7] No one can adequately plan an intricate order that involves millions of human free spirits.

There is relief provided by fact that large numbers of fairly rational free spirits are unlikely to parade lemming-like over the cliff. This is what the many traffic "doomsday" analyses miss. Employers and employees have strong incentives to co-locate to avoid onerous accessibility costs. While there are surely and inevitably outliers, always for peculiar and personal reasons, most commutes in many cities stay within a thirty-minute range. This is especially true where auto ownership levels are high. Recent U.S. data suggest a median below thirty minutes (FIG. 1). In fact, the thirty-minute limit has a remarkable history.[8]

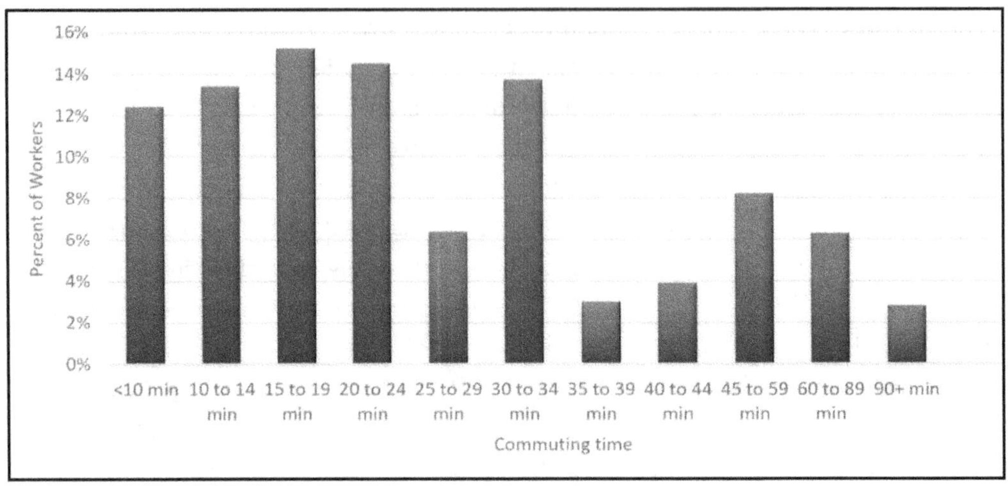

Figure 4.1: Proportions of American Workers with Various Commute Travel Times (all modes)

(Source: U.S. Census Bureau, American Community Survey, ACS 2018, 5-Year Estimates)

But the major Australian cities do not perform as well.[9] Wu and Levinson (2018) present data on thirty-minute commute accessibility for the major Australian metropolitan areas; Sydney and Melbourne each had less than 20 per cent of the jobs within a thirty-minute commute (all modes). What can be done? Improve access? Improve spatial organisation?

The latter is unlikely. What does it even mean? Spatial organisation is complex and best left to private choices. Intricate orders are just that – and simply beyond the capabilities of top-down planners to grasp or improve. That leaves improved access. Again, the answer seems too simple. Substantial mode shifts will not happen. Auto use is the overwhelming international favourite and that will remain. Yet, planners keep looking for ways to reduce auto use, not recognising that public transit, bicycling, and walking will remain marginal. The auto-highway system is dominant but underperforms in most cities because planners avoid time-of day pricing of roads or parking spaces. This means that default rationing must be by crowding (congestion).

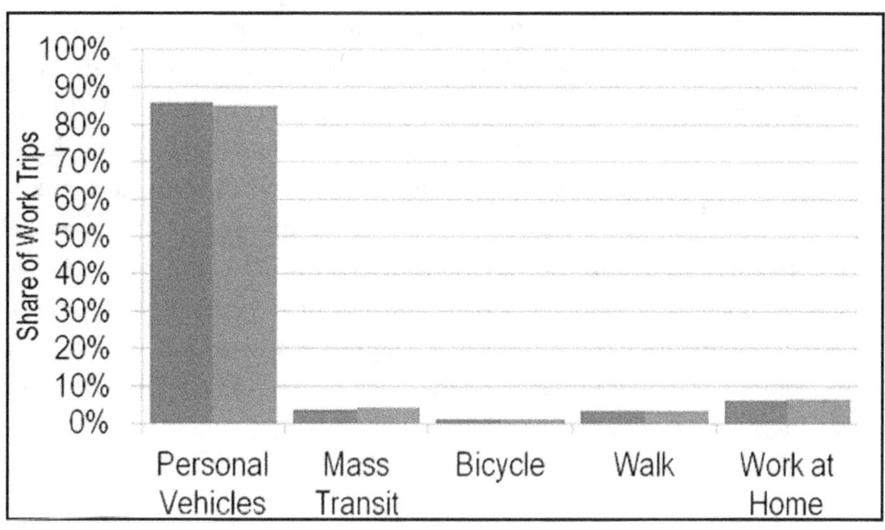

Figure 4.2: Work Trip Market Share: 2006-2011, Australia: Metropolitan Areas over 1,000,000

(Source: Demographia.com March 23, 2013)

When planners' reach exceeds their grasp, they seek simplifications to make their task manageable. "Compatible" land uses are one of planners' favourite fictions. The idea is that they can identify land uses that should be proximate. But reality is more complex. So the approach devolves into identifying broad land use categories (residential, industrial, commercial, etc.) and imagining that these can be somehow arranged by planners. But, in reality, location choice is complex. Large numbers of individuals are compelled to face this challenge and do the best they can. The results can be seen as "matching," or they can be seen as "compatible." These labels grossly over-simplify. The results come from people doing the best they can in the circumstances.

All this brings to mind the, by now apocryphal, story of the Soviet planner (or fellow traveller) who, visiting the West, asked "Who is in charge of bread distribution?" We may never know the look on the questioner's face when he heard the answer, "No one." How many consumers ever ask, let alone try to answer, the question? Some of them may suspect how much sustenance those living in planned-bread economies get. But no obesity worries.

Then there are those who do not comprehend the world but, nevertheless, are eager to change it. Planners and policy makers cannot change the world; utopians fail and/ or wreak havoc. These are not the visionaries we want.

What can plausibly be done? Where to start? An intriguing planning division of labour has been suggested by Professor Randall Holcombe.[10] Let the top-down planners plan all infrastructure; let bottom-up planners do all of the land use planning – taking all infrastructure, planned or in place, be the rules of the game. Let the "big picture" top-down planners as well as "skin in the game" developers (the bottom-up planners) specialise and join hands in this way. There is no blank slate of development, but perhaps we can get close. Vacant and undeveloped land should be freed from rules. Holcombe's suggested division of labour is most plausible on vacant and undeveloped land. It is unclear why these lands should be zoned in the first place. Unencumbered vacant land might be a good place to start. This is where the visionaries that are most needed, those ready to make bets with their own resources, might be encouraged to operate.

Endnotes

1   *The Economist,* 28 March 2020.

2   Paul Cheshire (2019) agreed. "My assessment is that cities are the most welfare enhancing innovation in human history: they empowered the division of labour, the invention of money, trade and technical inventions like the wheel - let alone government, the arts or culture."

3   Ridley, 2016.

4   London's and Stockholm's are not city-wide, but only inside a central area cordon.

5   Muller (2004) suggests "1. Walking-Horsecar Era (1800-1890) 2. Electric Streetcar Era (1890-1920) 3. Recreational Automobile Era (1920-1945) 4. Freeway Era (1945-present)" p. 29.

6   Nevertheless, Cox has shown that the six U.S."transit legacy cities" remain distinct.

7   Jacobs (p. 15, 1961). See also Bertaud (2018)

8   English (2019)

9   Wu and Levinson (2018)

10   Holcombe (2012)

References

Bertaud, Alain (2018) *Order Without Design: How Markets Shape Cities* The MIT Press

Cheshire, Paul (2019) "Paul Cheshire on Urban Economics" *The Unassuming Economist:* https://unassumingeconomist.com/2019/03/paul-cheshire-on-urban-economics/

English, Jonathan (2019) "The Commuting Principle That Shaped Urban History" *Bloomberg CityLab.* https://www.bloomberg.com/news/features/2019-08-29/the-commuting-principle-that-shaped-urban-history

Holcombe, Randall G. (2012) "Planning and the Invisible Hand: Allies or adversaries?" *Planning Theory,* 12(2), p. 199-210

Jacobs, Jane (1961) *The Death and Life of Great American Cities,* Random House.

Muller, Peter O. (2004) "Transportation and Urban Form: Stages in the Spatial Evolution of the American Metropolis" in S. Hanson (ed.) *The Geography of Urban Transportation* (3d ed.) New York: Guilford Press.

Ridley, Matt (2016) "The Evolution of Everything", *Cato Policy Report* (January/February).

Wu, Hao and David Levinson (2018) *Access Across Australia.* Sydney: University of Sydney.

5

Neighbourhood Essentials – the Importance of Local Shops and Services in New Suburbs

Robin Goodman and Annette Kroen

New suburbs built on the metropolitan edges of our cities are an important part of Australia's urban landscape, providing homes for a large proportion of new residents. In 2021, 20% of Australia's population was living in a "fast growing outer suburb" and between 2011 and 2016 those suburbs experienced an annual population growth rate of 3% which was nearly double the rate of Australia overall.[1] Growth in the outer suburbs has continued even during the migration restricted pandemic years of 2020-21, with Melbourne growth-areas adding an extra 36,600 in population while the overall metropolitan area declined by more than 60,000.[2] While planning policy tries to limit the outward expansion of cities, as long as new suburbs continue to be constructed it is vital that they provide the best possible living environments, in the most sustainable manner, for generations to come.

Much of the focus in planning new suburbs has been on housing and the basic layout of subdivision plans, with less attention paid to the provision of local shops, services and the detailed fine grain of community life. This is one of the factors that determines the higher cost of property prices in the inner areas, as people value the range of opportunities that a richer local environment can provide. Many new suburbs contain few places of employment, commercial or retail premises, particularly in the early years. Consequently, a high level of car dependence is built-in, with long delays in the arrival of any public transport infrastructure and services. Car dependency has many negative impacts, including traffic congestion, pollution, and poorer physical and mental health. While walking paths are generally constructed at the time of settlement, too little attention is paid to providing meaningful local destinations for people to walk to, from the outset.

This chapter describes how growth area residents experience the availability and accessibility of local destinations in their daily lives. After a brief overview of the current situation and published evidence we report on the lived experience of residents in two growth area suburbs in Melbourne, based on a survey questionnaire and interviews. The chapter concludes with some thoughts on how to enable the development of local destinations earlier in the lifetime of new suburbs.

Community, commuting and infrastructure in new suburbs

New suburbs are unlikely to offer many local jobs so most employed residents will need to undertake often quite lengthy commutes to get to work. Evidence shows that those who take public transport are more likely to incorporate walking into their daily journey than those who drive cars. However, public transport services are often provided to new suburbs years after residents move in, if at all. Residents can, and do, still walk for other purposes, and many new suburbs now offer pleasant paths and open space features which encourage leisurely strolls. However, having meaningful destinations such as shops, cafés, or community facilities will provide greater incentive for regular walking as part of healthy lifestyles, and therefore increase the amount of walking residents routinely do.

There has been some recent exploration of the lived experience of growth area residents in Melbourne investigating issues such as sense of community, costs of living, impacts on health and the transport situation.[3] Much of this research acknowledges the issue of a lack of infrastructure and services and the distance of existing amenities.

Affordability has been shown to be a key factor in the decision to move to the outer suburbs, closely followed by safety concerns, more spacious homes, and a family-centred environment with access to open and green space. Residents were found to be satisfied overall with their location, but were dissatisfied with the level of services, lack of infrastructure and the time needed for commuting. For example, there were tensions over developers failing to deliver infrastructure promises, such as a town centre, but also that residents were often unable to distinguish between private and public responsibility and services, for example whether the development of a park is a developer or council responsibility.[4] Some residents were also disappointed about the lack of community, particularly in relation to what had been promised through advertising, and because a lack of local facilities hinders the opportunity for a place-based sense of community.[5]

Residents are often committed to locality and would prefer to do more things locally.

So more local services are needed, and transport planning should focus on local mobility and not only on the journey to work.[6] One study points out the positive effect of the early establishment of a community centre in its case study but acknowledges that a community centre does not fulfil all needs for all residents so that the early provision of a range of spaces for residents to meet and interact is necessary.[7]

Planning for communities in growth areas

A large proportion of new fringe suburbs are planned as Master-Planned Estates (MPEs) or Master-Planned Communities (MPCs). These residential estates are generally of a larger size and plan for their own infrastructure and include a range of additional assets such as playgrounds, parks, schools, community hubs, and shops, providing a focus on local destinations. MPCs have often paid particular attention to building community and enabling local interaction, based on the idea that community can be facilitated through urban design, social amenities and places for social interaction.

State government planning for growth suburbs has become more focused on master-planning for mixed-use areas. In Victoria, Precinct Structure Plans are prepared by the Victorian Planning Authority (VPA) showing the layout of the prospective suburb including: housing lot yields; provision and location of employment land; transport networks; open space and natural systems; activity centres and community facilities. These plans create a structure for urban development and a framework for statutory planning controls so the differences between smaller-scale housing estates and larger-scale MPEs have become less pronounced.

The importance of local shops and services as destinations has been highlighted in recent "local living" planning concepts, such as the 20- and 30-minute neighbourhood in Melbourne and Sydney.[8] Several cities around the world have adopted similar concepts, and in general they refer to people being able to access (essential) daily services and amenities such as shops, schools, parks, public transport and jobs within the specified time limit (i.e. 15, 20 or 30 minutes) by walking. However, some cities, such as Sydney, also include public transport into the definition, while Melbourne, for example, specifies that the amenities should be accessible within a 20-minute *return* walk.

Yet, in many growth areas, town or community centres are one of the last things to be built, often because a certain size of population is needed for commercial viability. Residential densities have been increasing in growth areas but are generally still lower than in inner and middle suburbs, and development is staged and often starting with the lower density parts of the new suburbs. This means that quite a number of houses have to be built to achieve those sufficient customer numbers. At the same time developers often contend that external amenities need to be available to make smaller, medium density housing attractive to buyers. Supporting policies and improved coordination might be necessary to resolve this chicken and egg problem of densities and amenities.

The significance of local destinations for residents in two new suburbs in Melbourne

To understand the impact of development and planning in the growth areas on residents we conducted a study on two MPEs in the south-east and west of Melbourne. While the research covered a range of issues, here our focus lies on the significance of local destinations in the lived experience of growth area residents. We conducted a resident survey with 352 respondents in mid-2019 and follow-up interviews with 30 of the survey respondents later that year (see Kroen & Goodman 2022).[9]

The two case study estates each plan for about 1,300 houses, sites for schools and a town centre. Construction started in 2011/12 and the estates were mostly completed when the survey and interviews were undertaken, with the exception of the town centre in one of the estates, we will call Estate A. For this estate the two closest shopping centres were about 2.5km away for most residents and another one was about 4km away, while the other case study area, Estate B, had a small activity centre with a supermarket and other smaller shops (built around 2016).

The survey included questions about how important certain aspects were in residents' decision to move and how satisfied they were with aspects of their suburb. Perhaps unsurprisingly housing affordability featured highly in the decision to move with over 85% of respondents seeing it as very or quite important. However, access to destinations was also rated highly: living close to shops was very or quite important for 64% of respondents, followed by closeness to open space, 62%, and closeness to recreational facilities, 59%. Similarly, for 60% the ease of walking to places was very or quite important and for 68% the closeness to public transport.

This shows that the notion of the purely residential suburb and the belief sometimes expressed that residents who move to new suburbs do not mind a car-dependent lifestyle is not true. There will be some self-selection, i.e. people who strongly prefer walking and cycling will move to walkable inner and middle areas while people who do not care as much about walking and cycling move to outer areas. Yet, while affordability may have been the catalyst for moving, residents do still want to live close to shops, open space and recreational facilities and base their decision for a suburb on these aspects as well. Interviewees mentioned that they had specifically bought in their suburb because of the promise of a town centre even though this meant that prices were somewhat higher than in other areas. For other interviewees the access to shops and services had become more important since living in their suburb and experiencing a lack of access.

Most respondents expressed strong satisfaction with aspects of their neighbourhoods. In particular, 86% were happy with how easy and pleasant it was to walk around the neighbourhood, 77% with the number and quality of the parks in the neighbourhood. However, the highest levels of dissatisfaction were with time needed to travel to work (57%) and with the access to public transport (54%).

Unsurprisingly, satisfaction with access to shops and facilities differed quite strongly between the two case study areas (see Table 5:1), due most obviously to the differing level of service provision, as described previously. However, as might be expected, these attitudes within Estate B changed as services became available.

Table 5.1: Satisfaction with access to destinations

	Estate A		Estate B	
	Satisfied	Dissatisfied	Satisfied	Dissatisfied
Access to major roads/freeways	82%	13%	68%	30%
Access to public transport in my area	24%	73%	55%	39%
Access to fresh food shops	39%	57%	82%	14%
Access to cultural and recreational facilities	51%	40%	77%	9%
How easy and pleasant it is to walk in my area	87%	10%	95%	5%

Note: Missing percentages to 100% are respondents that have selected "neither". Satisfied = very or quite satisfied. Dissatisfied = very or quite dissatisfied.

Based on previous surveys[10], satisfaction with access to public transport increased between 2013 and 2015 when a bus started to run between the suburb and the nearest train station and shopping centre, and access to fresh food shops increased strongly between 2015 and 2019 after the retail centre with a supermarket and other smaller shops was built in the suburb.

The difference in access to destinations impacts on residents' daily lives (see Table 2). For Estate A nearly half (42%) of respondents who experienced travel restrictions had difficulties in going grocery shopping. In contrast, for Estate B only 24% of respondents who experienced travel restrictions reported difficulties with grocery shopping. Also, interviewees in Estate A stated that shops being further away combined with congestion meant that they shop less frequently and tend to do one large weekly shop by car. This meant that to some extent they bought less fresh food and got less physical activity from shopping, which could have an impact on their health and fitness. In contrast, interviewees in Estate B reported that they usually did one weekly shop with the car and then some local top-up trips, which were often by active transport.

Table 5.2: Did the transport restrictions you experienced make it hard for you to do any of the following?

	Estate A	Estate B
Participate in social or recreational activities	42%	39%
Visit a doctor or health professional	25%	30%
Go grocery shopping	42%	24%
Get to studying or training	25%	14%
Look for work or get to or from work	83%	82%

Residents stated that access to shops or a town centre in proximity is important to them because this offers the improved convenience of shopping more often and with this to buy more fresh food, the opportunity to walk to the shops or cafés, and potentially also the chance of community building through increased opportunities for (chance) meetings of other residents ("bumping into each other"). One further point mentioned in the interviews was access to ethnic specific food shops. Interviewees mentioned that they were going to a particular shopping centre because it had an Indian or Sri Lankan food shop, which may be something to consider for town centre development.

Interviewees in Estate A voiced their disappointment that certain infrastructure or services had not been delivered at the time of the interviews and after several years of having lived there. They emphasised in particular, the delay in arrival of the shopping centre, a bus service in the suburb, school and childcare. In that context, interviewees referred to perceived promises by the developer that had not been kept and cited the master plan that showed features such as bus routes or a shopping centre. Interviewees in Estate B referred to "broken promises" and "disappointment" to a lesser extent, which is very likely due to most infrastructure and services having been delivered at the time of the interviews. However, interviewees that had lived in Estate B for a longer time still mentioned that there were no shops or parks at the beginning.

It seems that the disappointment was caused by a combination of vague communication from the side of the developer and residents not verifying the timing of the infrastructure. Additionally, in the case of Estate A, the schedule had changed because the anticipated developer/supermarket chain of the shopping centre had pulled out.

This illustrates that better communication is needed about timing and that responsibilities and accountabilities need to be made clearer. It became apparent in the interviews that residents were not always sure who was responsible for which infrastructure and blamed either the developer for "dropping the ball" or council for not building certain infrastructure, and that they were also not clear about timing.

They did not necessarily expect the town centre and public transport in the suburb from day one, but they expected them to arrive soon after, stimulated by the perceived promises from the developer or real estate agents. Expectations of residents do also differ. While some residents expected "everything" to be there from early on, others expected that they will get "less" or will get some infrastructure or services later and they are comfortable with it, as this is also the reason why they paid less for a dwelling than elsewhere.

Translating principles into practice

Our research has shown that while access to a variety of destinations is one of the key elements considered when making the decision to move to a new suburb, it becomes even more important for residents once they have lived in the suburb for a while. It has also shown that the existence of local shops and services affects travel requirements and therefore residents' daily lives. We have seen that residents in the estate with an existing town centre were more satisfied with their access and reported shopping locally and walking to get there.

While this might not seem surprising, it is somewhat contrary to the general assumption often made that residents moving to those suburbs are prepared to drive everywhere and do not mind the car dependence of their suburb. When expectations of access to destinations felt to be necessary were not met, residents were dissatisfied and disappointed with the developer and/or the council. While our interviewees reported that they learned to adapt to the lack of access, it still had an impact on the feasibility of walking anywhere meaningful, and with this on their health and the volume of local car traffic. It should be noted that this research was undertaken before the COVID-19 pandemic and the lockdowns in Melbourne which saw many people working from home for long periods of time. It seems reasonable to assume that this experience will have strengthened the desire for more easily accessible local shops, services and other destinations to which one could walk or cycle.

Planning strategies support the further enrichment of local provision of mixed-use neighbourhood centres through the notion of the 20- or 30-minute city. However, planning practice, led as it is by an industry predominantly focused on residential housing, is slow to change. It is not only a question of a different design of those suburbs, but also of increased densities and more speedy and concentrated development to allow feasibility for business early on in the life of a new neighbourhood. All the elements needed for the 20-minute neighbourhood must be put in place as early as possible. The first residents should not have to wait for 5 or 10 years for their town centres and community spaces. While some of the negative impacts of a lack of infrastructure and services can be reversed, research suggests that travel behaviour patterns are shaped in the first 12-18 months.[11]

While place-based community has become somewhat less important for urban societies, it is still important, particularly for new communities where local networks and trust are still to be built, and also for recent migrants who are developing new social networks. More local facilities can improve community cohesion as residents have more informal interactions in local spaces. As earlier studies have pointed out, well-designed physical and social infrastructure can support informal and spontaneous social connection, facilitating a sense of belonging, while conversely in areas with inadequate infrastructure there is a higher likelihood for social isolation. Parks can play a similar role to town centres in community building through enabling informal interaction, and in our study residents were very satisfied with their local parks and the foot and cycle paths within those parks and open spaces overall. But not all residents will use parks and a variety of informal meeting spaces is needed.

Shops and services need a certain customer base to be viable. Increased densities and more speedy development, by concentrating on developing fewer areas at a time, would assist the achievement of this. Additionally, there is the need to think about alternative ways to provide and facilitate local facilities from the beginning. For some early services, temporary and/or adaptive structures could be utilised. For example, the developer's display centre can be combined with a café or convenience store or a community centre and a childcare centre. Other more creative possibilities could come from coordination and collaboration between those stakeholders and potentially also some easing of planning regulations.

Our research has shown that that there is extensive interest in increased coordination and collaboration for early delivery of services amongst the more innovative developers and state and local government planners. Improved coordination and staging of development would assist in earlier provision of services and clear communication of this could also help with confusion around responsibilities and expectations of residents towards infrastructure delivery. The creation of whole communities needs to be the stated aim, not just the provision of more affordable housing, vital though that is. This thinking about elements needed to make a thriving local community is there in our planning strategies, it now needs to appear on the ground, in the new suburbs we are now constructing which will last for generations to come.

Endnotes

1   id consulting (2018) *State of Australia's Fast Growing Outer Suburbs The economic & demographic transition of the Fast Growing Outer Suburbs.* Prepared for the NGAA; id consulting (2022) Australia Regional Profile and National Growth Areas Alliance Community Profile. Available at https://home.id.com.au/demographic-resources/.

2   Victorian Planning Authority, *Research Quarterly,* June 2022.

3   J. Smith, C. Waite, D. Lohm, M. Saberi, D. Arunachalam (2021) "Understanding the Lived Experiences of Housing and Transport Stress in the 'Affordable' Outer Ring: A Case Study of Melbourne, Australia", *Urban Policy and Research* (online); F.J. Andrews, L. Johnson, E. Warner (2018) "'A tapestry without instructions' Lived experiences of community in an outer suburb of Melbourne, Australia", *Journal of Urbanism: International Research on Placemaking and Urban Sustainability,* 11(3), 257-276; L. Nicholls, C. Maller, K. Phelan, (2017) "Planning for community: understanding diversity in residents experiences and expectations of social connections in a new urban fringe housing estate, Australia", *Community, Work & Family,* 20 (4), 405–423; L. Johnson, F. Andrews, E. Warner (2017) "The Centrality of the Australian Suburb: Mobility Challenges and Responses by Outer Suburban Residents in Melbourne", *Urban Policy and Research,* 35(4), 409-423.

4   D. Warr, B. Robson. (2013) "'Everybody's different': struggles to find community on the suburban frontier", *Housing Studies,* 28 (7), 971–992.

5   L. Buys, C. Newton, N. Walker (2021) "The Lived Experience of Residents in an Emerging Master-Planned Community", *Sustainability 2021, 13.*

6   L. Johnson, et al, op. cit.

7   L. Nicholls et al, op. cit.

8   *Plan Melbourne 2017-2050* and *The Greater Sydney Region Plan - A Metropolis of Three Cities*

9 A. Kroen, R. Goodman (2022) *The lived transport experience of residents in Melbourne's growth areas.* Unpublished Briefing Paper. RMIT University, Melbourne.

10 VicHealth 2016, *Planning and designing healthy new communities: Selandra Rise: Research summary,* Victorian Health Promotion Foundation, Melbourne.

11 S. Pemberton, A. Kroen, L. Gunn, R. Goodman (2021) *Behavioural change: Internal Working Paper for the 'Early delivery of healthy and equitable transport options in new suburbs' project.* RMIT Briefing Paper, RMIT University: Melbourne.

6

The Master Planned Community: Time for a Drastic Re-think

Peter Walters

Introduction

The Master Planned Community (MPC) is the latest manifestation of Australia's evolving outer suburban landscape. These large, single-developer housing estates are now the model for most greenfield residential development and offer the resident a relatively affordable home with the assurance of front-loaded retail, educational, and recreational amenities. A long-term commercial vision and an ongoing relationship with planning authorities over the life of an MPC development have delivered vastly improved outcomes for residents when compared with the MPC's piecemeal outer suburban predecessors.

While the MPC can be considered an improvement on the past, it is not a suburban revolution. In the first decades of the 21st century, Australians are facing the twin crises of housing affordability and climate change while fundamentally changing how they work and relate to their local environment. To meet these challenges, the state and the market need to combine for a radical rethink of the spatiality and built form of new suburbs. This includes how MPCs are constructed to deal with climate change and how our new "nation of renters" is treated and accommodated in what used to be considered the landscape of the homeowning Australian Dream. In this chapter, I will describe the MPC as a continuation of an Australian suburban tradition and outline its strengths and challenges. I will conclude with thoughts on how and why governments need to take radical measures to create a level playing field for more courageous developer innovation to underwrite the social, environmental and economic future of Australian suburbs and their residents.

The suburban dream

The Australian suburban dream runs deep in our national psyche. This cultural preference for a backyard, a garage and all they imply has strong historical and cultural origins – much of our national mythology is deeply suburban. Although the terrain is becoming more complex, the historical driver of housing growth on the fringe of Australian cities is still the sustained desire to live in a detached house in the suburbs.

The urban frontier, the edge of the metropolis, has traditionally been where Australians find the most affordable new home. Until the late 20th century, suburban development in Australian cities was comparatively piecemeal. Subdivisions of greenfield land were carried out by small-scale speculative developers, with much of suburbia until World War 2 developed by small-scale "do-it-yourself" operators, with residential architecture maintaining a local vernacular in response to climate, available building materials and localised builders.[1] By the 1950s, most Australians owned a car, and suburban development was now serviced by roads rather than strong public transport networks on the assumption that cars were the most efficient and preferable form of daily transport. This assumption began the car-based sprawl of Australian suburbia.

New outer suburbs in the second half of the 20th century began their lives as dirt-yard wastelands, where new homeowners had to wait patiently for the schools, shopping centres and sporting fields that followed settlement on the suburban frontier. As debt-wary local and State Governments became less willing to finance and subsidise infrastructure, living environments and amenities on the city fringe, new residential developments became places of low or slowly developing amenity. In many cases, efficient public transport would never be viable and never arrive.

The whole package?

Compared with 20th century suburban developments, the city's frontier is now less of a wilderness, with a far shorter wait for amenity for new residents. The outer suburban master-planned community (MPC) is the latest incarnation of the (relatively) affordable new suburban estate and now dominates this form of development in Australian cities. MPCs are built at scale by a single large developer on the greenfield urban fringe. Prominent market players have the resources to consolidate large enough parcels of land for development at a feasible price. The scale of the MPC allows developers, depending on size and resources, to offer new residents a more or less complete package of retail, recreational and educational amenities. Much of it is introduced in the early years to enhance the development's appeal and provides buyers with early investment security. Although MPCs are often built on a scale that can test the planning capacity of local governments, they are generally welcomed as a solution to the problem of housing and associated infrastructure provision at scale.

Restrictive building covenants, uniformity in landscaping design and clear entry statements provide the MPC with a coherent character that separates it from the surrounding suburbs, which are often older low-income suburbs and sites of disadvantage. This difference gives the new bounded MPC an air of exclusivity compared to its environs. Amenity is planned and coordinated in advance; the developer has long-term agreements with local councils and education providers. Mass production project home builders compete to offer the cheapest homes they can build. In this cutthroat world, competition allows the buyer the possibility of an affordable house and land, knowing that the developer will facilitate shops, schools, and green space in an acceptable timeframe. The coherence in street design, landscaping and the naming of neighbourhoods provides the new resident with the beginnings of a sense of place. Better-resourced developers employ community design specialists to stimulate a sense of community. They facilitate the establishment of community groups, sporting clubs and, in concert with marketing teams, a series of cyclical events and celebrations that provide the new community with a contrived sense of evolving place history. All this activity, wrapped up in sophisticated marketing campaigns, presents the new estate as a readymade community.

The MPC also differs markedly from its more piecemeal suburban predecessors in perceived and actual governance. Larger developments, such as Yarrabilba on the edge of Logan City or Aura on the Sunshine Coast, can take up to 30 years to be fully developed and sold. During this time, the property developer retains a high degree of control over the development type, scale and aesthetics. The high visibility of the developer, its efforts to create community and the constant associated marketing mean the development company comes to be seen as a de facto local authority, regardless of the role of the actual local government. This enduring presence gives these larger developments the impression of a highly privatised or commodified offering where the state's role becomes less visible than the role of the market, masking the extensive and ongoing negotiations between the developer and the legal planning authority.

The future is with us

While the MPC is a substantial improvement on its greenfield predecessors, there are some critical questions about whether this is a sustainable model for suburban development given the social, environmental, and economic challenges Australia is facing as a society now and into the future.

The first and perhaps most critical threat to the way of life of ordinary Australians is unaffordable housing. Australian suburbs transformed in the last decades of the 20th century. A combination of generous tax write-offs on residential investment property, capital-gains tax discounts, land supply shortages, high levels of immigration, increasing interest in housing from overseas investors and the knock-on effect of high demand for gentrifying inner-city property has led to a long and consistent speculator-led property boom since the 1990s. While this has been a bonanza for existing property owners generally those in the Baby Boomer and early Generation X cohorts, it has disastrously affected housing affordability for younger and more disadvantaged Australians. The median price of a dwelling in Australia's capital cities has grown in real terms by over 400 per cent since 1980, while the median wage has only doubled[2], creating a crisis in affordability for low-income Australians, many of whom are young. Although the outer suburban MPC is the cheapest way to buy a new house in Australian capital cities, Australia has the second worst income-to-house price ratios in the world.[3,4] Homeownership is now out of reach for many young people, with median house prices at multiples of between five- and nine-times annual median income.[5]

This long boom has shifted how people perceive their homes, and the house as an investment category now threatens our understanding of housing as somewhere to live. Stories of large windfall profits, encouraged by the real estate media and enabled by an accommodating tax regime, "flipping" homes for quick profits or buying multiple leveraged investment properties is a new marker of economic success. The discourse of property riches for the taking has been further reinforced by popular entertainment media, with television shows such as "Hot Property", "Auction" and "The Block" normalising and celebrating spectacular profits through astute property investment and home renovation.

Housing unaffordability means MPCs, contrary to historical stereotypes, are not the "mortgage belt" they once were. Housing unaffordability is slowly turning us into a nation of renters, with 30 per cent of Australian households renting, up from 20 per cent at the turn of the century. This figure rises to 60 per cent for those under 35.[6] Although renting your house is barely more affordable than buying it, renting is the only option for many who have little chance of accumulating sufficient capital for a deposit that will qualify them for a mortgage. Although historically, renters tended to concentrate in the inner city, they are now spread evenly across the metropolis, including outer suburban MPCs, where, depending on location, renters can comprise up to 50 per cent of residents.[7]

The nature of renting in Australia also means that leases are relatively short and can be terminated at short notice. This, combined with the more speculative nature of homeownership described above, means that population turnover in the outer suburbs can be high – more than 40% of Australian households reported moving within the last five years.[8] Strong vested interests and a lack of political will means there is little likelihood that housing will become more affordable for young and low-income Australians. There is a strong historical thread in suburban Australia of the dignity and independence of private home ownership.[9] As a legacy, contemporary research has shown that homeowners in the suburbs are still wary of renters and can view them as transient and unreliable, threatening the order of the suburb and property values.[10] This wariness can extend to homeowners' sense of reciprocity and shared understanding of belonging with renters, whom owners can view as somehow flawed in their pursuit of the Australian Dream.[11]

Developers and house builders have had to respond to price pressures and, more recently, the rapidly escalating building costs created by global supply chain challenges, resulting in cheaply built and environmentally unsustainable housing. Despite the provision of front-loaded amenity in MPCs, the quality of new housing has deteriorated to meet the limited purchasing power of new homebuyers. Smaller house blocks are filled with cheaply built project homes that will not stand the test of time. Builders cannot deliver environmentally sustainable housing in this market, so new homes are not designed for the climate in which they are located; instead, they are mass-produced across national markets. Houses have low ceilings, thin walls, a lack of space between them for natural ventilation or a tree canopy, and dark roofs without eaves. Builders are not able to position or design houses for passive solar orientation. Environmentally sustainable building measures are "add-ons" rather than inherent in the design of houses. New homes in MPCs are anything but climate resilient, requiring expensive additional heating and cooling depending on the climate.

While marketers liberally use the term "community" for all forms of new residential development, it has a particular role in the positioning and marketing of new MPCs. Much care is taken to present the development as an "already existing" community to buyers. Shapers of popular perceptions, particularly marketers and politicians, often position community in terms of strong bonds to a place, deep reciprocal relationships and an ethic of mutual care. This idea can be a desirable one. However, achieving this reciprocal care and responsibility requires a mutual need. Strong geographical communities have declined since the advent of the modern industrial city 150 years ago. The reality of contemporary urban life is that we have moved a long way from the village, where we relied on one another for day-to-day survival and wellbeing. The market and the government now take care of most of this on our behalf. We are free now to form strong networked communities that transcend place. It is no longer necessary to have a strong relationship with our neighbours to have a strong and supportive community. Our closest relationships are functions of work, school, sporting clubs, churches and other non-place based social histories before we move to a new suburb.

Having said this, we still desire a strong *sense* of community and belonging, which fulfils psychological rather than material needs. A sense of community develops over time and is related to feelings of security, trust in our lived environment, commonality, routine casual encounter, and a sense of shared destiny and accomplishment.

Work patterns and practices are changing rapidly. Suburbs are no longer the dormitories they once were, emptying during the day while adults lived their working lives far from home. The availability of cheap fast internet, secure communications and sophisticated networked applications have meant workers in white-collar and administrative roles have increasing freedom to work from home. The onset of COVID in 2020 forced a large section of the community back to their homes and neighbourhoods, and the practice of working from home has become normalised for at least part of the working week. A quick scan of Google Maps for any new suburban development reveals a myriad of home businesses embedded in the residential streets of new suburbs taking advantage of either advances in communications or the increasing number of clients in the local catchments for services like pet care, personal grooming and car repair.

Despite all this local activity during the day, the streets and small parks of new suburban developments remain largely empty during daylight hours, constrained by a spatial logic conceived for a life lived outside the suburb's boundaries during the working week. Retail is centralised, homogenous, primarily accessed by car and often hostile to casual encounter. Although developers are increasingly providing paths and trails for walking, due to the spatiality of the MPC, it does not offer viable point-to-point or function-to-function transport alternatives that entice residents out of their cars to accomplish everyday mundane tasks. Local parks designed for weekend recreation and the surveillance of children lack the nearby amenity to become effective third places where people can be "together alone" at different times of the day. This can mean people are confined mainly to the private realm of their homes during the week. New forms and rhythms of work mean the spatial logic of the outer suburb is becoming obsolete, missing the essential urban forms, use distribution and intimacy required to create a strong and welcoming public realm. In comparison, residents of wealthier older suburbs, designed in the 19th and early 20th century before universal car ownership, enjoy local, varied, and walkable amenities. In these older neighbourhoods, retail tends to be independent and idiosyncratic, with vibrant third places such as cafes, local libraries, public swimming pools and small parks in a truly "local" environment.

Bringing it all home

The market can now create coherent suburban master plans and work with local governments to implement a long-term vision to provide a high level of practical and social amenity in new greenfield suburban sites. Residents require less patience and pioneering spirit than they did a generation ago. The community building programs initiated by the more innovative developers can harness people's natural desire to connect socially and develop a sense of place and belonging.

However, the MPC is more of an improvement on the past than an urban revolution. Urban Australians, or in other words, most of us, are facing rapid social, environmental and economic challenges that require some more visionary decision-making and spending. Governments can no longer leave the heavy lifting of urban innovation to the market, constrained by current business models and risk appetite. Building more of what has historically delivered a commercial return may be sustainable in the short term. However, the quality of life for the average Australian, let alone those at the more disadvantaged end of the spectrum, is deteriorating.

Housing unaffordability is rapidly creating an underclass in Australia or severely limiting the life choices of those managing to keep up with their mortgage payments. In the short to medium term, the number of Australians renting their home will increase, and new housing developments need to be created with this in mind. There is still much that governments can do to create more direction and certainty in the market. For example, incentivising or subsiding build-to-rent developments as a part of a mixed tenure policy for all new developments while reforming tenancy laws to protect renters' long-term tenure, choice and security. Given that renters will continue to comprise a significant proportion of new suburban developments, any initiative to protect renter security and reduce housing mobility will make renters more invested in their communities. More secure, long-term residents contribute meaningfully to schools, associations and a general sense of place. The sustained presence of renters means the boundaries between renters and homeowners will blur, reducing the stigma of renting a home in the suburbs throughout the life course.

Central to promoting a sense of place and belonging is the recognition that suburbs are increasingly diverse places, expressed not just in housing tenure but culturally and occupationally. The flexibility to work and run small businesses from home is already transforming people's relationships with their local community. The traditional single-use zoning scheme applied to suburban developments needs to change if we hope for vibrant neighbourhoods rather than dormitories. The current model of developer-led, centralised and franchised retail in MPCs needs to be supplemented by more affordable, even subsidised, independent retail opportunities. This variety will create hyper-local amenity, particularly for its potential for third places such as cafes, community spaces, small bars and restaurants, which can spread throughout neighbourhoods. Meaningful local retail acts as a magnet for social interaction and casual encounter between residents, creating daily and weekly rhythms of local activity for people with diverse needs and timetables. None of this can happen without radical changes to how planning authorities conceive the way neighbourhoods are zoned. These changes need to be introduced at the inception of a master plan rather than retrofitted, generating acceptance and anticipation for new residents.

Finally, we can no longer ignore climate change in the name of commercial expediency. Communities without an adequate green canopy, houses without natural ventilation and passive solar orientation and the other structural necessities to build climate resilience means that communities designed to last for a hundred years will become uninhabitable. Once again, only governments can take the necessary measures to create a level playing field, allowing the commercial innovation required to make create communities where residents are comfortable and resilient in the 21st century.

Endnotes

1   R. Freestone, B. Randolph, and S. Pinnegar, "Suburbanisation in Australia", in *The Routledge Companion to the Suburbs,* B. Hanlon and T.J. Vicino, Editors. 2018, Routledge: Oxford. p. 72-86.

2   C. Murray. and J. Ryan-Collins, *When homes earn more than jobs: the rentierization of the Australian housing market.* UCL Institute for Innovation and Public Purpose, 2020. Working Paper Series (IIPP WP 2020-08).

3   IMF. *Global Housing Watch.* 2019 [cited 2020 20 April]; Available from: https://www.imf.org/external/research/housing/index.htm.

4   W. Cox, *Demographia.* 2018, Belleville: Demographia.

5   CoreLogic. *Mapping the Market.* 2019 [cited 2020 24 April]; Available from: https://www.corelogic.com.au/our-data/mapping-market.

6   AIHW, *Home Ownership and Housing Tenure.* 2022, Canberra: Australian Institute of Health and Welfare.

7   ABS. *Housing: Census.* 2021 [cited 2022 10 October]; Available from: https://www.abs.gov.au/statistics/people/housing/housing-census/2021.

8   ABS. *Housing mobility and conditions.* 2021 [cited 2022 10 October]; Available from: https://www.abs.gov.au/statistics/people/housing/housing-mobility-and-conditions

9   M. Rooney, *All give and no take? Social change, suburban life and the possibilities of sharing in Australia.* 2014, University of Tasmania.

10 ibid.

11 L. Cheshire, P. Walters, and T. Rosenblatt, "The Politics of Housing Consumption: Renters as Flawed Consumers on a Master Planned Estate", *Urban Studies,* 2010. 47(12): p. 2597-2614.

7

Enabling Australia's Next City

George Wilkinson III

Introduction

According to Mick Cornett in *The Next American City*, America's future belongs to mid-sized cities such as Oklahoma City, Des Moines, Indianapolis, Boise, Charleston, etc. These cities thrive in a crowded urban system, illustrating how smallness brings opportunity, that the success of one city does not preclude that of another. Naturally, Cornett is upbeat given America's glut of cities, including over 110 Metropolitan Statistical Areas (MSAs) with populations over 500,000.

Adopting similarly ambitious perspectives of the next Australian city, that is, one assuming mid-sized cities play a role, is challenging. Australia's urban system is small and its urban hierarchy largely frozen. As of the 2021 census, Australia was comprised of seven urban areas with populations over 500,000 and, as was the case during colonisation, the five largest cities are Sydney, Melbourne, Brisbane, Perth and Adelaide. Each state capital dwarfs its second city, standing uncontested in its respective state. Generally, Australia exhibits a remarkable scarcity of large non-capital cities.

While Australia's urban footprint is established it is not necessarily considered an optimal configuration. A recent Delphi study of planning experts conducted by the Australian Urban Design Research Centre found that decentralisation of population growth away from large centres is preferred, though opinions vary about alternative strategies (Bolleter et al. 2022). Recognising discontent with the current state, in 2019 the federal government launched a decentralisation policy to address unaffordable housing, congestion, and a lack of shared values in state capitals (Australian Government 2019). Despite an appetite for decentralisation, Australia's long history of unsuccessful new city proposals suggests decentralisation is easier said than done

(Bolleter 2018). The following chapter explores why this is the case. Specifically, this chapter examines Australia's unique settlement pattern, underlying drivers, and provides recommendations for enabling the growth of non-capital cities.

The Australian Urban Hierarchy

Over 60% of Australians live in six state capitals. Though Australia exhibits decentralised settlement nationally, upon "closer examination" states exhibit urban primacy (Short and PinetPeralta 2009: 1262). Primacy signifies centralised settlement, a polity dominated by its largest city and an absence of comparably large second cities. To contextualise primacy in states, Figure 7:1 presents measures where primacy equals the largest city's population as a proportion of total urban population (Mutlu 1989).

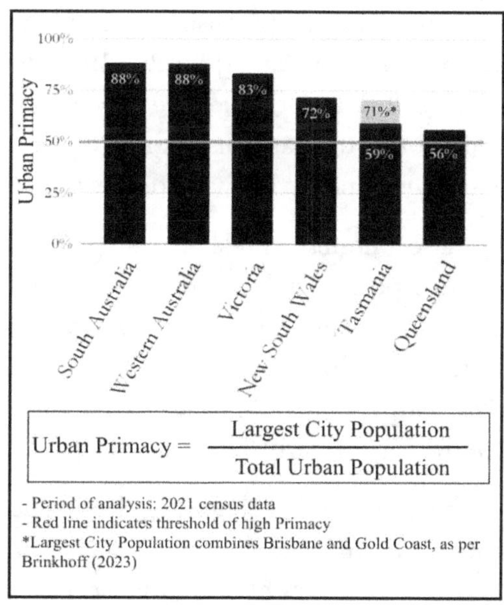

Figure 7.1: State Primacy Measures

Urban primacy is an enduring characteristic of Australian states, recognised during colonisation, observed for its persistence and extremity (Short and PinetPeralta 2009; Wilkinson et al. 2023). During the colonial period the high concentration of people in capitals was a subject of curiosity given Australia's development was expected to follow American decentralisation. According to Captain Vetch (1838: 158) "the ground requires less clearing and obstruction from the natives is less formidable," creating the "expectation that the population and the power of the Australians [might rival] the United States".

With experience, early expectations were tempered by disappointment and "surprise that so little [had] been made in the inland [country]" (Vetch 1838: 164). On the eve of Federation, it was contended that the capitals were congested cesspools with state centralisation being a regrettable outcome (Bolleter 2018). Recognising this, advocates of federation assured reluctant regions that federation would trigger decentralisation (Brown 2007b). Over a century later, primacy persists and the disproportionate growth of the capitals is projected to intensify in the 21st century (ABS 2013, 2017).

Explanations of Primacy in Australian States

20th century theories of primacy emphasise Australia's harsh environment (Rowland 1977) and the capitals' first-mover advantages (Johnston 1977; Neutze 1977) given they were relative oases cited by colonists and therefore served as logical hubs (Statham 1990). Still, Bird (1965) questioned the naturalist narrative given the founders' limited experience of Australia and the capitals' haphazard selection.

Taking a different tack, the economist Frank Stilwell (1974) attributed primacy to markets – capitalism favouring port capitals, exports favouring thin rural populations, modern technology enabling capitals to serve vast geographies, and urbanisation preceding rural development. Colonial administrative seaports, established in a modern era, centralised development, minimising the quantity of cities, state capitals prospering on account of their head starts (Brennan 1963).

There is also the matter of agglomeration economics, the location-specific advantages enterprises develop through proximity to complementary activities (Knox, Agnew, and McCarthy 2014). Cities are clusters of accumulated infrastructure, knowledge, capabilities, and activities from which savings derive (Coe, Kelly, and Yeung 2019). Theoretically, the gravity of agglomeration expanded with modernity (MacKinnon and Cumbers 2018). Thus, modernity expanded the capitals' reach, necessitating one city, closing the city-formation window. One problem, while agglomeration economics may explain the emergence of one city, it does not by itself explain a primate city's mutual exclusivity with other cities. Theories of primacy must do more than explain why cities grow; they must explain why only one city grows.

To address this, over the last 30 years economic geographers, urban economists, and political scientists have emphasised the ability of institutions to sculpt settlement (Ades and Glaeser 1995). Institutions constitute "the rules of the game" (North 1990: 3), the formal and informal practices that constrain and condition development (Glaeser et al. 2004; Huggins 2016). From the perspective of urban primacy, the institutional perspective posits that centralised settlement is symptomatic of centralised power (Galiani and Kim 2011). This follows the observation that primate cities are usually political capitals (Davis and Henderson 2003; Short and PinetPeralta 2009).

Interestingly, while primate cities are usually capitals, not all capitals are primate cities. Institutionalists attribute the variable population magnetism of capital cities to the balance of intergovernmental power therein (Henderson 2003; Kim and Law 2016). For example, in the countries and sub-national territories of North and South America, Sukkoo Kim and Marc Law (2012) measured strong capital city population magnetism where sub-national institutions were weak (e.g., Latin America). Within the sample, Canada and the United States stood apart for their strong subnational polities, decentralised national (and sub-national) settlement patterns, and many large non-capital[1] cities. Kim and Law (2012; 2016) attributed these features to British colonization and its permissive subsidiarity in the same way Latin American urban primacy is attributed to centralised Spanish colonisation (Aroca and Atienza 2016).

Australian scholars have not been silent about the role played by institutions. James Bird (1965), Richard Lonsdale (1972), Ronald Johnston (1977), and Graeme Neutze (1977) acknowledged, and in places emphasised, the centralising role played by institutions (e.g., weak localism). Still, these views were not popularly adopted. As AJ Brown (2003: 200) explained, it is "widely but inaccurately assumed" Australian state primacy was an economic outcome. Instead, "each centre used its political leverage to augment its control over associated territory, often against locational disadvantages and at the expense of [competitors]" (Brown 2003: 17-18). This author and colleagues (2022; 2022a, 2022b; 2023) tested elements of the institutional thesis in Australia and identified attributes of Australian federalism common to primacy internationally, including state centricity, weak localism, and fiscal centralisation. Wilkinson et al. (2023) linked primacy in states to a contentious balance of inter-governmental power that favours higher tiers and disables bottom-up drivers of economic development. That is, Australia's scarcity of large non-capital cities can be understood in terms of non-capital cities having limited and vulnerable existence as political, fiscal and administrative entities.

The suggestion that sub-state governments in Australia are weak is well examined in political science. According to Michael Jones (1993: 7-8), despite devolution being "a central element" of federal theory, in "Australia we apply the opposite theory." William Coleman (2016: 1) similarly derided Australian centralisation as "façade federalism." Critiques of federal centralisation also extend to states. Jones (1993: 13) likened Australian local governments to standing peacetime armies, "overmanaged, restless... waiting for a challenge." Indeed, political centralisation is well recognised, however its suppressive influence upon non-capital city regions is not.

Enabling Decentralisation

Alleviating regional disadvantages is a mainstay of Australian politics (Archer 2015). Population decentralisation has been justified in the name of national defence, regional improvement, and decongestion (Stilwell 1974). Still, decentralisation initiatives have largely failed, with the notable exception of Canberra (Bolleter 2018). This is likely because these initiatives rarely alter Australia's balance of intergovernmental power. For example, recent decentralisation appeals, such as Regions at the Ready (Drum 2018) and Regional Development and Decentralisation (Commonwealth of Australia 2017) emphasised the relocation of government offices, not institutional reform or subsidiarity (Eversole and Walo 2020).

Despite little effective redress of primacy, decentralisation retains relevance. The federal report, Planning for Australia's Future Population, aims to decentralise population from the capitals into regional centres through infrastructure investment (Australian Government 2019: 26). Recently, the Regional Australia Institute launched its *Regionalisation Ambition*, an initiative designed to "Rebalance the Nation" which has attracted considerable federal, state, regional, and local support (Regional Australia Institute 2022). Still, if current and future endeavours to decentralise population growth in Australia are to transcend lip service, they must engage with subsidiarity as a central tenet (Grant and Drew 2017), a focus that is not yet apparent.

Emphasis on subsidiarity is echoed in the federalism literature, notably by AJ Brown (2007b, 2002, 2007a), given the importance of subsidiarity in the Constitution. Brown (2002: 40) argues it is time to take "subsidiarity beyond political rhetoric... [and fully investigate a] long-term devolution of powers and responsibilities." Brown emphasises local capability building, the decentralisation of responsibility and risk, and the "relaxation of direct revenue-raising constraints on local government" (Brown 2007b: 248). Internationally, the merits of subsidiarity are recognised, with devolution of power being an integral component of reforms (Falleti 2005; Organization for Economic Cooperation and Development 2019). With this in mind, the following recommendations pose reforms which could enable decentralisation in the Australian context.

1. *Transcend the top-down paradigm:* A theme common to decentralisation initiatives in Australia is the idea that a centralised top will orchestrate decentralisation, a conceptually flawed logic. Instead, Dennis Rondinelli and colleagues (1989) highlighted the importance of commitment by higher tiers of government to lead a transfer of power, to support the participation of lower tiers, to patiently enable the building of capability and competence in subsidiaries. While Australia's public sector needs to engage with subsidiarity, this first requires culture change and steadfast, long-term commitment to a new operating model.

2. *Earned here, stays here:* Australian public finance is renowned for vertical fiscal imbalance, meaning the federal government collects taxes well in excess of federal expenditures and as a result lower tiers of government have few own source revenues and are highly reliant upon top-down grants and transfers (Burton, Dollery, and Wallis 2002). The Goods and Services Tax (GST), for example, is a federally implemented sales tax distributed in full to states and territories. However, federal to state, also state to local, distributions are governed by the principle of effort neutrality. That is, distributions are determined by per-capita need, not local productivity. Whilst egalitarian in orientation, effort neutrality disincentivises local performance. For example, if a local government implements a tourism strategy drawing in crowds, it derives little direct financial benefit while incurring many direct costs. Indeed, local businesses benefit from growth in tourism, however the absence of an "earned here, stays here" sales tax isolates the local government from measurable elastic incomes and therefore dampens incentives to continuously pursue such endeavours. It is recommended a component (e.g., 10%) of federal-to-state and state-to-local distributions be effort derived, thereby supporting an equality of opportunity.

3. *Decouple local and state balance sheets:* In Australian public finance, local failure equals state failure because state and local government balance sheets are legally intertwined. Local governments are creatures of states. Were a local government to incur debts and default, its respective state would be liable. To move away from this, it is recommended states provide an oversight model to qualifying local governments that legally isolates the local government from its state and set the basis for its fiscal autonomy. In the United States, a hotbed of subsidiarity and the most decentralised economy in the world, local autonomy is achieved through

instruments called "home rule charters", effectively individually negotiated local government constitutions that protect local rights, responsibilities, and fiscal autonomy (Dollery, O'Keefe, and Crase 2009; Grant and Dollery 2012). Such a practice would not exonerate states from all responsibility should a local government fail, but would contain local risk and elements of state responsibility, allowing qualifying local governments to better leverage their credibility and engage with higher risk-reward.

4. *Streamline, Simplify sub-state governance:* Using Western Australia as an example, Figure 7:2 illustrates the need for public sector simplification. The figure conveys the tangled and duplicitous current state, where federal and state governments both manage regional entities and the state endures a heavy management burden over 147 dependents. Were such a management structure applied to individuals within a corporation, for example, the absence of middle management would be an obvious weakness. Interestingly, this structure differentiates Australia from Canada and the US where counties serve as intermediaries between local governments and states/provinces. To address this, Figure 7:2 proposes a future state where chains of command are streamlined, with each tier having fewer direct reports, a more manageable distribution of responsibilities. Importantly, this recommendation is not proposing growth in the size and scale of the public sector, but a reconfiguration and better usage of existing resources.

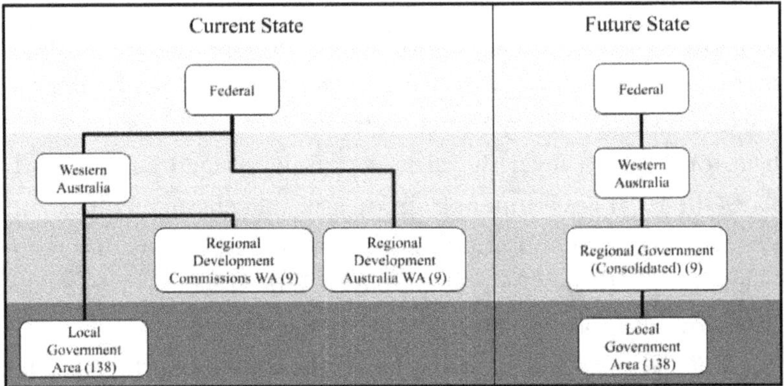

Figure 7.2: WA Operating Model

5. *Pick winners and formalise regional capitals:* One challenge in regional development is picking winners because selecting regions for investment is fraught with controversy and competition. Despite this, there is evidence to suggest State Governments are growing comfortable with the designation of regional centres as strategic centres or regional capitals, such as Western Australia's Regional

Centres Development Plan Framework, (Government of Western Australia 2015). This formalisation should continue and the legislative gravity of what it means to be a regional capital expanded and legally protected. One of the primary benefits of the nomination and formalisation of regional capitals is that it provides states with focused engagement and investment centres in the same way state capitals are focal points for Canberra.

Conclusion

This chapter examined Australian settlement, factors that sculpt it, and provided recommendations for enabling Australia's next city. The recommendations are by no means comprehensive or simple. They are provided at a high level to spark a conversation about ways of formalising, extending, and protecting the political, fiscal and administrative powers of sub-state governments. Naturally, there will be hesitation to implement specific recommendations such as choosing winners because then there will be losers. Or there will be concerns that effort derived federal-to-state and state-to-local distributions will further disadvantage already disadvantaged regions whilst others thrive. These concerns should be tempered by acknowledgement of the current state - Australian states represent some of the most extreme examples of regional inequality and uneven development on Earth, both in magnitude and scale. The public sector's risk aversion and "obsession" with an equality of outcomes (Jones 1993: 9) has not prevented inequality nor supported a fair go for regions. On the contrary, while the capitals are highly liveable centres, high primacy in all states signifies an *extreme* diversity of outcomes, vast territories where the capital takes all and non-capital cities are deprived of the agency to self-start. Thus, if Australia's next city is to be as bold a concept as it is in the United States, then we must accept that its birth requires fundamental reforms that change what it means to be a city in Australia.

Endnotes

1   Neither national nor subnational capitals (e.g., Los Angeles, Chicago, Dallas, Montreal, Vancouver, Calgary, etc.).

References

Ades, Alberto F., and Edward L. Glaeser. 1995. "Trade and circuses: explaining urban giants", *The Quarterly Journal of Economics,* 110: 195-227.

Archer, Jack. 2015. "Population Dynamics in Regional Australia." In. Canberra: Regional Australia Institute.

Aroca, Patricio, and Miguel Atienza. 2016. "Spatial concentration in Latin America and the role of institutions", *Investigaciones Regionales*, 36: 233-53.

Australian Bureau of Statistics. 2013. "3222.0 Population Projections Australia, 2012 (Base) to 2101" In. Canberra: Government of Australia.

———. 2017. "3222.0 - Population Projections, Australia, 2017 (base) - 2066" In. Canberra: Government of Australia.

Australian Government. 2019. "Planning for Australia's Future Population" In. Canberra: Department of the Prime Minister and Cabinet.

Bird, James. 1965. "The foundation of Australian seaport capitals", *Economic Geography*, 41: 283-99.

Bolleter, Julian. 2018. *The Ghost Cities of Australia: A Survey of New City Proposals and Their Lessons for Australia's 21st Century Development* (Springer: Perth).

Bolleter, Julian, Nicole Edwards, Robert Freestone, David Nichols, and Paula Hooper. 2022. "Evaluating scenarios for twenty-first-century Australian settlement planning: a Delphi study with planning experts", *International Planning Studies:* 1-22.

Brennan, T. 1963. "The pattern of urbanization in Australia", *International Journal of Comparative Sociology*, 4: 152-61.

Brown, AJ. 2002. "Subsidiarity or subterfuge? Resolving the future of local government in the Australian federal system", *Australian Journal of Public Administration*, 61: 24-42.

———. 2003. *The Frozen Continent: the Fall and Rise of Territory in Australian Constitutional Thought 1815-2003* (Griffith University).

———. 2007a. "Federalism, Regionalism and the Reshaping of Australian Governance" in Alexander Jonathan Brown and Jennifer A Bellamy (eds.), *Federalism and Regionalism in Australia - New Approaches, New Institutions?* (ANU Press: Canberra).

———. 2007b. "Reshaping Australia's federation: The choices for regional Australia", *The Australasian Journal of Regional Studies*, 13: 235.

Burton, Therese, Brian Dollery, and Joe Wallis. 2002. "A century of vertical fiscal imbalance in Australian federalism", *History of Economics Review,* 36: 26-43.

Coe, Neil M, Philip F Kelly, and Henry WC Yeung. 2019. *Economic geography: a contemporary introduction* (John Wiley & Sons).

Coleman, William. 2016. *Only in Australia: The History, Politics, and Economics of Australian Exceptionalism* (Oxford University Press: Oxford Scholarship Online).

Commonwealth of Australia. 2017. "Issues Paper: Select Committee on Regional Development and Decentralisation." In. Canberra: Parliament of the Commonwealth of Australia.

Davis, James C, and J. Vernon Henderson. 2003. "Evidence on the political economy of the urbanization process", *Journal of Urban Economics*, 53: 98-125.

Dollery, B., S. O'Keefe, and L. Crase. 2009. "State oversight models for Australian local government", *Economic Papers: A journal of applied economics and policy*, 28: 279-90.

Drum, Damian. 2018. "Regions at the Ready: Investing in Australia's Future." In. Canberra: House of Representatives Select Committee on Regional Development and Decentralisation, Parliament of the Commonwealth of Australia.

Eversole, Robyn, and Megerssa Walo. 2020. "Leading and following in Australian regional development: Why governance matters", *Regional Science Policy & Practice*, 12: 291-302.

Falleti, Tulia G. 2005. "A sequential theory of decentralization: Latin American cases in comparative perspective", *American political science review*, 99: 327-46.

Galiani, S., and S. Kim. 2011. "Political centralization and urban primacy: Evidence from national and provincial capitals in the Americas" in Dora Costa and Naomi Lamoreaux (eds.), *Understanding Long-Run Economic Growth: Geography, Institutions, and the Knowledge Economy* (University of Chicago Press: Chicago).

Glaeser, Edward L, Rafael La Porta, Florencio Lopez-de-Silanes, and Andrei Shleifer. 2004. "Do institutions cause growth?", *Journal of Economic growth*, 9: 271-303.

Government of Western Australia. 2015. "Regional Centres Development Plan Framework" In, edited by Department of Regional Development. Perth.

Grant, Bligh, and Brian Dollery. 2012. "Autonomy versus oversight in local government reform: The implications of 'home rule'for Australian local government", *Australian journal of political science*, 47: 399-412.

Grant, Bligh, and Joseph Drew. 2017. *Local Government in Australia: History, Theory and Public Policy.* (Springer: Singapore).

Henderson, J. Vernon. 2003. "The urbanization process and economic growth: The so-what question", *Journal of Economic growth*, 8: 47-71.

Huggins, Robert. 2016. "Capital, institutions and urban growth systems", *Cambridge Journal of Regions, Economy and Society*, 9: 443-63.

Johnston, Ronald J. 1977. "Regarding urban origins, urbanization and urban patterns", *Geography*, 62: 1-8.

Jones, M.A. 1993. *Transforming Australian Local Government: Making it Work* (Allen & Unwin: St Leonards).

Kim, Sukkoo, and Marc T Law. 2012. "History, institutions, and cities: A view from the Americas", *Journal of Regional Science*, 52: 10-39.

Kim, Sukkoo, and Marc T. Law. 2016. "Political centralization, federalism, and urban development: Evidence from US and Canadian capital cities", *Social Science History*, 40: 121-46.

Knox, Paul, John Agnew, and Linda McCarthy. 2014. *The geography of the world economy* (Routledge).

Lonsdale, Richard E. 1972. "Manufacturing decentralization: the discouraging record in Australia", *Land Economics*, 48: 321-28.

MacKinnon, Danny, and Andrew Cumbers. 2018. *An Introduction to Economic Geography: Globalisation, Uneven Development and Place* (Routledge).

Mutlu, Servet. 1989. "Urban concentration and primacy revisited: an analysis and some policy conclusions", *Economic Development and Cultural Change*, 37: 611-39.

Neutze, Graeme Max. 1977. *Urban Development in Australia: A Descriptive Analysis* (Allen & Unwin Australia: Sydney).

North, Douglass C. 1990. *Institutions, Institutional Change and Economic Performance* (Cambridge University Press: Cambridge).

Organization for Economic Cooperation and Development. 2019. *Making Decentralisation Work: A Handbook for Policy-Makers* (OECD Publishing: Paris).

Regional Australia Institute. 2022. "Regionalisation Ambition 2032 - A Framework to Rebalance the Nation." In. Canberra: Regional Australia Institute.

Rondinelli, Dennis A, James S McCullough, and Ronald W Johnson. 1989. "Analysing decentralization policies in developing countries: a politicaleconomy framework", *Development and change*, 20: 57-87.

Rowland, D. T. 1977. "Theories of urbanization in Australia", *Geographical review*, 67: 167-76.

Short, *John Rennie, and Luis Mauricio Pinet-Peralta. 2009. "Urban primacy: Reopening the debate", Geography Compass,* 3: 1245-66.

Statham, Pamela. 1990. *The Origins of Australia's Capital Cities* (Cambridge University Press: Cambridge).

Stilwell, Frank. 1974. *Australian Urban and Regional Development* (Australian and New Zealand Book Co: Sydney).

Vetch, Captain. 1838. "Considerations on the Political Geography and Geographical Nomenclature of Australia", *The Journal of the Royal Geographical Society of London*, 8: 157-69.

Wilkinson, George, Fiona Haslam McKenzie, and Julian Bolleter. 2022a. "Federalism and urban primacy: Political dimensions that influence the city-country divide in Australia", *International Journal of Urban Sciences*, 26.

——. 2022b. "Why does Perth stand alone? Interviews with subject matter experts about the drivers of settlement in Western Australia", *Australian Geographer*, 53: 183-200.

Wilkinson, George, Fiona Haslam McKenzie, Julian Bolleter, and Paula Hooper. 2022. "Growth Dynamics and Municipal Population Change in Australia, 1911-2016", *Australasian Journal of Regional Studies*, 27: 285-305.

——. 2023. "Political Centralisation, Federalism and Urbanization, Evidence from Australia", *Social Science History*, 47.

8

The Canadian Suburban Experience:
Sprawl is Bad. So Why do We Keep Building It?

Antony P. Lorius and Laura E. Taylor[1]

Nothing unites land use planners in Canada quite like their disdain for "urban sprawl". Everyone (and not just planners) is against sprawl – publicly at least – and who can blame them? Sprawl is an issue that literally causes people to take to the streets, placards in hand, to protest the injustice.[2] Fuelling this contempt for sprawl, in part, is the term itself, which has now come to signify any type of expansion of the urban area at the rural margin, under any circumstance.

Of course, the traditional definition of sprawl is more specific, referring to forms of urban growth that are variously described as haphazard, disorganised, uncontrolled, unrestricted[3], poorly serviced, and largely unplanned. Problematic, yes: no question. However, by this traditional definition, there is very little "sprawl" in Canada, especially in the major growth centres.

The Greater Toronto and Hamilton Area (GTHA) for instance is one of the most densely built urban areas on the North American continent, even with a population of seven million and a perennial growth rate of more than one per cent. In this huge urban area, new urban development lands are carefully studied, planned, serviced, and used very efficiently. Regional planning across the GTHA has sought for decades to protect the countryside, promote intensification, increase residential density, and encourage mixed-use, compact, transit-supportive, and pedestrian-oriented communities. New suburbs are denser now than they have been at any time since the 1950s.[4] In the city of Toronto alone, more than 250 high-rise towers are under construction, which is more than New York, Boston, Los Angeles, Seattle, San Francisco, and Washington. D.C. combined.[5] Transit is being built in the form of busways, light rail, interregional commuter rail and subways, and bike lanes are being extended everywhere, all in hopes of getting people out of their cars.

Wouldn't you think the GTHA would be held up as a model for smart growth? Nope. The negative image of urban growth as noxious sprawl persists. A 2021 "value for money" audit of planning in Ontario laments difficulties in "curbing" urban sprawl around Toronto, defined – incorrectly, again – as "generally unplanned, scattered development characterised by low density, haphazard, and disorganised settlement patterns [that are] inefficient to service". Most communities have fallen short of mandated intensification targets, the audit also points out, creating further sprawl.[6]

A bit catchier than an audit are the narratives of suburban growth provided by local community and other organised interest groups: most typically along the lines of an outdated, car-dependent, greenspace-destroying, financially unsustainable conspiracy that is "rigged" to enrich land speculators and exclude new households from the walkable and transit-friendly existing neighbourhoods where people *really* want to live and work. Heady stuff. Eventually, the argument goes, the path of sprawl ends at a climate change catastrophe from which there is no return.

So, according to the narratives, the only prudent path forward is to stop entirely the expansion of urban areas. And in the Toronto area, some community groups have been successful in convincing their local elected representatives to do just this: vote against sprawl, i.e., against any expansion of the existing urban area.[7] After all, who in their right mind would support a pattern of urban growth and development that:

- Bulldozes large amounts of farmland and natural areas to build isolated homes in neighbourhoods far away from where people work and shop;
- Forces people to drive to get around which means owning expensive vehicles and being trapped in a landscape dominated by large amounts of road infrastructure, highways, and parking lots;
- Allows land developers to keep making profits by destroying farmland and natural areas;
- Significantly raises property taxes, makes energy bills and fuel costs higher, pollutes the air and, in turn, worsens the climate crisis; and (among others)
- Destroys our ability to feed ourselves. Once built on, farmland is lost forever and we lose access to fresh, healthy local food. We become more reliant on imported food as the climate crisis increases global food scarcity.[8]

The solution, it would seem, is obvious: all growth should be accommodated within existing urban areas. All new housing, in particular, to accommodate growth should be provided through the intensification of existing lands already designated for urban development where there is plenty of potential for new units. In the court of public opinion, the verdict is in. And within the planning industry itself, we are not aware of many qualified experts (if any) who do not publicly promote the curtailing (or even stopping) of urban sprawl as anything less than central to ensuring the development of healthy and sustainable communities.

On the flip side, arguments in favour of sprawl (or at least questioning the suburbs' underlying negative image) are much fewer in number and typically dismissed in the broader debate as either: irrelevant given the sheer scale of attendant negative social, environmental, and economic impacts; or, little more than advocacy (or worse) on behalf of private development interests.[9] In short, it would seem, everyone agrees that sprawl is bad. Plain and simple. The case could not be stronger.

There is just one small problem: *we keep building it* in Canada, the United States, Australia, and elsewhere around the world. In Europe, for example, sprawl has increased rapidly in many areas including those traditionally held up as examples of "smart growth" or sustainable (i.e., better planned) forms of urban development (Paris, London, the Netherlands).[10] And we have all been doing it for a long time. In Canada, for instance, when Don Mills, the first large-scale comprehensively planned suburban community in the Toronto area[11] began development in the early 1950s, the voices of disapproval arose almost immediately: "a ghastly mess... Mile upon mile it sprawls, subdivision after subdivision, as long as times are prosperous there is no sign it will stop".[12]

And so began the great repudiation of the suburban growth model, across Canada and many other communities around the world. And what has changed since the 1950s? Interestingly, very little. Rather than leading to a nuanced discussion of the externalities of suburban development and a reflection on suburban design, the Don Mills model was copied for decades all around the Toronto area and many other major urban centres.[13] Canadians still love living in the suburbs and planners who claim to know better keep complaining about it. And largely irrespective of location, the standard list of problems laid at the feet of the suburbs tends to be about the same as identified in 1954.[14]

The problems wrought by "sprawl" are serious, clearly.[15] And yet, inexplicably, we have still become a nation of suburbs. As of 2016, more than two-thirds of the country lives in the suburbs and the share is proportionally higher in larger metropolitan areas.[16] There is no evidence that this trend is slowing rapidly or significantly.[17] On the contrary, the COVID pandemic has had the effect of accelerating trends of growth outside major urban centres since 2021 in both the United States[18] and Canada.[19]

Some of this pandemic-related "flight" to the suburbs has since moderated but the underlying and long-standing economic and demographic drivers remain in place. People still want homes in suburban areas, housing developers keep building them, and local elected officials keep approving applications for more. What, then, one might ask, is going on? It certainly begs the question: if the evidence is so clear, the case against sprawl so strong, the opposition so vocal and consistent...how does this keep happening?

Part of the explanation is that – contrary to popular myth – land use *planners don't actually approve anything*. In Canada, at least, approving plans for new suburban development is the job of local municipal councils: a group of elected officials who are responsible for making decisions about municipal financing and services, including development approvals.[20] People are often surprised to learn that planners don't actually plan the city, *per se*: they advise. And planners certainly don't build the city. Ultimately, it is up to the locally elected officials to decide collectively what is in the best interests of the community, including the location and extent of new urban areas, and the type and density of new development being put forward by developers within those areas. Even the planners working for developers don't always make the plans that are ultimately built. All completed projects, in the end, reflect myriad negotiations and changes over time, often settled through litigation.[21]

As it turns out, the "planner as city builder" is one of several myths that has been perpetuated as part of the primarily negative stereotype of suburban growth. Other myths, as we discuss below, are about cars vs transit, density vs intensification vs affordability, and about boomers vacating their suburban homes for younger folks. "It just *has* to change...": it has been said now for close to 100 years.[22] And we agree that much *should* change, but we don't believe the suburbs are going anywhere. For context, we are writing from our position as planners watching the dynamics of the sprawl debate in the GTHA unfold over the past 20 years. On one hand, we take seriously the externalities and impacts of suburban development, especially climate change, and we have supported professionally "good planning principles" aimed at encouraging intensification and more compact urban forms. On the other hand, we both live in single detached homes in leafy central Toronto neighbourhoods, each with three kids and a car in the driveway.

Reflecting on our experience as planners, we have seen that the anti-sprawl agenda in the GTHA has been so successful over the past 20 years that provincially-led planning policies, regulations, and processes changed dramatically during that time. In 2006, a Provincial "growth plan" was put in place with mandated population and employment forecasts and, more importantly, a set of density and intensification targets that defined the envelope within which new development was allowed. *A Place to Grow: The Growth Plan for the Greater Golden Horseshoe* covers an area even larger than the GTHA. The *Growth Plan* was accompanied by the *Greenbelt Plan* within which urban growth was not permitted. The combined objective of these two plans was to limit the amount of new greenfield lands designated for urban development through compact urban form.[23] Although never explicitly stated, the underlying policy mechanism to achieve urban containment goals was to shift the price structure of new housing to make lower-density forms (i.e., conventional suburban houses) more costly, thereby encouraging more compact (i.e., more apartment-based) development.

The *Growth Plan* has been successful in moving the needle towards achieving its goals, including a huge shift to intensification. However, new suburbs continue to be built: either at higher and higher densities or in communities at the edge of the commuter shed beyond the reach of the *Growth Plan* and its mandated targets. Accompanying this growth has been a considerable escalation in housing prices, which has been well-documented, beginning with the detached housing market. In response to the affordability crisis (of which the *Growth Plan* framework was partly but not wholly responsible), the new Provincial government regime in 2023 is proposing to collapse the *Growth Plan* into a new Provincial Planning Statement, which changes how growth planning will be carried out. Most importantly, the former stringent policy tests applied to urban expansion – a fundamental aspect of growth management and long-range planning in Ontario for nearly 20 years – will come to an end.

We are now facing a more laissez-faire suburban future, which has already started to appear with the rollback of two decades of strict provincially-mandated growth management policies. It seems we have come full circle. And what this recent (and somewhat unsettling) experience has shown, in our view, is that the language of "sprawl" leaves little room for nuanced consideration. The complex discussions we ought to have been having about cars and transit, density and intensification, demographics, affordability, and market forces did not take place, at least in the mainstream public forums.

Rather, the discourse has been dominated by the voices of the people who believe that the suburbs should simply be eliminated, perpetuating myths about land use planning and misunderstandings about who – at the end of the day – is responsible for the decisions we make.

Sadly, land use planners are often left holding the bag.[24] This remains the case even though planners have very little ability to force delivery of the preferred outcomes, including the ability to stop expansion of the urban area. To provide some insight into this curious situation, below we pay more attention to what is myth and what is reality in the sprawl debate. Our purpose here is to unpack the sprawl debate in order to provoke more realistic discussion about some of the most entrenched myths involved. We begin with the following list of seven myths. Of course, you may be able to think of more. Each myth is briefly introduced and contextualised with a few thoughts about the reality. Might it be possible to move beyond entrenched myths about urban sprawl to talk about the world in which we actually live and plan? We certainly hope so.

The Myth: Cars Are An Irrational Obsession

It has been said that the suburbs are a self-fulfilling prophecy. Car ownership makes suburbs possible, and the suburban form makes cars necessary. Where it gets tricky is in explaining how, exactly, this happened in the first place.[25] The popular view is that people have an irrational obsession or "love affair" with cars: if only people knew better, the story goes, they wouldn't drive so much and would (presumably) just find some other way to get around. Suburban design problem solved.

The Reality: Cars Are Super Convenient

The reason people like cars is because cars are convenient and generally make life easier (if you can afford them), like fridges, stoves and washing machines. And with cars it's even more than convenience: people generally like to be independent. Cars provide the opportunity, freedom and convenience to go where you want, when you want. On demand.

Cars are so convenient, in fact, that even in mature Canadian urban areas where transit is well-served, the modal split is still dominated by the private auto. In the City of Toronto, for example, which is widely recognised as having one of the most extensive transit systems in Canada[26], only 25 per cent of total trips to work (commuting) are taken by transit. The majority of trips (roughly 60%) are taken by car with the balance (a little under 15%) by walking, biking and other methods.[27]

Mobility goals are also more universal than most people think. Looking around the world it would appear as soon as a person or household has enough money, the mobility upgrade takes place: a scooter, or e-bike and eventually a car. And from a social equity perspective, it has been said that "the shortest distance between a poor person and a job is along a line driven in a car".[28] It is correct to observe that the cost of owning and operating a car is a huge barrier to entry, but in this case the time *is* money.

There is nothing irrational about our "obsession" with cars. Cars provide a huge comparative advantage over other forms of mobility (especially transit) and are the only path to economic opportunity for many. Which is not to say that we should stop trying to reduce everyday car use as much as possible, as there are big attendant problems associated with cars that we should seek to address – public health, public space, emissions, among others: this is clear. However, cars are here to stay until transit can provide a comparable level of convenience.

The Myth: Transit Can Serve All Trips At All Times

One of the recurring themes in contemporary planning practice is the need to encourage more transit-oriented development. The theory is that a symbiotic relationship exists between density and public transit whereby more compact urban forms encourage the provision of transit and vice-versa: transit works to encourage intensification within existing urban areas and facilitate better suburban design. Suburban design problem solved (again) with the added benefit of accommodating more trips on transit which, in turn, means fewer greenhouse gas emissions for the "win" on climate change.

The Reality: Transit Works Very Well In Some Situations, And Not So Well In Others

Implicit in this myth are two specific expectations. First, that transit-oriented suburban design will be accompanied by actual transit investment and second, that just getting more trips on transit will make suburbs act/seem less like suburbs. In reality, belief in both outcomes is aspirational (at best) considering actual travel patterns and the potential costs involved.

In most Canadian cities commuting patterns moved away from the "central city" model long ago – the one where most work trips are back and forth from the surrounding areas to a central business district, like a bullseye. The trip to work today has proportionally fewer suburb-to-central (i.e., downtown Toronto) trips and more suburb-to-suburb trips, more like a spider web.[29] Over time more "central place" functions are being provided locally within suburbs, further dispersing trip patterns.[30] And while Toronto's downtown, for example, remains a major source of economic activity, it is no longer the only game in town (so to speak). Significant concentrations of jobs in the various "mega zones" of employment have grown in suburban areas around Toronto.[31] Within this evolving urban structure, we are all taking more trips in more directions for an increasing variety of reasons to get to higher-order shopping centres, community recreation facilities, health care, places for entertainment and others.

And – minor detail – turns out that transit costs a lot of money. In Toronto, building subways today costs far more now in real dollars than decades ago, even though the latest projects have fewer stations, traverse simpler, less-dense contexts, and have been delivered with record-low borrowing costs (at least until recently).[32] In the Toronto area, the capital costs of transit are borne through a complex negotiation between the various levels of government, including municipal development charges, and operating costs are largely expected to be covered by user fees. And in the end, after decades of debate and service delivery challenges, the results are mixed as relatively few kilometres of transit have been built and paid for.[33]

So why, again, is this happening? Surely the transit "experts" must have accountability in all this. But again, nope. The reality is that transit is not capable of servicing increasingly dispersed patterns of travel demand across the metropolitan area. The most successful systems are about accommodating trips most likely be attracted to transit, not spreading it around everywhere. Transit works best where destinations include concentrated employment opportunities, like downtown Toronto through Union Station, and others where transit can provide a fast, comfortable service.

The problem is that we are not having a conversation about the idea of hybrid mobility: people don't want to talk about a world with cars, only a world without them. Planners go along with the policy expectation that for many trips, transit can greatly ease the need for cars. Transit-oriented policies are thus the focus of official plans. But the reality is that cars are here to stay. "Complete streets" and similar creative approaches are a step in the right direction but are less common policy approaches in suburbs. The discussion we should be having is how to focus investment in transit on locations where it is likely to be most successful, along with the private auto and other forms of personal mobility.

The Myth: Density Is A Virtue And Can Solve All Of Our Problems

Planners are gifted at writing "good planning principles" with great words and broad-based references to laudable goals like sustainability, resilience, compact urban form, complete communities, transit-oriented development, and the list goes on.

What these principles have in common though is that it's all mostly about residential density. The "central city" ideology prevails; everything that is dense, served by transit and generally crams the greatest number of people on the smallest land base is good. Everything else (i.e., sprawl) is bad, and is thus a problem to be converted to the good.[34]

The Reality: Residential Is Only One of Many Uses Within The Urban Area

The reality is that the net density of new residential areas in most new Canadian communities is already very high. Plus, residential is not the only land use in cities. In the City of Hamilton, for example, only about a third of all urban land is for residential use.[35] The proportion is somewhat lower for communities with more industrial land, like the City of Mississauga, home to Toronto Pearson International Airport, where the share of lands occupied by residential is around 30 per cent.[36] In any event, lands in other uses make up the largest proportion of the total urban area, including open space, institutional, transportation and utilities, and employment.

Moreover, while net residential densities have been increasing through smaller lot sizes and more row houses and condo apartments, increasing standards for public open space and more stringent environment protection and requirements have balanced these gains, resulting in neighbourhood-wide densities similar to the good old-fashioned large-lot suburbs of the 1950s. Indeed, under current planning requirements the older denser leafy communities in central Toronto or lower Hamilton would not be allowed to develop today because of increased environmental protection and higher standards for stormwater, parks, and schools.

Wait, what? The total area of environmentally sensitive lands protected from development in new suburban areas is *more than it was back in the 1950s*? Believe it: there are actually areas in the older City of Toronto where brass plaques can be found laid in the concrete sidewalks to commemorate watercourses that were buried to make way for new development.[37]

The focus on residential density and growth patterns diverts attention away from issues related to the broader structure of new urban areas, and the sacrifices we are prepared (or not) to make in order to compact (literally) urban form, i.e., compress the total amount of lands used. It also means that everyday access to nature, overall liveability and quality of life gets lost in the debate.

The Myth: Intensification Is "Free" Or At Least Costs Way Less Than Suburban Growth

It is often suggested that new suburbs are expensive. Rather, intensified urban forms are not as "costly" as new urban growth areas since they rely on existing services, and do not require immediate investment in new infrastructure to serve growth in people and households. As a result, the prevailing narrative is that intensification is preferred because it is less "wasteful" and more efficient from service delivery and municipal finance perspectives. Seems like a no-brainer, yes?

The Reality: Intensification Still Requires Expensive Infrastructure

It is not always the case that intensification costs less. Broadly speaking, it is primarily the cost of "linear" or spatially driven services that is affected by the form of growth. The cost of "people-oriented" services tends to be less affected as these are required regardless of form. Services for which delivery is affected by spatial factors do tend to have lower per unit costs. Fire protection is a good example. Similarly, road repairs and winter maintenance are also good examples of the type of linear service for which costs are driven by spatial factors and may be lower for intensification.

Unlike linear services, however, the costs of "people-oriented" services are driven by user demand. Libraries, recreation facilities schools and parks are good examples of services that need to be provided regardless of population density, unit type or built urban form. Some services can be provided more cost-effectively at higher densities, yes, but only if capacity is available. For instance, with greater intensification there will be more high-rise buildings, suggesting a need for specialised high-rise firefighting equipment. The local road (and transit) network will also be used more intensely, which generates new costs and service needs to maintain a state of good repair.

Community services also tend to be more challenging, complicated, and costly to deliver within an intensified urban environment. Conflicts over traffic, dog-walking, park space, and entertainment uses only compound this challenge. More intensified patterns of development do tend to yield higher revenues, especially with respect to property taxes. However, the need to upgrade existing infrastructure often creates additional costs that were not anticipated.

The reality is that the high-rise residential condo boom of the last 20+ years in the City of Toronto has led to a critical shortage of park space, necessitated massive investments to upgrade old and under-sized water and sewer infrastructure, and has created an environment where the provision of new community facilities is hugely expensive, especially recreation centres and schools. In many of the more successful locations for intensification in central Toronto new projects are now posting warnings to buyers that there likely will not be space for their children in local schools and they may need to attend (i.e., and ironically, get bused out to) more distant facilities.[38]

Intensification, like all types of urban development, is not cheap. And the overall fiscal impacts of intensification are far more complex than simply making "better" use of existing infrastructure. In the City of Toronto, for example, much of the initial capital cost of infrastructure upgrades is passed on to the end-user, which some have argued has the effect of worsening (not improving) affordability.[39] Also turns out, as noted above, that it is surprisingly easy to overwhelm local servicing capacity like schools and piped services. In the end, it all costs money, and somebody has to pay. So, intensification is not *de facto* cheaper than other forms of growth, although it does offer many other benefits that of course need to be weighed along with the bottom line. The conversation planners should be having is about the full costs of all types of development, financing options and situations where – on a city-wide basis – intensification may actually be more expensive than traditional suburban growth.

The Myth: Downsizing Will Save Us from Sprawl

This is an increasingly common argument against any type of urban expansion: as baby-boomers age they will downsize. Grandparents will vacate their large existing homes to make room for younger generations. Since there are so many boomers, the argument goes, this shift will generate significant new housing supply, and in particular it will free up an amount of existing single-family homes that will be so large as to reduce or eliminate the need for any urban expansion.

The Reality: Ageing In Place Is Here To Stay

Like most myths, this one is compelling until we look at the data. In Canadian cities at least, there is no indication widespread downsizing is happening.[40] The evidence seems to be the opposite. Most ageing boomers – like 90 per cent! – are looking to stay in their homes for as long as possible and for very good personal reasons. Seniors as a group are less likely to move than other groups like Millennials, because of the additional costs of moving, access to health care, the stress of decluttering required for downsizing and adjusting to condo living, among other factors.[41]

Downsizing does occur, but on average much later in the demographic cycle or in response to negative events such as divorce, major illness, and widowhood. The pattern we are seeing overall is that most older Canadians are doing what their parents did: choosing to remain in their house.[42] And for households that need the money for retirement? Other options such as reverse mortgages or accessory units (i.e., basement apartments) are usually more convenient. The reality is that downsizing is often not a very good deal unless it is either to a much smaller space or to a less expensive location at the urban fringe.

And even if we can agree that downsizing should occur, how would one even structure a public policy response to compel that shift? Create a tax or other penalty that forces seniors out of their homes the moment they are empty-nesters and deemed to be "over-housed"? Make suburban seniors move when they turn 70? Putting aside the implicit social judgement involved (that one is morally obliged to live in a pre-ordained maximum amount of space) the solution is far from an easy fix. As with many well-intentioned planning ideas, what in theory may seem plausible in practice is often not realistic.

So, if downsizing is not occurring, then we must deal with the demand for new homes that will continue to be strong. The conversation we should be having is about retrofitting the suburbs for ageing in place, planning for growth, and not waiting for boomers to bequeath their backsplits to the Millennials.

The Myth: Housing Affordability Is Improved In An Intensified Environment

It is often suggested that housing affordability is improved through an intensified urban environment, including the addition of the popularised "missing-middle" forms such as multiplexes, laneway houses, and other accessory forms. This affordability argument is a long-standing myth that has become more fashionable recently with the rise of "densification" in Canada.[43]

The Reality: Affordability Is A Challenge Under Any Scenario

While clearly a convenient and persuasive position for opponents of urban expansion, the relationship between intensification and affordability is far from straightforward. On one hand, imposing limits on new growth areas works against affordability by constraining conventional suburban homebuilding and pricing more people out of the ground-related housing market.[44] Other factors such as the rate of growth, incomes, borrowing capacity of developers and homebuyers, and development approval timing also have an effect. House prices have escalated across North America, including communities without comparable constraints to land supply such as in the Dallas-Fort Worth area in Texas.

On the other hand, increased intensification makes it look like more affordable housing is being built but only because the new units are smaller, cheaper apartments. Larger "family-sized" apartment units remain extremely expensive relative to comparably sized ground-related homes, since high-rises cost more to build per square foot. Similarly, providing more "missing middle" housing may contribute to improving affordability by providing more apartments, but again only because these units are small. And, other things being equal, developers will tend to price most new units at the maximum the market will bear, suggesting that housing affordability overall is not necessarily improved by an intensified urban environment. More units for more people, yes, but not more accessibly priced.

Moreover, as a relatively new concept, the impact of "up-zoning" on affordability remains the subject of debate.[45] There is some evidence, for example, to suggest that building missing middle housing has the effect of raising prices in localised markets through accelerated gentrification because most of the new units are high-end custom builds. Others have suggested that on a city-wide basis up-zoning tends to improve affordability through the "filtering" process - in which existing households move into new units thereby freeing up older and lower-cost units elsewhere. Others argue that the filtering process is too slow to meaningfully improve affordability for those with lower incomes.[46]

The conclusion to be drawn here is that there is no clear evidence that housing affordability will necessarily be improved under any urban growth scenario. Housing affordability is a complex issue with many factors involved, of which the relationship to intensification is but one. The reality is that affordability is likely to remain a challenge no matter how much intensification we have. Historically in Ontario, significant house price corrections have only occurred in response to declines in demand, not excess supply.[47]

And on the demand side, not much seems to be changing. Like it or not, the dream of home ownership is alive and well.[48] There is no question that living a dense urban lifestyle with access to swanky amenities is great (if you can afford it) but this does not mean it is therefore a priority or even a real option for most people.[49] The old adage "drive until you qualify" is apt as ever in the Toronto area where new suburban homes at the outer edge of the commuter shed are more affordable and much more spacious than new high-rise condominiums even in redeveloping suburban areas.

The Myth: If Only We Had The "Right" Planning Policies In Place, There Would Be No Sprawl

From a broader perspective, much of the popularised opinions about how we must "build our cities differently" often focuses on the need for new planning policy tools or approaches: almost as if there is some secret policy algorithm that has yet to be discovered.

More specifically, an implicit assumption exists that there is a one-to-one trade-off between urban expansion (i.e., greenfield development) and intensification. That is, if we only put in place purposeful zoning and planning policies, growth would automatically be redirected into more intensification. Similarly, there is a pervasive view that ever more aggressive planning interventions, including fixed urban boundaries, are required to support this approach. Or, in other words, discovering the magic policy combination will stop sprawl.

The Reality: Planning Policy Does Not Build the Suburbs

The reality is that this is not how cities work, nor how land use planning as a legislative instrument is structured. Most of the clarion calls for significant change to the way we grow tend to ignore the scale of social and economic transformations required – like changing the structure of the economy to get more jobs into office towers (and other higher density job spaces) or changing housing preferences to get a lot more people (i.e., middle income families) into apartments. And face it: land use planning is a blunt tool for that kind of work. Tax policy? International trade regulations? Huge financial subsidies for electric vehicle plants and associated supply chain investments? Sure. Money talks.

But planning policy? Not as much. Planning can remove barriers and encourage more intense forms of development but cannot force a particular type of development to happen in a particular place. From an employment perspective, planning cannot control the economic sectors likely to invest in a community or job densities once a place is built. Ironically, some of our most pressing economic development imperatives – like accelerated technological innovation and productivity growth - are by their very nature labour-saving and act in spatial terms against objectives to increase employment density.[50] So while planning policy might include job density targets - other things being equal – no municipality is going to turn away investment in industrial and business parks no matter how many jobs are created.

And from a residential perspective, it is crucial to recognise that the pattern of household formation and demand for space are fundamentally social constructs. Demand for housing is about *what people want* as they grow up and work to put a roof over their heads and food on the table. And vote in local elections. Across the broader population irrespective of the wide diversity of cultural backgrounds and life experience, people are still choosing to live together, get married, have children, buy houses with backyards, commute to work, and in some cases downsize. Not everyone follows these lifecycle patterns, but most of us do.

The market, after all, is "us": not some abstract concept but rather the collective result of millions of real people from all walks of life making countless choices day in and day out, to make their lives as comfortable as possible. The reality is that the settlement forms we see in city-regions across Canada, the United States and around the world are co-created by an array of economic, demographic, institutional, political, and cultural systems: not planning policy.

The Need for a New Dialogue

It has been said that if you ask ten economists the same question you will get ten different answers. Ask most land use planners (and pretty much anyone else it seems) about top issues facing Canadian cities and you will get similar answers: urban sprawl is *the* problem, captured by alarming statistics on loss of prime agricultural land, destruction of natural habitats and biodiversity, auto-dependency, congestion, air pollution and comparisons to the oil sands industry in Alberta.[51] Yet even more so today than when the "ghastly mess" was first observed in Toronto in 1954, we keep building it and as long as times are prosperous there is no sign it will stop.

What is to be made of all this? One conclusion we can draw is that planning to stop sprawl does not stop sprawl. Suburbs are being planned and sold as fast as we can build them. Constrained urban boundaries, while a persuasive concept in theory, have proven difficult to implement. Politics is part of the difficulty, but there is also the real risk that constrained boundaries in high-demand urban areas will act to redirect growth elsewhere: often to proximate ex-urban and rural communities that are not nearly as well-suited to accommodate it.[52]

Is this good planning? Probably not, at least insofar as we believe that growth should be concentrated in the areas best suited to handle its demands. And to be clear, these would be the major metropolitan areas that have the urban structure, strategic location, and developed multi-modal transportation connections within the broader economic region. Small towns and rural areas are not, in our view, suitable major growth nodes.

Is the solution to avoiding this problem to *over-designate* new lands for greenfield development? This would certainly remove some of the incentive for speculation at the rural margin and hand control back to the local municipality, who can then manage growth pressure through the phasing of approvals and infrastructure investment. After all, the designation of urban lands for development, in and of itself, does not "make" the market. But maybe we're not quite ready for that one just yet.

So, returning to the question again if suburbs are so bad, why do we keep building them? Our answer is that perhaps we have been having the wrong conversations. Where we may have failed as land use planners is to guide a more productive and helpful narrative with the public about the impacts of our lifestyle choices and how the decisions about accommodating those choices get made. Cities and suburbs in Canada are driven by a powerful set of forces and operate within a (relatively) free market and (relatively) democratic decision-making system. Planning policy is a part of how cities work, no doubt about that, but is far from the determining factor that much of the popular discourse would have one believe.

We need to have different conversations. The myths we explore above are some of the areas where "good planning principles" are in direct conflict with people's lifestyle choices. With high levels of national immigration, in Canada at least, continued urban growth is inevitable. Intensification is important, yes, but not to everyone. By some accounts, the next wave of growth in a "post-urban" economy may be even more dispersed, localised, and home-based, enabled by the growth of green battery technology, the Internet of Things, autonomous vehicles, and entrenchment of remote work models.

Does this mean that we should throw up our hands and abandon all hope of compact suburban forms and rejuvenated and revitalised urban cores? Certainly not. As with most public policy debates, the resolution falls somewhere in the middle. To this end, we urge planners and decision-makers to challenge the standard and simplistic narrative that suburbs are bad, and to test the myths more openly around key elements of the sprawl debate.

We should be accepting that urban, suburban, central city and rural value-systems are all integral parts of city-regions, and are co-produced through demographic and market forces, finance, servicing, democratic decision making, and yes – planning.[53] To ignore these realities only perpetuates the negative image of urban growth in general, along with the "failures" of land use planning to deliver change needed to save suburban populations from the consequences of their own choices. In our view, it's time to correct these misperceptions with more serious and evidence-based discussions about the suburban worlds we inhabit.

Endnotes

1   We are indebted to Ray Simpson (in memoriam) and Russell Mathew for inspiration underlying the ideas in this chapter over the years.

2   Saira Peesker, "'You can't eat money': Residents protest urban sprawl on eve of public input deadline", *CBC News,* July 22, 2021, https://www.cbc.ca/news/canada/hamilton/urban-boundary-expansion-1.6112983#:~:text=Hamilton-,%27You%20can%27t%20eat%20money%27%3A%20Residents%20protest%20urban,influx%20of%20future%20home%20buyers.

3   Larry Bourne, "The urban sprawl debate: Myths and realities and hidden agendas", *Plan Canada* 41, no. 4 (2001): 26-28.

4   On average, lot sizes for ground-related housing have been declining for decades. Lot sizes for single and semi-detached units in the suburban areas of the GTHA declined to under 400m^2 in the 2006 to 2011 period. For detail see https://www.ontario.ca/document/performance-indicators-growth-plan-greater-golden-horseshoe-2006. New residential communities since 2011 have become even denser, in the City of Brampton for example, with lot sizes for single-detached units as low as 260m^2 which equates roughly to a 32-foot lot frontage.

5   Michael Ranger, "Toronto has more cranes in use than most U.S. cities combined", *CityNews*, April 14, 2023, https://toronto.citynews.ca/2023/04/14/toronto-cranes-construction-north-america/. And that's just the City of Toronto. According to City of Mississauga Mayor Bonnie Crombie at the 2023 ULI Spring Meeting, this 50 year-old bedroom suburb that was "the capital of urban sprawl" now has 36 towers downtown and 35 towers elsewhere in the city ranging in height from 30 to 56 storeys, with an 81-storey tower under construction (see "M City" https://urbantoronto.ca/database/projects/m3-m-city.34084), with 116 towers proposed to be built in next 20 years.

6   Office of the Auditor General of Ontario, *Value-for-money audit: Land-use planning in the Greater Golden Horseshoe*, December 2021.

7   The City of Hamilton in the Toronto area is one good example of several, with Council ultimately voting to not follow the recommendations of consultants (including one of this chapter's authors) and its own staff to expand the urban boundary to accommodate growth over the period to 2051. See Samantha Craggs, "Hamilton councillors vote down a massive expansion to the city's urban boundary", *CBCNews*, November 19, 2021. https://www.cbc.ca/news/canada/hamilton/urban-boundary-1.6255120.

8   Adapted from Environmental Defence Canada which is a leading Canadian environmental advocacy group. https://environmentaldefence.ca/the-big-sprawl/ The list of attendant social and economic consequences attributed to sprawl is well-documented and tends to be consistent from an environmental advocacy perspective.

9   Todd Litman, "Urban Sprawl Is Not More Affordable: Influential Housing Report Supporting Suburban Expansion is Little More Than Propaganda", *The Tyee*, March 23, 2018, https://thetyee.ca/News/2018/03/23/Urban-Sprawl-Not-More-Affordable/

10   European Environment Agency (EEA) and Swiss Federal Office for the Environment (FOEN), *Urban sprawl in Europe* (2016), https://www.eea.europa.eu/publications/urban-sprawl-in-europe. The Netherlands, in particular, is often held up as the gold standard for innovative approaches to urban development yet is at the top of the list of major clusters with high sprawl values.

11   John Sewell, "Don Mills: E.P. Taylor and Canada's first corporate suburb", *City Magazine* 21, no. 2 (1977) 28–38.

12   John Gray, "Why live in the suburbs?", *Maclean's* 67, no. 17 (1954) 7–11, 50–52.

13   In spite of the valiant efforts of Andres Duany and the rest of the New Urbanists, who have produced many guides to suburban design practice (see the near-perfect *Charter of the New Urbanism*). The Toronto area boasts several communities designed and influenced by Duany and New Urbanism (notable, among others: Cornell in Markham, River Oaks in Oakville, and Niagara-on-the-Lake), but these remain isolated examples in a sea of suburban design indifference.

14   Peter Shawn Taylor, "Canadians love living in the suburbs so why aren't we building more of them?" Report on Business, *The Globe & Mail*, October 17, 2018, https://www.theglobeandmail.com/business/rob-magazine/article-canadians-love-living-in-the-suburbs-so-why-arent-we-building-more/.

15   Canadians for a Sustainable Society, "Stop sprawl", 2023, https://sustainablesociety.com/research-material/urban-sprawl/

16   David Gordon, *Still suburban? Growth in Canadian suburbs, 2006–2016*, (Council for Canadian Urbanism. Working Paper #2, 2018), https://www.canadiansuburbs.ca/wp-content/uploads/2022/03/Still_Suburban_Monograph_2016.pdf

17   Generally, the pattern remains according to the 2021 Canada Census. Details can be found at a high level here: Peter Holle and Wendell Cox, "Canada: Suburbs Dominate Growth - 2021 Census", *Frontier Centre for Public Policy*, February 16, 2022, https://fcpp.org/2022/02/16/canada-suburbs-dominate-growth-2021-census/.

18   Patrick Sisson, "How the pandemic supercharged sprawl", *CityLab Bloomberg*, January 5, 2022 https://www.bloomberg.com/news/features/2022-01-05/a-supernova-of-suburban-sprawl-fueled-by-covid.

19   Statistics Canada, "Canada's large urban centres continue to grow and spread", *Statistics Canada* Catalogue 11-001-X, February 9, 2022, https://www150.statcan.gc.ca/n1/en/daily-quotidien/220209/dq220209b-eng.pdf?st=PRX2L9rp.

20   Association of Municipalities of Ontario (AMO), "How local government works", 2023, https://www.amo.on.ca/about-us/municipal-101/how-local-government-works. In Canada, planning and development decisions are also made through various quasi-judicial boards and tribunals. In this case, the role of planners (amongst other professionals) is to provide objective opinion-based evidence, led and cross-examined by lawyers, that is considered by tribunal members who ultimately render the decision.

21   The influence of lawyers on city-building and urban expansion is extensive - they run the show when planning approvals and negotiations get tough. Their impact is woefully understudied, see Deborah G. Martin, , Alexander W. Scherr, a. W., & Christopher City, "Making law, making place: lawyers and the production of space", *Progress in Human Geography* 34 no. 2(2009): 175–192, https://doi.org/10.1177/0309132509337281.

22   Thomas, J. Nechyba and Randall P. Walsh, "Urban sprawl", *The Journal of Economic Perspectives* 18, no. 4 (2004): 177–200, https://www.jstor.org/stable/3216798. According to the authors, the term sprawl was first coined 1937 with the major outlines of current debates coalescing in the post-World-War-II era.

23   Ontario Ministry of Municipal Affairs, *A Place to Grow: Growth Plan for the Greater Golden Horseshoe* (Queen's Printer for Ontario, 2017). Intensification targets have changed with the various versions of the *Growth Plan* (the first plan in 2006 and the "last" in 2019, as the plan is expected to be superseded). In 2017, for example, urban growth centres corresponding with

the downtowns of each of the major suburban cities in the GTHA were to be planned for a minimum density target of 200 residents and jobs per hectare. New greenfield areas were to be planned for a minimum of 80 residents and jobs per hectare. The intensification targets have also been increased, from the original 40% of new units in the existing built-up area to 50% of new units in the more recent versions, and the density target has ranged from 50 to 80 residents per hectare. Note employment areas are treated separately in the updated plan, recognising challenges in shifting job density through planning policy.

24   Christopher Hume, "Ontario's Growing Environmental Crisis is Largely the Fault of Bad Urban Planning", *Storeys*, February 25, 2020, https://storeys.com/hume-bad-urban-planning-environment-neighbourhoods/.

25   Alan Walks (ed.), *The Urban Political Economy and Ecology of Automobility: Driving Cities, Driving Inequality, Driving Politics* (London: Routledge, 2015).

26   Emily Hochberg, "Redfin Unveils the Best Canadian Cities for Public Transit in 2019", *Redfin*, March 11, 2019, https://www.redfin.com/news/best-cities-canada-public-transit-score/.

27   Statistics Canada, 2021 Census of Population. Details available at: https://tinyurl.com/5y8cm869

28   Joel Kotkin, "Autonomous cars are about to transform the suburbs", *Forbes*, February 21, 2018 (reprinted as Chapter 17 in this book). More recent work has shown that in the U.S. access to jobs is far greater by private automobiles than transit, as measured by 30-minute trips: Wendell, "30-minute commute access: Theoretical and actual", NewGeography.com, April 19, 2022, https://www.newgeography.com/content/007423-30-minute-commute-access-theoretical-and-actual.

29   Katherine Savage, "Results from the 2016 Census: Commuting within Canada's largest cities", *Statistics Canada*, Catalogue 75-006-X, May 29, 2019. https://www150.statcan.gc.ca/n1/pub/75-006-x/2019001/article/00008-eng.htm and noting that the long-term impact of the pandemic on commuting is still to be seen.

30   Pierre Filion, "The mixed success of nodes as a smart growth planning policy", *Environment and Planning B: Planning and Design*, 36, no. 3 (2009): 505–521, https://doi.org/10.1068/b33145. Also, southern Peel and Halton Regions, for example.

31   Sophia Thornley, "Globalization and the economic geography of the GGH", *NeptisGeoWeb*, January 16, 2021, https://www.neptisgeoweb.org/stories/126. This is also the case for many large U.S. metropolitan areas, in California for example, where the vast majority of jobs are located in suburban areas not the downtown or Central Business District (CBD), see Charles Blain, Wendell Cox, Joel Kotkin, Alan M. Berger, Tory Gattis, Zina Kapper, and Alicia Kurimska, *The Next American Cities* (Urban Reform Institute, January 2022), https://urbanreforminstitute.org/wp-content/uploads/2021/12/The-Next-American-Cities.pdf. It is also worth noting that the evolution of the integrated region in the GTHA is the direct outcome of conscious land use planning efforts to put in place a structure of nodes and corridors to direct growth throughout the metropolitan region. And as a result of this very successful approach, as many people now travel between suburban communities as to the downtown core.

32   Stephen Wickens, *Station to Station: Why Subway-Building Costs Have Soared in the Toronto Region* (Residential and Civil Construction Alliance of Ontario, April 2020). Other transit projects in Toronto have also been delayed and over budget, most notably the Eglinton Crosstown Light Rail Transit line. See Anna Hardie, "Why does it cost so much to build transportation

in Canada? An Analysis of the Eglinton Crosstown", *Public Policy and Governance (PP+G) Review*, University of Toronto Munk School of Global Affairs, February 7, 2023, https://ppgreview.ca/2023/02/07/why-does-it-cost-so-much-to-build-transportation-in-canada-an-analysis-of-the-eglinton-crosstown/.

33   Stephen Spencer Davis, "Who Broke the TTC?" *Toronto Life*, July 6, 2023, https://torontolife.com/deep-dives/who-broke-the-ttc-inside-torontos-public-transit-disaster/#:~:text=In%20June%201995%2C%20Mike%20Harris,in%2Dprogress%20Eglinton%20West%20line.

34   Naama Blonder and Andrea Yu, "Urbs vs. Burbs: 'My parks are nicer than your backyards'", *Toronto Life*, May 4, 2023, https://torontolife.com/real-estate/my-parks-are-nicer-than-your-backyards-an-architect-explains-why-young-families-should-live-downtown/.

35   Data provided by the City of Hamilton as part of the assessment of land needs to 2051.

36   City of Mississauga, "Existing Land Use 2020", https://mississauga.maps.arcgis.com/apps/dashboards/2652bb0ffb2f4cc0b09e4b41bbbc4000.

37   There are places in historic central Toronto, for example, where existing natural features were wiped off the landscape to make way for development, a practice which would not be allowed today. One example is in Trinity Bellwoods Park in Toronto's west end, where Garrison Creek (which used to run through the park) is now buried as a sewer pipe. Taddle Creek is another buried river, now partially restored along Philosopher's Walk by the Royal Conservatory of Music with a nice little parkette closer to the water. The City is also embarking on a multi-billion dollar "renaturalisation" of the lower Don River, which during the late nineteenth and early twentieth century was straightened and channelised to facilitate development of the Port Lands.

38   Salmaan Farooqui, "Leslieville just one of several Toronto neighbourhoods with a shortage of schools", *Toronto Star*, September 4, 2017, https://www.thestar.com/news/gta/leslieville-just-one-of-several-toronto-neighbourhoods-with-a-shortage-of-schools/article_6063f9cc-ec90-5d0a-b76f-644d83f522d2.html.

39   Steve Lafleur and Josef Filipowicz, "Opinion: Toronto's development charge increase will make housing even less affordable", *Toronto Star*, November 18, 2022, https://nationalpost.com/opinion/opinion-torontos-development-charge-increase-will-make-housing-even-less-affordable. Note that the City of Toronto can grow only through intensification as the land area is hemmed in on all sides by surrounding municipalities and Lake Ontario.

40   Jason Heath, "The retirement downsizing myth: No, seniors aren't moving in droves - and that will affect the housing market", *Financial Post*, October 20, 2020, https://financialpost.com/personal-finance/retirement/the-retirement-downsizing-myth-no-seniors-arent-moving-in-droves-and-that-will-affect-the-housing-market.

41   Matthew Halliday, "Why downsizing your home in retirement may not be as simple as you think", *The Globe & Mail*, March 9, 2022, https://www.theglobeandmail.com/investing/article-why-downsizing-your-home-in-retirement-may-not-be-as-simple-as-you/.

42   Kerry Gold, "Housing scarcity won't be fixed by expecting seniors to downsize, experts say", *The Globe & Mail*, July 31, 2021, https://www.theglobeandmail.com/real-estate/vancouver/article-housing-scarcity-wont-be-fixed-by-expecting-seniors-to-downsize.

43   David Ley, "Massive densification will not solve our housing affordability problem", *Vancouver Sun*, June 21, 2022, https://vancouversun.com/opinion/david-ley-massive-densification-will-not-solve-our-housing-affordability-problem.

44   As explained in the *City of Hamilton Residential Intensification Market Demand Analysis* (Lorius and Associates consulting, March 2021) by limiting the available greenfield land supply, the *Growth Plan* has the effect of further shifting the price structure of housing to make lower-density forms relatively less attractive and thereby encouraging a more compact urban form (https://pub-hamilton.escribemeetings.com/filestream.ashx?DocumentId=250989).

45   In this case the term "up zoning" refers generally to a change in zoning rules to increase density in neighbourhoods where only detached or semi-detached houses were permitted and may include duplexes, triplexes, town houses, or small apartments, and other similar "missing middle" housing forms.

46   Though largely focused on the U.S. experience, for a helpful overview of the main points of debate see: Brian Doucet, "Simply adding supply won't solve our housing crisis", *TVOToday*, December 15, 2021, https://www.tvo.org/article/simply-adding-supply-wont-solve-our-housing-crisis; and Todd Litman, "The Housing Supply Debate: Evaluating the Evidence", *Planetizen*, May 13, 2021, https://www.planetizen.com/blogs/113295-housing-supply-debate-evaluating-evidence.

47   Evidence from previous Toronto area housing bubbles (1974 and 1989) show that house price corrections only occurred when high borrowing costs combined with an economic recession led to a large decline in demand. In neither case was affordability restored by a large supply of housing (of any type) coming to market and depressing prices. For detail, see Hemson Consulting Ltd., *How Many Homes Do We Need, Built Faster? Review of Ontario's "1.5 Million Homes"*, (Regional Planning Commissioners of Ontario, March 2023), https://rpco.ca/how-many-homes-do-we-need-built-faster/.

48   CIBC, "Canadians' dream of homeownership persists, despite affordability concerns: CIBC Poll", *Cision*, June 5, 2023, https://www.newswire.ca/news-releases/canadians-dream-of-homeownership-persists-despite-affordability-concerns-cibc-poll-808717195.html.

49   Alex Cyr and Andrea Yu, "Urbs vs. Burbs", *Toronto Life* July 2023, https://torontolife.com/real-estate/urbs-vs-burbs-six-families-defend-their-visions-of-the-ideal-life-in-and-around-the-gta/.

50   Antony Lorius, "The Evolution of Employment Land", *Plan Canada* 61, no. 1 (Spring 2022): 28–32.

51   Dianne Saxe, "Why urban sprawl is Ontario's oil sands", *OPPI Planning Exchange Blog*, 2019, https://ontarioplanners.ca/blog/planning-exchange/february-en/why-urban-sprawl-is-ontario's-oil-sands.

52   Of particular concern in the Toronto area is the risk of negative regional impacts on Prime Agricultural areas where growth migrates away from land-constrained (and expensive) housing markets to more dispersed and smaller urban communities with lower density and intensification targets (if any), meaning that for the same number of new housing units proportionally more greenfield lands are consumed. In our view this is less than ideal. For more on exurban issues, see Laura Taylor, & Patrick Hurley (Eds.), *A Comparative Political Ecology of Exurbia: Planning, Environmental Management, and Landscape Change* (Springer, 2016), https://doi.org/10.1007/978-3-319-29462-9_1.

53   The discussion about the complexity of suburbs has definitely started in academia, see for example, Roger Keil, *Suburban Planet* (Cambridge: Polity, 2017).

References

Association of Municipalities of Ontario (AMO), "How local government works", 2023, https://www.amo.on.ca/about-us/municipal-101/how-local-government-works.

Blain, Charles, Wendell Cox, Joel Kotkin, Alan M. Berger, Tory Gattis, Zina Kapper, and Alicia Kurimska, *The Next American Cities* (Urban Reform Institute, January 2022), https://urbanreforminstitute.org/wp-content/uploads/2021/12/The-Next-American-Cities.pdf.

Blonder, Naama and Andrea Yu, "Urbs vs. Burbs: 'My parks are nicer than your backyards'", *Toronto Life*, May 4, 2023, https://torontolife.com/real-estate/my-parks-are-nicer-than-your-backyards-an-architect-explains-why-young-families-should-live-downtown/.

Bourne, Larry. "The urban sprawl debate: Myths and realities and hidden agendas", *Plan Canada* 41, no. 4 (2001): 26–28.

Canadians for a Sustainable Society, "Stop sprawl", 2023, https://sustainablesociety.com/research-material/urban-sprawl/

CIBC, "Canadians' dream of homeownership persists, despite affordability concerns: CIBC Poll", *Cision*, June 5, 2023, https://www.newswire.ca/news-releases/canadians-dream-of-homeownership-persists-despite-affordability-concerns-cibc-poll-808717195.html.

Cox, Wendell, "30-minute commute access: Theoretical and actual", NewGeography.com, April 19, 2022, https://www.newgeography.com/content/007423-30-minute-commute-access-theoretical-and-actual.

Craggs, Samantha, "Hamilton councillors vote down a massive expansion to the city's urban boundary", *CBCNews*, November 19, 2021, https://www.cbc.ca/news/canada/hamilton/urban-boundary-1.6255120

Doucet, Brian, "Simply adding supply won't solve our housing crisis", *TVOToday*, December 15, 2021, https://www.tvo.org/article/simply-adding-supply-wont-solve-our-housing-crisis.

Environmental Defence, "The Big Sprawl", https://environmentaldefence.ca/the-big-sprawl/.

European Environment Agency (EEA) and Swiss Federal Office for the Environment (FOEN), *Urban sprawl in Europe*, 2016, https://www.eea.europa.eu/publications/urban-sprawl-in-europe.

Farooqui, Salmaan, "Leslieville just one of several Toronto neighbourhoods with a shortage of schools", *Toronto Star*, September 4, 2017, https://www.thestar.com/news/gta/2017/09/04/leslieville-just-one-of-several-toronto-neighbourhoods-with-a-shortage-of-schools.html.

Filion, Pierre, "The mixed success of nodes as a smart growth planning policy", *Environment and Planning B: Planning and Design*, 36, no. 3 (2009): 505–521, https://doi.org/10.1068/b33145.

Gold, Kerry, "Housing scarcity won't be fixed by expecting seniors to downsize, experts say", *The Globe & Mail*, July 31, 2021, https://www.theglobeandmail.com/real-estate/vancouver/article-housing-scarcity-wont-be-fixed-by-expecting-seniors-to-downsize.

Gordon, David, *Still suburban? Growth in Canadian suburbs, 2006–2016*, (Council for Canadian Urbanism. Working Paper #2, 2018), https://www.canadiansuburbs.ca/wp-content/uploads/2022/03/Still_Suburban_Monograph_2016.pdf.

Gray, John, "Why live in the suburbs?", *Maclean's* 67, no. 17 (1954): 7–11, 50–52.

Halliday, Matthew, "Why downsizing your home in retirement may not be as simple as you think", *The Globe & Mail*, March 9, 2022, https://www.theglobeandmail.com/investing/article-why-downsizing-your-home-in-retirement-may-not-be-as-simple-as-you/.

Hardie, Anna, "Why does it cost so much to build transportation in Canada? An Analysis of the Eglinton Crosstown", *Public Policy and Governance (PP+G) Review*, University of Toronto Munk

School of Global Affairs, February 7, 2023, https://ppgreview.ca/2023/02/07/why-does-it-cost-so-much-to-build-transportation-in-canada-an-analysis-of-the-eglinton-crosstown/.

Heath, Jason, "The retirement downsizing myth: No, seniors aren't moving in droves - and that will affect the housing market", *Financial Post*, October 20, 2020, https://financialpost.com/personal-finance/retirement/the-retirement-downsizing-myth-no-seniors-arent-moving-in-droves-and-that-will-affect-the-housing-market.

Hemson Consulting Ltd., How Many Homes Do We Need, Built Faster? Review of Ontario's "1.5 Million Homes", (Regional Planning Commissioners of Ontario, March 2023), https://rpco.ca/how-many-homes-do-we-need-built-faster/.

Hochberg, Emily, "Redfin Unveils the Best Canadian Cities for Public Transit in 2019", *Redfin*, March 11, 2019, https://www.redfin.com/news/best-cities-canada-public-transit-score/.

Holle, Peter and Wendell Cox, "Canada: Suburbs Dominate Growth - 2021 Census", (Frontier Centre for Public Policy, February 16, 2022), https://fcpp.org/2022/02/16/canada-suburbs-dominate-growth-2021-census/.

Hume, Christopher, "Ontario's Growing Environmental Crisis is Largely the Fault of Bad Urban Planning", *Storeys*, February 25, 2020, https://storeys.com/hume-bad-urban-planning-environment-neighbourhoods/.

Keil, Roger, *Suburban Planet* (Cambridge: Polity, 2017).

Kotkin, Joel, "Autonomous cars are about to transform the suburbs", *Forbes*, February 21, 2018.

Lafleur, Steve and Josef Filipowicz, "Opinion: Toronto's development charge increase will make housing even less affordable", *Toronto Star*, November 18, 2022, https://nationalpost.com/opinion/opinion-torontos-development-charge-increase-will-make-housing-even-less-affordable.

Ley, David, "Massive densification will not solve our housing affordability problem", *Vancouver Sun*, June 21, 2022.

Litman, Todd, "The Housing Supply Debate: Evaluating the Evidence", *Planetizen*, May 13, 2021, https://www.planetizen.com/blogs/113295-housing-supply-debate-evaluating-evidence.

Litman, Todd, "Urban Sprawl Is Not More Affordable: Influential Housing Report Supporting Suburban Expansion is Little More Than Propaganda", *The Tyee*, March 23, 2018, https://thetyee.ca/News/2018/03/23/Urban-Sprawl-Not-More-Affordable/.

Lorius and Associates consulting, *City of Hamilton Residential Intensification Market Demand Analysis*, March 2021, https://pub-hamilton.escribemeetings.com/filestream.ashx?DocumentId=250989

Lorius, Antony, "The Evolution of Employment Land", *Plan Canada* 61, no. 1 (Spring 2022): 28–32.

Martin, Deborah G., Alexander W. Scherr, a. W., & Christopher City, "Making law, making place: lawyers and the production of space", *Progress in Human Geography* 34 no. 2(2009): 175–192, https://doi.org/10.1177/0309132509337281

Mississauga, City of, "Existing Land Use 2020", https://mississauga.maps.arcgis.com/apps/dashboards/2652bb0ffb2f4cc0b09e4b41bbbc4000.

Nechyba, Thomas, J. and Randall P. Walsh, "Urban sprawl", *The Journal of Economic Perspectives* 18, no. 4 (2004): 177–200, https://www.jstor.org/stable/3216798. According to the authors, the term sprawl was first coined 1937 with the major outlines of current debates coalescing in the post-World-War-II era.

Office of the Auditor General of Ontario, *Value-for-money audit: Land-use planning in the Greater Golden Horseshoe*, December 2021.

Ontario Ministry of Municipal Affairs, *A Place to Grow: Growth Plan for the Greater Golden Horseshoe* (Toronto: Queen's Printer for Ontario, 2017).

Peesker, Saira, "'You can't eat money': Residents protest urban sprawl on eve of public input deadline", *CBC News*, July 22, 2021, https://www.cbc.ca/news/canada/hamilton/urban-boundary-expansion-1.6112983#:~:text=Hamilton-,%27You%20can%27t%20eat%20money%27%3A%20Residents%20protest%20urban,influx%20of%20future%20home%20buyers.

Ranger, Michael, "Toronto has more cranes in use than most U.S. cities combined", *CityNews*, April 14, 2023, https://toronto.citynews.ca/2023/04/14/toronto-cranes-construction-north-america.

Savage, Katherine, "Results from the 2016 Census: Commuting within Canada's largest cities", *Statistics Canada*, Catalogue 75-006-X, May 29, 2019. https://www150.statcan.gc.ca/n1/pub/75-006-x/2019001/article/00008-eng.htm and noting that the long-term impact of the pandemic on commuting is still to be seen.

Saxe, Dianne, "Why urban sprawl is Ontario's oil sands", *OPPI Planning Exchange Blog*, 2019, https://ontarioplanners.ca/blog/planning-exchange/february-en/why-urban-sprawl-is-ontario's-oil-sands.

Sewell John, "Don Mills: E.P. Taylor and Canada's first corporate suburb", *City Magazine* 21, no. 2 (1977) 28–38.

Sisson, Patrick, "How the pandemic supercharged sprawl"; *CityLab Bloomberg*, January 5, 2022, https://www.bloomberg.com/news/features/2022-01-05/a-supernova-of-suburban-sprawl-fueled-by-covid.

Spencer Davis, Stephen, "Who Broke the TTC?" *Toronto Life*, July 6, 2023, https://torontolife.com/deep-dives/who-broke-the-ttc-inside-torontos-public-transit-disaster/#:~:text=In%20June%201995%2C%20Mike%20Harris,in%2Dprogress%20Eglinton%20West%20line.

Statistics Canada, "Canada's large urban centres continue to grow and spread", *Statistics Canada*, Catalogue 11-001-X, February 9, 2022, https://www150.statcan.gc.ca/n1/en/daily-quotidien/220209/dq220209b-eng.pdf?st=PRX2L9rp

Statistics Canada, *2021 Census of Population*, https://tinyurl.com/5y8cm869

Syed, Fatima and Emma McIntosh, "Appeals not allowed, again: Ontario orders Waterloo to sprawl into farmland", *The Narwhal*, April 13, 2023, https://thenarwhal.ca/ontario-waterloo-sprawl-farmland/.

Talen, Emily (ed.), *Charter of the New Urbanism* (New York: McGraw Hill, 2013).

Taylor, Laura E. and Patrick T. Hurley (Eds.), *A Comparative Political Ecology of Exurbia: Planning, Environmental Management, and Landscape Change* (Springer, 2016), https://doi.org/10.1007/978-3-319-29462-9_1

Taylor, Peter Shawn, "Canadians love living in the suburbs so why aren't we building more of them?" Report on Business, *The Globe & Mail*, October 17, 2018, https://www.theglobeandmail.com/business/rob-magazine/article-canadians-love-living-in-the-suburbs-so-why-arent-we-building-more/.

Thornley, Sophia, "Globalization and the economic geography of the GGH", *NeptisGeoWeb*, January 16, 2021, https://www.neptisgeoweb.org/stories/126.

Walks, Alan (ed.), *The Urban Political Economy and Ecology of Automobility: Driving Cities, Driving Inequality, Driving Politics* (London: Routledge, 2015).

Wickens, Stephen, *Station to Station: Why Subway-Building Costs Have Soared in the Toronto Region* (Vaughan, ON: Residential and Civil Construction Alliance of Ontario, April 2020).

Part Two:
Contemporary Suburban Development in Australia

9

The Regulation of Residential Development in New South Wales

Gary A Shiels AM

Introduction

Town planning in New South Wales (NSW) has undergone evolutionary change from regional planning to local council controls, and back to a regional/metropolitan approach, the latter being in response to the population growth. Since the introduction of the first Town Planning Act and the County of Cumberland Plan, there has been phenomenal growth in population and car ownership. In the past seven decades, we have seen the population grow from 1.7 to 5.3 million, with car ownership increasing from 522,000 to over 2 million, resulting in a dramatic expansion of Sydney's Central Area. The population in the whole of NSW is now over 8 million. Population growth, fed by migration, has produced an insatiable demand for housing, which has resulted in the spread of urbanisation to the north, west and south. The emerging built form has resulted in a need to embrace environmentally sustainable development and the provision of infrastructure in the planning of Sydney. Accordingly, the latest Plan for the Metropolis identifies the growth of Sydney into three cities, and seeks to guide the emerging pattern of development in a planned and orderly manner. In this chapter, I will discuss the key milestones in the evolution of town planning in NSW from the Cumberland Plan to the Three Cities Plan over the past 77 years.

The Town and Country Planning Amendment Act (Part 12A)

It is somewhat serendipitous that in the year I was born (1945), the Town and Country Planning Amendment Act (The Amendment Act) was gazetted and was included as part of the Local Government Act (LGA), 1919. The LGA was gazetted in response to *The Royal Commission for Improvement of Sydney and Suburbs*, which was undertaken following the outbreak of the Bubonic Plague in Sydney. The stated purpose of the Amendment Act was, *to make better provision for and in relation to town planning and country planning* (Local Government Amendment Act, No. 21, (Part 12A) 1945). The Amendment Act identified the powers of State and local government to carry out town and country planning functions. The Amendment Act also established the qualifications of town planners, which was the *Town and Country Planners Certificate (Ordinance 4)*. To be a qualified town planner in NSW, you needed to be certified. Some said, if you were a town planner, you deserved to be certified! As there was no real knowledge of what a town planner was supposed to do, this qualification was largely foisted upon State and local government. At a local level, this Ordinance 4 qualification was gifted to the resident engineer in the respective councils. At State level Ordinance 4 was either absorbed or disregarded by State Government. The County of Cumberland Council (the Council) was the authority recognised by the Amending Act. The Council was busily preparing the County of Cumberland Plan for Sydney.

County of Cumberland Plan

The County of Cumberland Plan, formulated in the early 1940s and gazetted in 1951, marked an important milestone in town planning, and was arguably the first plan for Sydney since Captain Arthur Phillip's Plan, in 1792.

The County of Cumberland was described as, *a natural setting for one of the world's great cities* (Winston 1957, p.6). The plan covered an area of 1630 square miles, comprised the City of Sydney and its environs. The aim of the County Scheme was simply stated, *To make the County a pleasanter place to live in, more efficient for business, and a healthier, safer place for children to grow up in* (Winston 1957, p.39). The plan had only one residential zoning, *Living Areas*, which permitted all forms of residential development. To address the challenges of urban sprawl into the suburbs, a green belt was part of the zoning plan, an idea borrowed from the U.K., to separate the existing metropolitan area from rural lands. Extensions to the metropolitan area would occur through the creation of new garden suburbs or satellite towns, also an idea inspired by the new towns in the U.K. such as Welwyn. The County Plan also comprised a Planning Scheme, which gave it statutory force, and contained some early planning terms and broad zoning definitions. Although lawyers and planners have sought to wordsmith those definitions, many still survive today, in various forms of legislation.

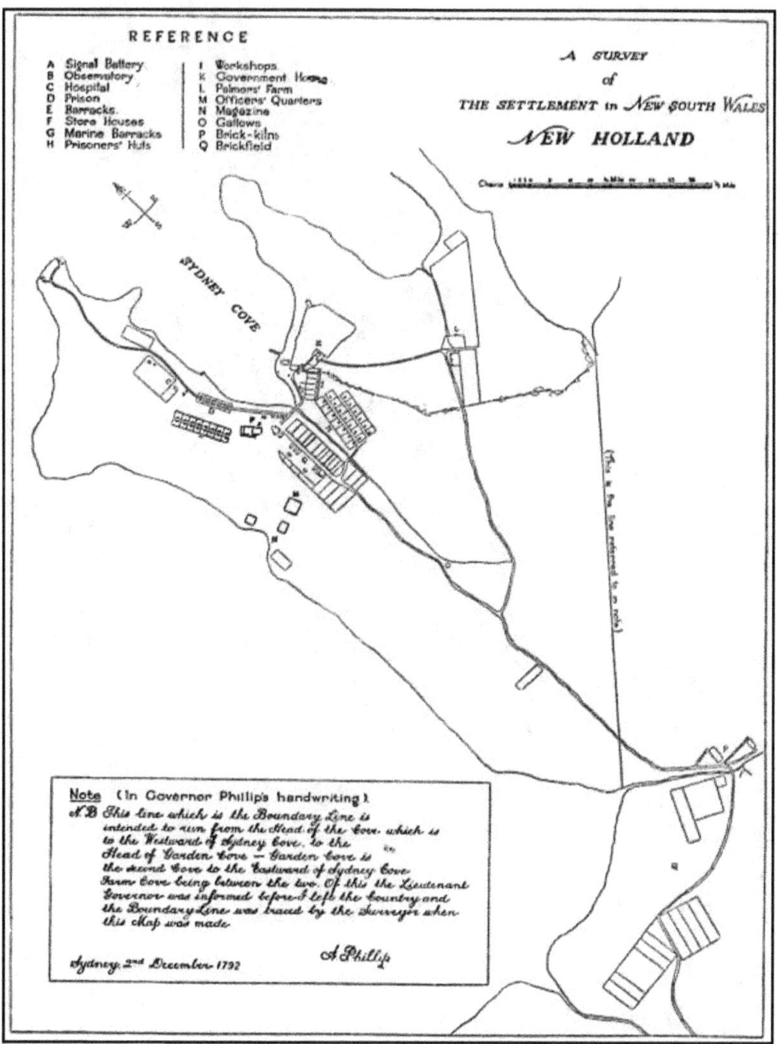

Figure 9.1: Australia's First Town Plan: Plan for Sydney prepared by Governor Phillip, 1792.
(Original in Mitchell Library, Sydney)

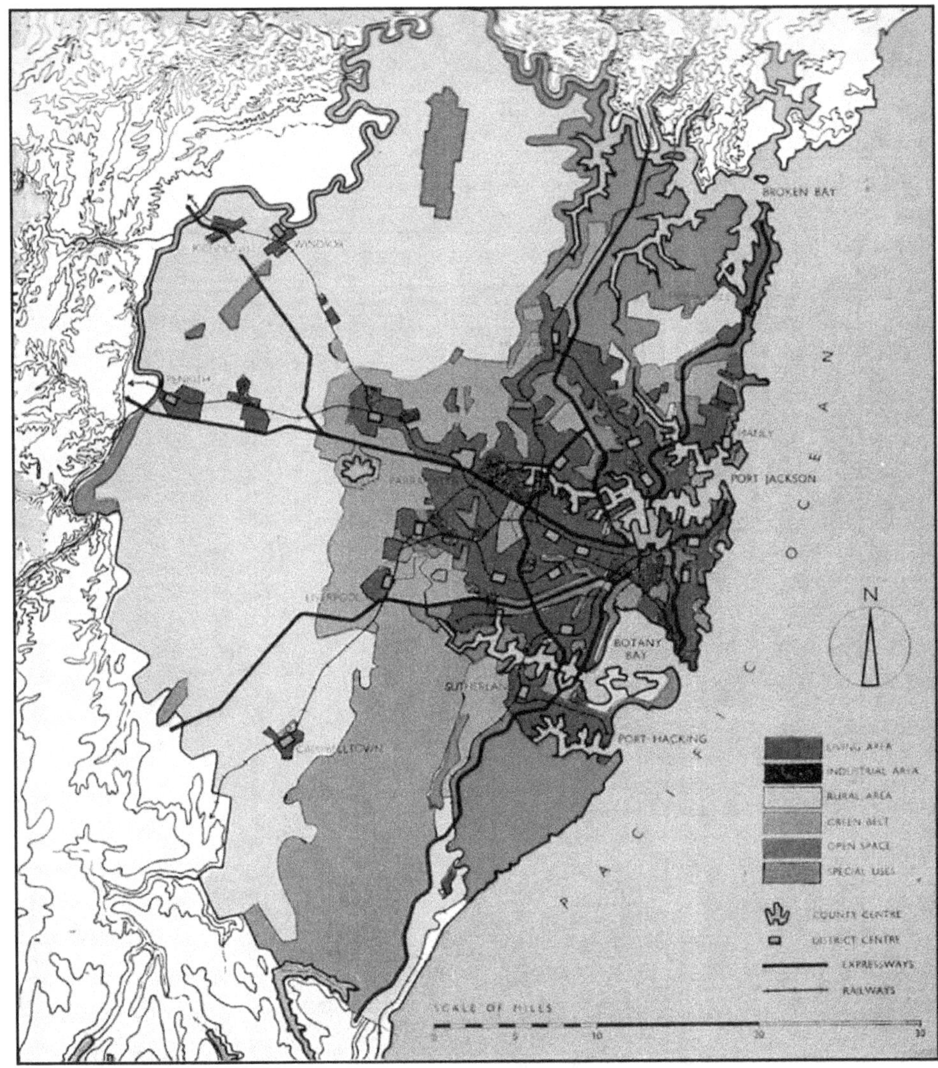

Figure 9.2: The County Plan
(from Denis Winston, *Sydney's Great Experiment*, Angus & Robertson, 1957)

Sydney Region Outline Plan

In the post-war era, the focus of town planning shifted towards accommodating the growing car culture and suburbanisation. The Department of Main Roads (DMR) had become the de facto planning authority by the strenuous designing and building of a road program, which was providing the blueprint for development to follow. The extent of work being undertaken is highlighted in the DMR Annual Report in 1959, when they advised, that the bitumen surfacing of 442 miles of Main Roads had been completed, 44 bridges had been constructed, and 100 miles of deteriorated bitumen surfaces had been repaved. The Report also advised that several other projects had been completed, which included work on the Sydney Harbour Bridge and considerable work on surrounding regional roads. These road works were encouraging development areas where infrastructure was not always available. To guide development and strengthen regional planning, The Sydney Region Outline Plan (SROP) 1970-2000 was published in 1968 by the, then, State Planning Authority (SPA) and it was described as *a strategy for development* (SPA,1968). While the Plan had considerable merit, it failed to achieve its objective to guide development, due to development pressures and a lack of statutory force.

Local Planning Scheme Ordinances

The introduction of local zoning plans further separated land uses and placed greater emphasis on local planning. Residential flats and houses were in separate zones and some councils had five or more residential zones. Similarly, commercial and industrial zones were subdivided to segregate noxious and hazardous uses from residential dwellings. Zoning plans were accompanied by Local Planning Scheme Ordinances (LPSOs), which aimed at reinforcing spatial order and separating incompatible land uses. The planning function was beginning to overshadow the previous approving group in councils, which was the Building Department. Initially, building inspectors had little regard for town planners as they were intruding on the building inspectors' *turf*. I recall in one of the first councils I worked, there was a sign in the building department stating, *If you can read and write you can plan, and even if you can't you can!* Town planners had a lot of work to do, to prove that they were adding value to the development process. Some developers still mount the negative argument about town planners today, particularly if they are having difficulty gaining approval for an *ambit claim* development application (DA). The growth in LPSOs moved the planning emphasis back to the local areas and further diluted the regional considerations contained in SROP. LPSOs were prepared by each of the, then, 42 local councils for their local government areas (LGAs) that comprised the metropolitan area. There was little regard to the SROP or regional planning.

The Environmental Planning and Assessment Act 1979

In 1979, The Environmental Planning and Assessment Act (EP+A Act) was gazetted to introduce *environmental sustainability* and to rationalise the parochial content in local plans. There was a fanfare by the Minister for Planning, telling everyone that the new Act would streamline and revolutionise planning in NSW. The EP+A Act was accompanied by other Acts, and introduced: State Environmental Planning Policies (SEPPs); Regional Environmental Plans (REPs); Ministerial Directions (MDs); and Development Control Plans (DCPs). Planners had become the masters of the acronym. Existing LPSOs, became (Deemed) Local Environmental Plans (LEPs), on the basis they would be updated in a few years. Zoning tables with the identified permissible uses, now had an increasing number of development standards, creating two levels of prohibition for a proposed development. Development standards included: maximum height; maximum floorspace ratio; and minimum landscape area, just to name a few. A proposal had to be permissible in the zone and satisfy the development standards before moving to the next level of assessment. These controls were so inflexible, that State Government introduced an enabling instrument (SEPP No.1 Variation) that allowed the standard, not the zoning, to be varied. While a flexible interpretation was adopted initially to numeric variations, the Land and Environment Court decisions have resulted in rigorous guidelines to satisfy the legal protocol. If the statutory controls could be negotiated, the next level of assessment was the Development Control Plan(s), the contents of which related to the LGA. Finally, there is the involvement/objections from the community that councils must consider.

Instead of rationalising and streamlining the planning system, it became more complicated and bureaucratic. There were now State, Regional, and local planning policies, statutes and controls that needed to be considered with every development application. The convoluted nature of the planning controls has perpetuated a growth in town planning consultants, with developers and residents needing assistance to negotiate the planning process. Although the EP+A Act has had many iterations, it remains, arguably, the most complicated piece of planning legislation in Australia, when compared to other States and Territories.

The Changing Role of Town Planners

As a young planner I observed the emergence of the Engineer/Town Planner in the 1960/70s. These appointed persons inevitably had an engineering bias, and planning was a secondary function. In the 1970/80s, planners obtained planning qualifications via either the Ordinance 4 examination process or the emerging planning degrees at universities. Planners have always been in the inevitable position of managing councillors, responding to developers, and addressing the increasing needs of the community, whose expectations seem to be increasingly demanding. The growth in technology has placed greater demands on council planners to co-ordinate various disciplines. Councils were beginning to recognise that planners had the variety of skill sets to manage multi-disciplinary teams. In several councils, the Director of Planning oversaw the Health, Building and Engineering Departments. I experienced this evolution of the planner's role, firsthand, in the early 1980s, after being appointed Director of Planning at Leichhardt Council. Twelve months after my appointment, there was a management review at council and I became the Director of Planning and Community Development, in charge of strategic, statutory, and social planning. The Social Planning Department embraced childcare, long day care, aged care, and several other activities. My staff increased from 20 to 120 and it was a particularly steep learning curve. My role had evolved from being a planner, to being a manager of a mega-department. This trend has further evolved in State and local governments, with managers, not necessarily qualified planners, managing planning departments.

Evolution of Town Planning at a Local Level

Although there have been many changes to town planning at a local level, there are three key milestones which have occurred in the past two decades. These milestones, which were all introduced by State government, were not well received by councils. First, local councils have been required to go through a process of voluntary and forced amalgamations, and there has been a varying degree of success. State government argued that there would be substantial cost savings and efficiencies in processing DAs. This proved to be a painful process, with many staff members, including General Managers and Planning Directors, being retrenched. Amalgamated councils frequently have different planning controls from three or more LGAs, making life difficult for assessment planners, developers, and decision makers alike. To my knowledge, there is limited documented evidence on the cost savings and improved efficiencies resulting from these amalgamations. As of January 2023, there were a total of 33 local councils in the metropolitan area, with a total 128 councils throughout NSW. There are also 12 regions in regional NSW.

The second change was to the decision-making process in local councils. Historically, councils would consider planning matters and DAs at a committee level then the full council, both of which had the elected councillors as the decision makers. The council committee would make the recommendation, which would be endorsed or changed by the full council. State Government introduced regional and local planning panels to take over the decision-making power of councils and councillors.

Regional planning panels determine matters over $30 million, while local planning panels determine matters below that level. Panels comprise a chair, two experts and a community representative. Local councillors no longer have a role in determining DAs. Disputes against the determination by a regional or local planning panel are to the Land and Environment Court. Merit appeals are normally heard by a commissioner, while matters involving legal issues are heard by a judge.

The final milestone, also foisted on local councils, was the requirement to prepare *a local strategic planning framework*, for their LGA. These frameworks are to guide long-term planning decisions at a regional or metropolitan level. These strategic planning frameworks were required to consider factors such as population growth projections, infrastructure needs, environmental protection, and social equity. These strategic frameworks were seen by many as a pathway back to regional planning.

The Greater Sydney Regional Plan

In recent years, there have been calls for town planning to respond to pressing global challenges, such as climate change and resilience. Planners are now considering strategies to mitigate and adapt to climate impacts, including flood management, sustainable energy systems, green infrastructure, and the protection of natural resources. This shift reflects a growing understanding of the need for place making and planning for affordable housing, while addressing environmental sustainability and providing resilient cities.

In recognition of these challenges for resilient and sustainable cities, and pressures for development in western Sydney, the previous State Government moved the planning emphasis back to regional planning, with the establishment of the Greater Sydney Commission. The Commission had a vision for Greater Sydney, where residents live within 30 minutes of a city, with access to their jobs, education, health facilities, services, and great places. The Greater Sydney Regional Plan pursued that vision with a Metropolis of Three Cities Regional Plan. The regional plan identifies the Eastern Harbour City, the Central River City, and the Western Parkland City. The Plan would then be linked with five district plans, which in turn would be linked to the local plans in each council area.

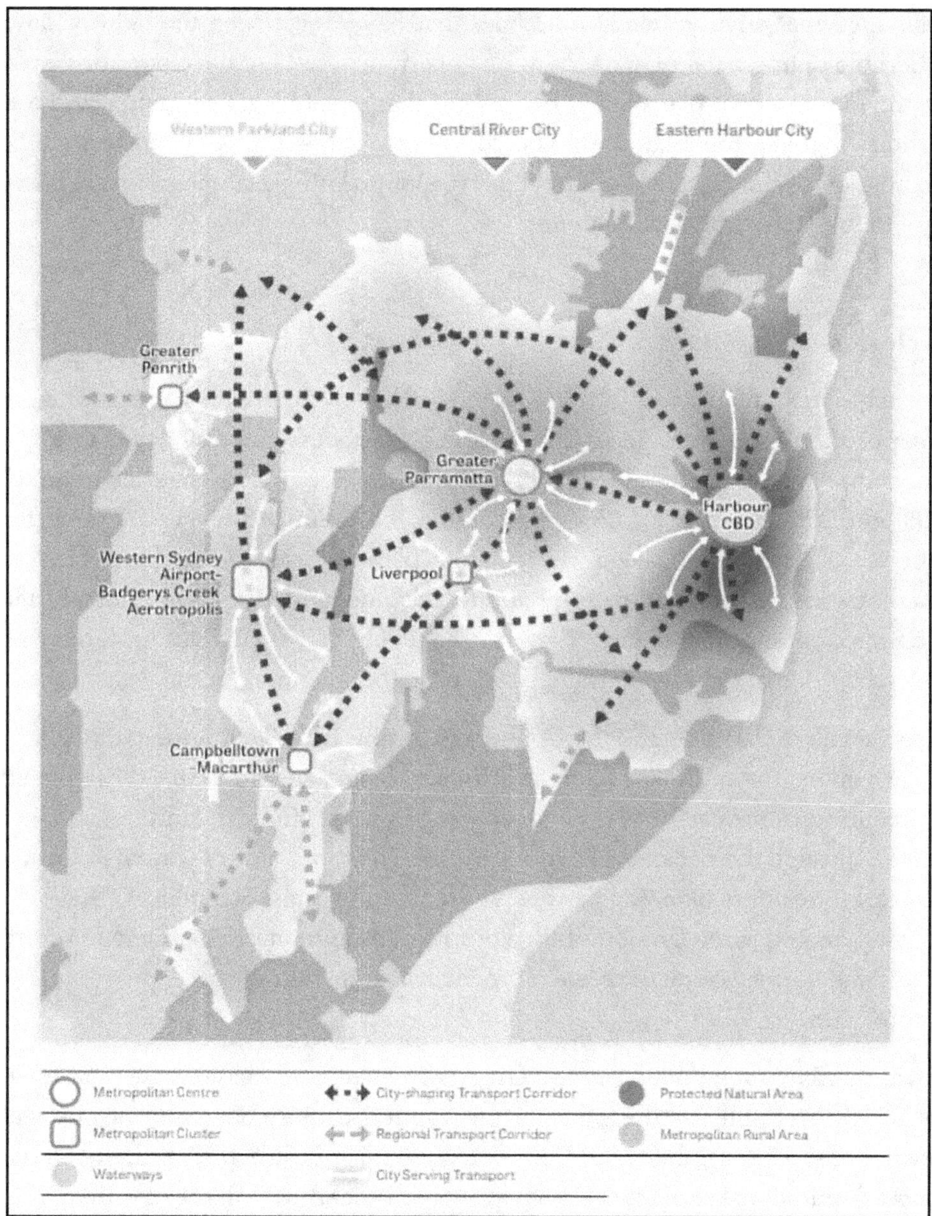

Figure 9.3: Sydney Three Cities Diagram

(Greater Sydney Regional Plan 2018, Greater Sydney Commission)

The Greater Sydney Regional Plan has considerable potential; however, its success will depend on whole of government support, and financial commitment for transport and infrastructure by State and local government. It is one thing to prepare a plan, it is another thing to implement it. Planning shelves are littered with numerous plans containing great environmental outcomes that have never seen the light of day. In my humble opinion, the plan needs to be government led not developer driven. The two previous regional plans failed because of inadequate legal substance and a lack of whole of government support. The NSW Government announced in June 2023 the abolition of the Greater Sydney Commission to bring planning control back in-house to the Department of Planning.

Conclusion

In conclusion, I feel incredibly privileged to have experienced the evolution of town planning and technology from circa 1960s to the present day. During that time, computer mainframes have evolved from the size of a large office to a laptop or iPhone. The potential of iPhones seems to be unlimited, everyone is addicted to them, and they have become a valuable planning tool. Also, the evolution of technology in the preparation of planning documents defies description. Multiple copies of plans and documents, requiring the felling of a small rainforest, have been replaced by digital data being transferred through a planning portal.

When we talk of Part 12A and the County of Cumberland Plan, present day planners look at you as if you are speaking in a foreign language. However, these planning documents were the catalyst for town planning in NSW. Indeed, land use zoning has survived through the decades in various forms. The move from regional to local and now back to regional planning has been welcomed by most planners. This evolution of town planning is recognition of the complexities and interdependencies of urban systems and the aspiration to create more inclusive, sustainable, and environmentally friendly cities.

Notwithstanding the abolition of the Greater Sydney Commission, the Three Cities Plan for Sydney still has the potential to respond to the challenges of population growth, housing affordability, and the demands for infrastructure, if there is holistic support from all stakeholders. Governments will need to balance the demands of spatial strategies, quality urban design, sustainability, community engagement, smart city technology, and climate resilience. City sizes and population growth need to be based on objective, sustainable, data-driven decision-making and not on political whims that more people and housing is necessarily needed or desirable. Town planning still has some way to go to fully utilise the principles of smart city technology and built environments where people want to live.

In my time as a planner, I have prepared and seen many plans initiated, with very few being implemented. As I am the eternal optimist, I believe that Sydney will continue to grow and flourish in an orderly and cohesive manner, hopefully driven by an endorsed regional plan that is based on a sustainable level of population and housing growth.

References

ABS (2023) *Population New South Wales*, 2023 Australian Bureau of Statistics

ABS (2023) *Motor Car Ownership in New South Wales* Australian Bureau of Statistics

Cumberland County Council (1951) *County of Cumberland Planning Scheme*

NSW Government (1945) Local Government Amendment Act, No. 21, (Part X11A) Town and Country Planning Schemes

State Planning Authority (1968) *Sydney Region: Outline Plan 1970-2000 A.D.*, A Report by the State Planning Authority of New South Wales, March, 1968

Winston, Dennis (1957) *Sydney's Great Experiment. The progress of the County of Cumberland Plan*, Angus and Robertson, Sydney

NSW Government (1979) *The Environmental Planning and Assessment Act* 1979

Greater Sydney Planning Commission (2018) *The Greater Sydney Regional Plan: A Metropolis of Three Cities*, State of New South Wales

Koziol, Michael and McGowan, Michael (2023) "Minns Abolishes Sydney Planning Agency to Bring Control Back In-house", *Sydney Morning Herald* (23 June 2023)

10

Contemporary Suburban Development in Victoria

Peter Seamer

Two years after John Batman founded Melbourne in 1835, central Melbourne was laid out by the surveyor Robert Hoddle. Melbourne grew rapidly beyond the Hoddle grid, and with the discovery of gold in the mid 1850s, the metropolis and the State boomed. The structure of the city was set by its geography, soil and climatic conditions and the growth of rail, under the direction of such characters as Tommy Bent. An amazing character, he was a developer, long time Mayor of Brighton, an arguably unscrupulous Rail Minister, and was generally regarded as corrupt. After that, amazingly, he became Premier of Victoria.

Melbourne CBD, unlike some other Australian cities such as Sydney, because of its geography, is highly central to its suburbs, and relatively, to the whole of the State. Its radial road and rail network have driven a CBD-centric city, which in turn has led to many suburban areas being relatively poorly served by services and employment.

For much of its life Melbourne's growth was managed by the Melbourne and Metropolitan Board of Works (MMBW), essentially an engineering organisation responsible for surveying, the provision of water supply, sewerage, main drainage and being the main city planning organisation and main road builder. Its excellent visionary 1929 plan was followed over the years by a series of plans allowing the city to adjust to growth.

Most notable among these was the wide-ranging 1954 plan which set out directions for the CBD, major suburban centres, and main road proposals. The concept of a multi nodal metropolis has remained a fundamental part of all metro planning strategies but has achieved patchy success. District centres, transit cities, activity centres, clusters, high technology precincts have all been part of it: plenty of strategies but, at least until COVID we remained a CBD centred metropolis.

However, the MMBW was relatively independent of Government, and was headed up by Council representatives who, in effect had little say over its direction. The key players in planning the metropolis rested with a series of powerful chairmen who oversaw Melbourne's growth for a century. Many see it as unfortunate that this technically led body was disbanded as the principal planning body in 1992, and its role was narrowed to a role as a water authority. The power shifted back to the State Government, its politicians and its bureaucracy, which was probably more democratic but arguably less efficient and more open to both political and private interference.

The Planning System

Planning in Victoria is overseen by the Minister of Planning and his chief instrument is the Planning and Environment Act. There are a wide range of policy documents and planning procedures which are nothing if not complex and highly layered. For example, the official guide to "Using Victoria's Planning System" runs to 278 pages. There have been many attempts to rationalise the system but often overly legally focused reviews have generally only made it worse.

The tool the Minister uses is the Planning Scheme, which zones land for particular uses. Only the Planning Minister can zone or rezone land, or delegate the right to propose an amendment to the planning scheme. Much of the day-to-day planning and administration of the planning scheme including planning permits for development is undertaken by local Municipalities. In some cases, the Department or other bodies such as the Victorian Planning Authority (VPA) can undertake this role. Additionally, the various utility providers have strong powers. However individual permits (DAs in some States) can be contested at the Victorian Civil and Administrative Tribunal (VCAT) and it is VCAT that generally has the final say.

Melbourne's Growth, its Suburbs, and its Growth Areas

The series of MMBW plans set the direction for the growth of the suburbs, including its road network and centres of business activity, while more recently the 2002 "Melbourne at 2030" provided a comprehensive high level direction for growth. Being one of the world's large but lowest density cities at around 1500 people per square kilometre, a primary principle was the creation of a more compact city including building up activity centres which can provide a wide range of services, local employment and housing.

While the document was attempting to be broadly aspirational, perhaps its biggest impact was on the creation of an urban growth boundary to limit the spread of Melbourne. In 2005 the publication of "A Plan for Melbourne's Growth Areas", led to the establishment of the Growth Areas Authority (GAA) in 2006. It oversaw the growth of new suburbs on the Metropolitan fringe, through a structured planning approach using Precinct Structure Plans (PSPs) to replace previously used broad area zoning and, often, ad hoc growth on a site-by-site basis.

In this way Melbourne has been able to develop integrated suburbs that are built around functioning town centres and local school sites, with excellent public open space, fit for purpose roads, bike paths and correctly planned utilities, and to an extent, built to maximise access to employment, while still protecting culturally or environmentally sensitive areas.

In 2014 the then Liberal Government produced a major review of planning for the city, and to some extent the State, with "Plan Melbourne". This was later "refreshed" by the Labor Government with "Plan Melbourne 2017-2050". The role of the GAA was expanded to include non-growth area precincts by becoming the Metropolitan Planning Authority and then after the change of Government at the 2014 election, the Victorian Planning Authority. Its primary role is in creating integrated suburb plans for selected parts of Victoria that must be enacted by the Minister of Planning by amending the Victorian Planning Scheme.

Melbourne's Growth Areas are ringed by an Urban Growth Boundary, with areas in affected Municipalities outside this ring, being zoned "Green Wedge" and which are not able to be developed or even rezoned without the approval of both houses of Parliament. While much of the land inside the Green Wedge Zone is not particularly green and certainly not a wedge, the term evoked the memory of the then Premier Dick Hamer's creation of radial undevelopable wedges: "Melbourne's Green Lungs". Areas inside the boundary are zoned Urban Growth Zone which require a PSP to allow development.

This system has avoided mistakes which previously created isolated and underserviced developments not fit for future resident's needs.

Another reason for the creation of the GAA was to control the growth of housing. Contested planning matters had led to very long gestation periods for the approval of new suburbs and the rolling out of an extensive program allowed more housing to become available in well planned suburbs. The 80 or so PSPs (equating approximately to a similar number of suburbs), had an early effect on stabilising lot prices and for several years kept prices well below some other States, and Sydney in particular. Relatively affordable housing was probably one of the main reasons behind rapid population growth in Victoria in the pre-pandemic years.

An arguably somewhat slower roll out of PSPs, and delays in projects being approved by Councils has seen supply shortages and with high levels of demand, a parallel increase in housing costs. However, these prices, combined with arguably the world's longest pandemic lockdowns and the resulting loss of overseas students has seen Melbourne's population growth rate slow, although this did not immediately result in a drop in housing demand which in early 2022 was at all-time highs in the growth areas. However, the combination of significantly greater taxes on development and housing over a decade and customer anxiety about jobs, international security and inflation and developer difficulty with staffing and material supply have led to a sudden demand slump in mid 2022, the long-term effects of which are still unknown. However high-level political statements about the need to increase immigration suggest that this slump will be temporary.

Home Ownership

Housing ownership has always been a cornerstone of "the Australian Dream" but by world standards Australia (along with New Zealand, the UK, and the USA) is only middle level by world standards on the extent of home ownership to total housing, at around 65%. By contrast in China and Russia have levels around 90%, albeit with there being dissimilarities on their land ownership systems.

The Australian Institute of Health and Welfare, however, shows there are changes in homeownership. For example, 30- to 34-year-olds in 1971 had a homeownership rate of 64% which by 2016 had fallen to 50%. Similarly, overall ownership is falling: in 1994 71% of households owned their own home but by 2019 this had dropped to 66%. Victoria has a slightly higher rate than the average with 68% which may reflect somewhat lower house prices than NSW, possibly resulting from better availability of sites for development.

The standout difference between renters and owners is in housing affordability. Owners without a mortgage have their housing cost to gross household income being 3%. Renters by comparison pay 20% for their housing.

There are a number of schemes to support people getting into the housing market. These change from time to time, depending on market conditions and elections. Most of these are federal but Victoria has a plethora of additional schemes. A $10,000 grant ($20,000 in the regions) is available for first home buyers purchasing a home of less than $750,000. Similarly, there is a 50% stamp duty exemption for houses valued below $600,000, and partial concessions for houses valued up to $750,000.

As well as these there are concessions for off the plan purchases, pensioner exemptions, young farmer concessions, and a principal place of residence concession with restrictions to stop double dipping.

The Rental Market

There is a serious problem emerging with the supply of rental properties. While vacancies peaked at 5.2 per cent during the pandemic, this dropped to just 1.8 per cent across the city in March 2022.

In the outer suburbs, where renters are more likely to be families with children, the shortage is even more acute, with for example, just 0.4 per cent of properties being available for rental in the Cardinia council area in Melbourne's outer south-east.

The publication "Domain" quotes overall outer suburban local government areas having vacancy rates of 0.6 and 0.7 per cent. ("The Age" 8 April 2022).

Renters in the middle ring areas face better odds with vacancy rates above 2 per cent.

The most dramatic change to Melbourne's rental landscape was in the city centre, where rental vacancies were at just 1.5 per cent in March 2022, down from more than 11 per cent a year before.

While Melbourne has the highest vacancy rates of all capital cities, new minimum standards for rental accommodation imposed by the State Government in March 2021, along with the level of land tax, and currently high returns for landlords selling rather than renting, make rental a decreasingly attractive proposition for landlords. This is likely to lead to more acute housing problems for renters with all the predictable negative outcomes, particularly for families, when parents must move their children out of schools when they are forced to relocate.

Victoria's low rental vacancies will result in more people dropping out of rental altogether with consequent effects on public housing waiting lists and homelessness.

This situation might be rectified by the growth of "Build to Rent" housing, and possibly even a community recognition that landlords play a critical role in housing Australians rather than the usual demonisation that we often see in the press. Government actions to encourage the development of rental properties as well as their existing support for house purchasing may be a partial answer as will Victoria's "Big Housing Build".

Population

While Victoria's growth rate was higher than all other States from 2015 to 2019, this has rapidly reversed with the onset of COVID and its associated lockdowns, particularly with the loss of overseas students. Victoria was the only State with negative population growth in 2020 and 2021.

	Population at 31 Dec 2021 ('000)	Change over previous year ('000)	Change over previous year (%)
New South Wales	8,095.4	11.2	0.1
Victoria	6,559.9	-3.5	-0.1
Queensland	5,265.0	73.7	1.4
South Australia	1,806.6	9.6	0.5
Western Australia	2,762.2	30.5	1.1
Tasmania	569.8	4.3	0.8
Northern Territory	249.3	0.2	0.1
Australian Capital Territory	453.3	1.9	0.4
Australia (a)	25,766.6	128.0	0.5

Table 10.1: Population Change in Australia 2020-21

Housing Growth and Supply

In Victoria there was steady growth of new housing, even strong growth until the mid to latter part of 2022 which saw a dramatic slump in sales, presumably due to uncertainty in the world generally, interest rates, and a shortage of tradespeople and materials. Approvals for units plummeted by over 40% in July 2022 across Australia which in turn will further weaken the rental market in particular.

State/Territory	Private sector houses	Total unit approvals
New South Wales	2215	3571
Victoria	3208	4236
Queensland	2054	2837
South Australia	949	1149
Western Australia	1099	1204
Nationally	9937	13595

Table 10.2: Building Approvals Data, July 2022 *(Source: Building Approvals Australia, July 2022, ABS)*

The latest ABS figures show Victoria is leading the way for overall approvals with South Australia leading the way in percentage growth. New South Wales and Western Australia are underperforming at present.

Employment

Unemployment fell in every State or Territory except Western Australia and is lowest in the ACT (3.1 per cent), Victoria (3.2 per cent), New South Wales (3.3 per cent) and Western Australia (3.4 per cent, up from 3.1 per cent in May) in mid 2022.

However, where jobs are in different suburbs to where people live, major problems arise with transport to those jobs, in terms of commuting time and cost, congestion and infrastructure cost.

Self-containment is the percentage of people who work in the same area that they live in. You would expect smaller cities to have a higher percentage than larger cities. In the chart below the pre COVID results show that Melbourne fares reasonably well in this regard, despite the highly centralised role played by the CBD.

GCCSA	2011	2016	Difference
Greater Sydney	44.1%	43.4%	-0.7
Greater Melbourne	51.8%	51.8%	0.0
Greater Brisbane	47.6%	46.9%	-0.7
Greater Adelaide	56.0%	54.9%	-1.1
Greater Perth	52.6%	52.5%	-0.1
Greater Hobart	97.5%	97.1%	-0.4
Greater Darwin	96.1%	96.5%	0.4
Australian Capital Territory	96.7%	96.2%	-0.5

Table 10.3: Changes in self-containment by greater capital city statistical areas (GCCSA), 2011 and 2016

(Source: ABS Census of Population and Housing, 2011 and 2016, 2071.0.55.001)

However, since the pandemic things have shifted. Across Australia many people are working from home with the peak being around 40% at the height of the lockdowns.

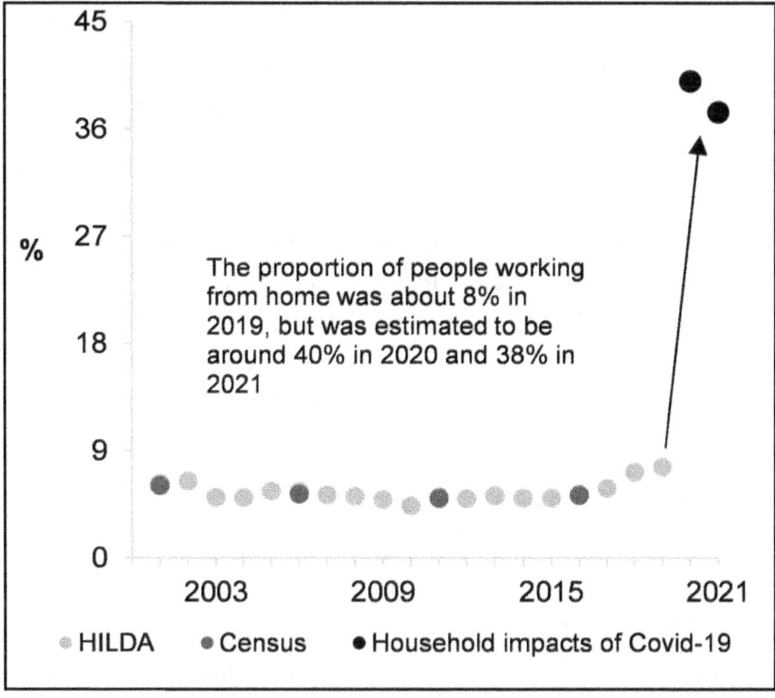

Figure 10.1: Working From Home (*Working from Home Productivity Commission Research Paper*, 2021)

Office Occupancies

In September 2022 the Property Council's latest occupancy survey showed that Brisbane enjoyed the largest rise, with occupancy jumping from 57 to 70 per cent, while Adelaide saw occupancy increase from 71 to 78 per cent and occupancy in Perth lifted from 69 to 76 per cent. Occupancy rates in Sydney remained steady at 52 per cent. In Canberra occupancy dropped from 64 to 54 per cent.

While occupancy rose in Melbourne from 39 to 41 per cent, Victoria has fared the worst in Australia, possibly due to our extended lockdowns changing people's habits, as well as population shrinkage partly due to our high levels of overseas students prior to the epidemic.

With the reduction in controls around the pandemic there will undoubtably be a partial reversion to pre pandemic patterns. The question is how much our work patterns have changed permanently.

Liveability in the new suburbs

In the inner areas virtually all new housing is in apartments, which vary greatly in quality and size. Some of the worst outcomes have been where very large developments have been parachuted into existing areas without providing parallel increases in public open space, or road and public transport capacity.

In the growth areas there are other problems. Planners have been pushing for higher densities. Land is increasingly expensive and developers are trying to reduce the size of sites. The width of roads and overly zealous utilities greatly limit where canopy planting can occur. Home buyers are less interested in gardens and more interested in butler's pantries. Therefore we are seeing large houses on small blocks with little private open space and planting. The result is large areas of often mono-dimensional housing with no planting, and little capacity for avenue planting.

That said, there is a much greater emphasis on the size of public open space and land protected for environmental reasons.

The Forces Driving Change

For many years the main force driving change in Melbourne has been growth, partly due to relative housing affordability and student accommodation. Housing growth has been concentrated in high rise apartments in the inner City and more conventional housing in the Growth Areas.

There are many people that have been pushing for greater suburbanisation of employment, with policy support at both State and Local Government level but until recently the needs of the CBD have been generally given priority for major projects. The Victorian Government has shifted this prioritising somewhat with more funding towards suburban projects, particularly transport, but it is COVID that has brought about the step change that has been needed. With COVID, working in, and commuting to the CBD is less desirable. This has seen more business activity in the suburbs, and in particular has seen a shift to working from home. Consequently there is a need to have more space in the home (especially during lockdowns) which has led to disproportionately high levels of growth in conventional housing in the outer areas. Unfortunately housing in the growth areas has become more expensive, largely due to an imbalance between supply and demand and significantly increasing Government charges.

The world is changing and while efforts are being made, Melbourne like other cities in the world must face up to the challenges of climate change, decreasing international security, staff shortages, inflation, the cost of living and possibly decreasing confidence from the public in our institutions.

Melbourne and its suburbs, and all Victoria faces a wide range of planning challenges, and some of these are:

- The price of buying a dwelling, where increasingly large numbers of Victorians are locked out of the market.
- A significant and growing shortage of rental accommodation.
- A shortage of quality jobs in the middle and outer suburbs thereby making congestion and commuting time worse and forcing people to live in areas they can ill afford. Put simply we still have too many jobs in the wrong places.
- Some of the newest infill developments are not achieving good urban design outcomes with some inner-city apartments being overly dense and not having requisite open space, while in the growth areas we see some developments having mono-dimensional housing with little private or street tree planting. Both these shortfalls may result in these being poor areas to live in the future.
- Finally, despite some positive efforts by Government, the disparate growth of the city has resulted in rich, well-serviced and expensive inner areas, and less well-off outer areas. We are creating a city of the haves and the have nots.

That said many new innovative developments, and better planning have led to a wider range of housing outcomes, better environmental sustainability and probably a stronger focus on the needs of the wider community.

In closing Melbourne may no longer be ranked by *The Economist* as the world's most liveable City (it's number 10 in 2022) but it is an excellent place to live, and this has been driven by a strong planning tradition allowing its growth to be well managed.

11

The Queensland Suburb:
A Singular Vision

Laurel Johnson and Stephanie Wyeth

The desire for low-density suburbs of single detached homes has strongly influenced Queensland's planning policies and metropolitan development. In this chapter, we map major milestones in the State's development and planning history and find that the dominant aspiration for suburban living heavily influences State and Local Governments, the development industry and communities. We conclude that a singular vision of suburbia remains influential in the State, though the combined challenges of population change (high growth and ageing), low housing availability and affordability, increasing costs of living, economic uncertainty, growing intergenerational inequity and climate change are working to unsettle that vision.

History's Imprint

This exploration of suburban development begins with a review of selected historical events. Reflecting on its settlement history helps the reader to understand the mindset that influences the State's unique pattern of suburban development. The figure below shows some of the development and planning milestones that are explored in this chapter.

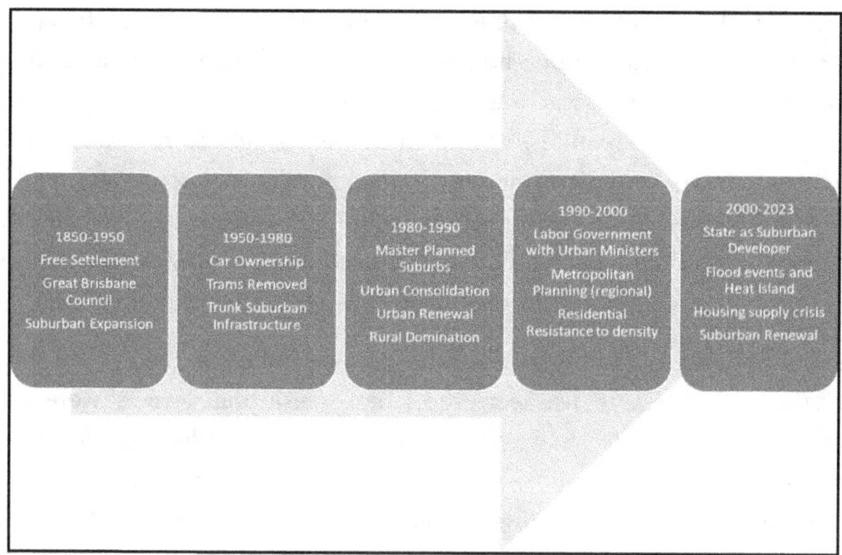

Figure 11.1: A potted history of Queensland suburban development milestones

Resistance and Roads

Brisbane was established as a penal colony outpost by the New South Wales Government in 1825. The Brisbane settlement was a prison for recidivist convicts and considered the most brutal prison in Australia. As in other colonial settlements, the treatment of Indigenous occupants of the area descended from a relatively amicable mutual curiosity and the trading of knowledge, food and goods to a resistance to colonisation and resultant murder, displacement and dispossession (Aird, 2001). It would be over a century until Aboriginal people were freely able to return from the regional missions to settle in Queensland's suburbs and even then, they were often "fringe dwellers", occupying areas at the edge of settlements (Aird, 2001).

Free settlement commenced from the 1840s and the development of road corridors was inevitable, and those corridors unsurprisingly followed the tracks of First Nations people. Examples of these are Waterworks Rd built on a Turrbal pathway leading to Mt Coot-tha – a place of the honeybee dreaming and the Old Northern Rd pathway to the triennial Bunya feast in the Bunya Mountains (Cole, 1984).

A Poor Country Town

After the Second World War, suburban development was rapid as residents fled the decaying inner-city areas that were perceived as dirty and unsafe and the Federal Government's War Service Homes Scheme provided returned servicemen with finances to build detached homes (Gleeson, 2006, p.15). Suburbs comprising rudimentary and uniform timber homes were often "home built" and the design and materials reflected post-war austerity (Gleeson, 2006, p.16). The homes were relatively small and on separate lots and most were single storey "tin and timber" constructions built above the ground, on wooden and later concrete stumps. Though Brisbane City Council is the largest municipality in Australia, its early development was marred by its limited financial base and subsequent inability to effectively service its new suburbs with sealed roads, water and sewerage infrastructure.

Despite the fast pace of post-war suburban development, by the end of the 1950s, only one-third of Brisbane was sewered, many suburban streets were unsealed and homes relied on individual water tanks. Lines of outdoor toilets in wooden boxes dominated backyards in the suburban landscape and the modern capital was mocked as being a "sentry box" town (Cole, 1984, p. 206). The lack of sewered land did not inhibit the suburban development but it did lead to resident protests based on a concern for public health. The popularity and longevity of Lord Mayor Clem Jones (1961 to 1975) is largely based on him having "sewered Brisbane".

Revenue and Infrastructure Limits

While suburban development tended to follow the railway and tram lines (Melville and Minnery, 2015), the availability of affordable private vehicles enabled residential development "in the wedges" between the public transport networks. Inevitably, this led to more cars than the basic suburban roads could handle and the traffic congestion resulted in a conflict between cars, trams, and buses. Between 1949 and 1963, car registrations in Queensland increased by over 200,000 and related to this, tram patronage dropped by over 30% (Cole, 1984, p.263). As trams were seen to compound traffic congestion and cause accidents involving pedestrians, they were removed from service in the late 1960s. Traffic congestion and the competition between transport modes continue to plague the city and influence resident resistance to infill development where increased traffic and car parking are common sources of resident objection to new higher-than-usual density development in the suburbs.

Despite the simple nature of most of the homes (styled as "workers' cottages") and the lack of sewerage and reticulated water and unsealed, congested roads, Brisbane residents chose the suburban lifestyle. Between 1996 and 2005, Brisbane was Australia's fastest growing city, and most of that expansion was suburban (Felton, 2011). In 2005, Australian demographer Bernard Salt described Brisbane as "Australia's most suburban city" (Salt 2005 in Felton, 2011, p.1).

Suburban Development: From Ad Hoc Incrementalism to Master-plan

After WW11, suburban development was ad hoc and incremental with limited rules. Integrated master planning became a popular approach when large-scale, private development companies moved to Queensland from the 1990s. The first master-planned, developer-led suburban community was the Centenary Suburbs at the southwest edge of Brisbane. Others followed including Robina and Varsity Lakes at the Gold Coast, Forest Lake in Brisbane, Greater Springfield in Ipswich, and North Lakes in the north of the metropolis. These master-planned suburbs were generally centred on an artificial lake with integrated services, open space and mobility networks, a range of housing lot sizes and price points. The first wave of master-planned developments challenged the State Government to deliver infrastructure such as public transport, schools, health and other community facilities to the new suburbs in a coordinated and timely way.

The Queensland Government: From Disinterest to Developer

The removal of the National Party Government and the population pressures in the south east in the 1990s were impetus for the State to initiate regional growth management for south east Queensland. The main population pressures were on the coastal strip in the corridors from the New South Wales border in the south to Noosa on the Sunshine Coast in the north. Another growth corridor followed the western axis to Ipswich and beyond to Toowoomba. Fears of the 200km city stretching from the Gold Coast to Noosa inspired regional metropolitan planning (Spearritt, 2009).

The recently released Draft *ShapingSEQ* 2023 Update (Queensland Government, 2023) increases the targets for both the number and the diversity of new dwellings in the growing south east. The revised plan hopes to shift the dwelling growth ratio for new residential development from 60% consolidation and 40% expansion to 70% and 30% respectively. The State Government requires that urban Local Governments increase the representation of attached dwellings in their Local Government areas to grow the supply of low and high rise (above 8 storeys) attached homes. There has been variable success for Local Governments in achieving dwelling diversity as community resistance to higher than usual density housing is potent and political and investor interest in the development of detached housing in existing suburbs is variable. Some Local Governments (with the support of the State) are incentivising higher density residential development with streamlined planning processes (such as Temporary Local Planning Instruments that remove community consultation requirements), car parking relaxations, no height limits and infrastructure discounts for high rise development. Others are taking a critical eye to the barriers for infill development and are commissioning specialists in community engagement, communication, design and development to promote place-based responses that support urban change.

Urban Consolidation

As well as engaging in planning at the regional scale, the State has more recently involved itself in local planning and development through its powers under the State's *Economic Development Act 2012*. The next section provides an overview of the State's approach to planning and its current role as an active master-planner of new greenfield and infill suburban development.

The Evolution of Queensland Planning

For decades, urban planning was viewed by the State as another of Local Government's regulatory responsibilities. The State Government was slow to leverage the power of urban planning for its own purposes though it maintained the right to rezone land (through Ministerial intervention) and approve Local Government planning schemes and amendments. The State was disengaged from urban planning, which was Local Government's role, though the State had considerable power in the planning system that it could use with limited exposure to public scrutiny or transparency.

Performance-Based Planning

The performance-based approach is not clearly defined and in practice, the Queensland system is part performance-based and part prescriptive. For example, if it can satisfy the prescriptive "rules", then many developments do not require a planning approval. That means that, if a development proposal follows the "rules" for that development type and is unconstrained by planning overlays, then no planning approval is needed. This is an incentive for business-as-usual development, particularly in suburban areas. New detached suburban homes are mostly developed as prescribed in the dwelling code and this generally results in a uniform suburban landscape that meets the expectations of suburban residents. On the other hand, in inner areas undergoing significant urban change, height limits are routinely breached as developers obtain approvals based on the "performance" of the project or via negotiated trade-offs for other alleged community benefits.

The State as Suburban Developer

There is a paradox in Queensland's planning system. The paradox is that the State has established its own land use planning and property development agency. The State introduced powers under the *Economic Development Act 2012* to effectively usurp the land use and regulatory controls that are administered within the planning system that it designed. Economic Development Queensland (EDQ) is a suburban property developer with its own planning powers.

The State nominates land for priority development (known as priority development areas or PDAs), and this land is removed from the authority of the relevant Local Government for a period of time in order to fast track new development at particular locations "to deliver significant benefits to the community" (EDQ). At the time of writing, there were 34 PDAs in the State, representing an ultimate new residential population of over 400,000 in predominantly greenfield suburban locations. The idea of the PDA is to ensure that the State can coordinate infrastructure, create development plans and approve development so that new master-planned suburbs come to market relatively faster in order to address housing supply and housing affordability pressures.

A Housing Supply Crisis

Figure 11.2 shows the pressure on Queensland from unexpected interstate migration since the initial wave of the COVID pandemic in 2020.

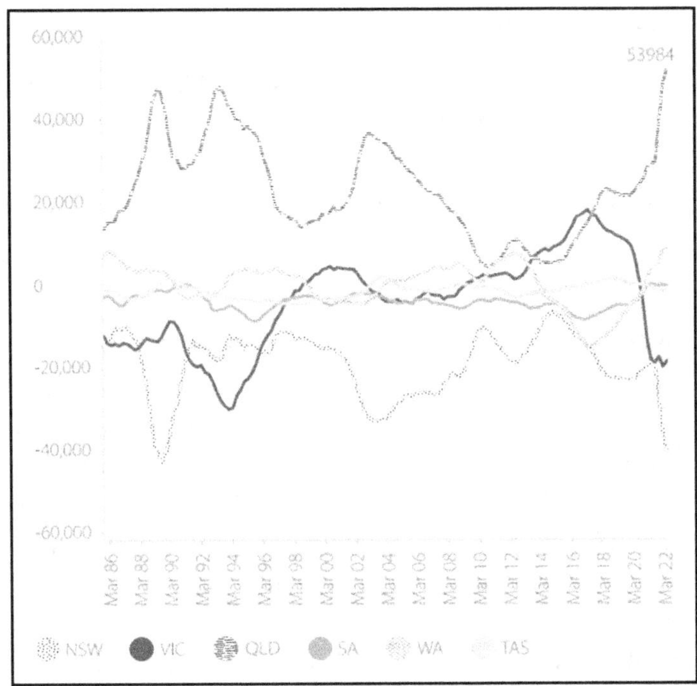

Figure 11.2 Annual, Rolling Interstate Migration (ABS, CoreLogic)

Figure 11.3 shows the reduced supply of rental vacancies as a result of the high demand generated by this population growth. In addition to increased demand, we know that, on the back of heavily inflated property values since the pandemic, many rental properties have been sold and others are flood affected. The constraint in supply and high demand impacts rental affordability across the State (Pawson, et. al., 2023).

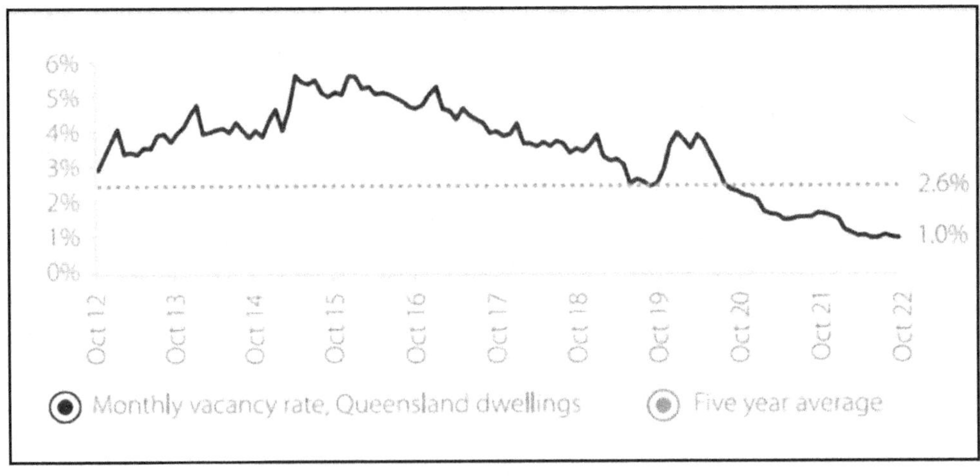

Figure 11.3: Monthly Rental Vacancies, Queensland, 2012-2022 (Source: CoreLogic)

The attraction of the sub-tropical metropolis (particularly post-COVID) has a disastrous effect on housing affordability and availability in the region (Pawson, et.al, 2023). The recent announcement by the Queensland Government that the urban footprint that is available for new greenfield development is 40% less than expected due to a range of infrastructure, flooding and koala protection constraints (among others) could result in an expanded urban footprint and/or more pressure on existing suburbs to densify and diversify.

Suburban Solutions

In the context of resident resistance to densification in existing suburbs and the urgency for more housing, different strategies have been trialled to increase densities in the suburbs. This section briefly considers suburban transit-oriented development and the recent emergence of suburban renewal and gentle density solutions.

Suburban Transit-Oriented Development

The resistance in the middle-ring suburbs results in the clustering of medium density housing on greenfield sites at the edge of the metropolitan area, where residential resistance is less likely. Unfortunately, many of these developments are incremental and imprinted with the historical lag in the provision of State and local infrastructure such as schools, parks, bikeways, health and community facilities to new suburban areas. There are many instances of this approach across South East Queensland, where incremental "gated" townhouse development has now cemented the role of these new suburban homes as the 21st century "worker's cottage".

Suburban Renewal

The ability to advance suburban consolidation as a policy agenda is challenged by a range of factors including lack of lots suitable for redevelopment into "missing middle" product, fragmented land ownership, and the "blunt nature" of the planning policy, zoning regimes and regulations to deal with "fine grain" infill projects (Gallagher, et. al., 2020). Where these factors are more favourable, projects have flourished often transforming the built environment and local communities.

To address these issues, the Brisbane City Council has initiated a policy of "suburban renewal", whereby planning interventions will occur in identified suburban precincts (mostly underutilised industrial areas) to unlock the potential for higher density, mixed use suburbs. This approach of selective suburban renewal identifies areas for planned intervention for high density, mixed development and introduces precinct level development plans as the vehicle to achieve it.

Gentle Density

Queenslanders have been slow to shift from separate homes to higher density housing forms. Recent changes by the State Government to second dwelling provisions is one of the many "gentle density" strategies for more housing in existing suburbs that is likely to be compatible with suburban values. Design guidelines for suburban development, public and active transport investment, and major suburban tree planting initiatives each contributes to suburban life and potentially addresses the issues that foster resident resistance to mixed density suburbs. The State Government's strategy to enable "granny flats" (second dwellings) to be privately rented is one way that the suburbs of Greater Brisbane are likely to change.

The Context for Future Suburbs

Culture and Choice in the Suburbs

The expectation of a peaceful suburban life has led to the regulation of home businesses and more recently, complaints and resultant regulation of the use of suburban homes for Airbnb. While regulation to encourage a mix of land uses at suburban activity centres has had some success, there appears to be little appetite for entrepreneurial activity in suburban streets. Despite this, there is evidence of small businesses operating from homes (some unlawfully), particularly in the more culturally diverse suburbs.

Climate Resilience

A major challenge for Queensland is the resilience of the suburbs to a changing climate that results in flooding, extreme weather events and hotter and longer summers. Future-proofing the design of the suburbs and suburban homes and the preparedness of suburban communities for the climate risks underpin their capability to withstand new weather patterns and respond to disasters.

Mobility

When it is complete, Brisbane's Cross River Rail project will allow more frequent suburban train services in the metropolitan south-east. A system of regional bikeways extends the active travel network across suburbs and to the city centre. In addition to this infrastructure, personalised transport including e-bikes and e-scooters have the potential to improve access and convenience for suburban residents. Personal mobility and a complementary network of active transport paths to stations and activity centres could shift the entrenched mobility challenges for many suburban residents and address their concerns that increased density equates to more traffic congestion and on-street parking pressures.

The Queensland Suburb as a Solution

Queensland suburbs are adapting. There is evidence of activity at the suburban scale to address the local impacts of Global challenges, including the housing crisis. Localised food production and distribution, the collective planting of verges to cool streets and provide for wildlife, the electrification of transport charged at home and the rapid take-up and sharing of solar energy, reconciliation action in local community organisations and groups, the development of second dwellings in suburban backyards and new tenure options such as co-housing and build to rent are each evidence of the adaptability of the Queensland suburb and suburban residents.

The carbon-positive 2032 Brisbane Olympics will demonstrate creative and innovative ways to achieve carbon-positivity in the built environment and those lessons will extend to the State's future suburbs. The Queensland suburb is a potential solution (not just a contributor) to the multiple crises. Partnering with suburban residents who seek local solutions is a way forward for Governments, businesses, developers, built environment professionals and non-Government organisations to realise the potential of the suburb as a solution.

References

Australian Bureau of Statistics (ABS) *Snapshot of Queensland* Australian Bureau of Statistics (abs.gov. au). Accessed 9 March 2023

Australian Bureau of Statistics (ABS) *Census of Population and Housing: Time Series 2011 – 2021*, Dakabin SA2 (31421576), Accessed 19 March 2023

Cole, J., R. (1984). *Shaping a city: Greater Brisbane 1925-1985*. William Brooks. Eagle Farm. Queensland

CoreLogic. (2022). *Queensland: ANZ Corelogic Housing Affordability Report 2022*. Accessed at Queensland: ANZ CoreLogic housing affordability report 2022

Felton, E. (2011). "Brisbane: Urban Construction, Suburban Dreaming", *Journal of Media and Culture*. Vol. 14. No. 4 B

Gallagher, R., Sigler, T., Liu, Y. (2020) "Targeted urban consolidation or adhoc redevelopment? The influence of cadastral structure and change on the urban form of Brisbane, Australia", *Urban Geography*. 41:2. Pp.183-204

Gleeson, B. (2006). *Australian Heartlands: Making space for hope in the suburbs.* Allen and Unwin. Crows Nest. New South Wales

Melville, E, and Minnery, J. (2015). "Public Transport, urban form and urban structure: the example of Brisbane's tram system", *Australian Planner*, Vol. 52, No. 2, 156-168

Pawson, H., Clarke, J., Moore, J., van den Nouwelant, R., Ng, M. (2023). *A blueprint to tackle Queensland's housing crisis.* UNSW City Futures Research Centre. UNSW.

Queensland Government. (2023). Draft Shaping SEQ: South East Queensland Regional Plan 2023 Update, Queensland Government, Brisbane, accessed 16 October 2023. DSDILGP_Draft_ShapingSEQ_Regional_Plan_A4.pdf (amazonaws.com)

Spearritt, Peter (2009). "The 200 KM city: Brisbane, the gold coast, and sunshine coast", *Australian Economic History Review*, 49 (1), 87-106. doi: 10.1111/j.1467-8446.2009.00251.x

12

Suburban Development Through a WA Lens

Ray Haeren

Arguably WA has Australia's strongest suburban heritage. Perth (the capital and home to nearly 80% of the State), is a very suburban city stretching 180 kilometres along the coast. This relates to the timing of Perth's growth which has been substantially post war and therefore aligned with the rise of the private motor vehicle. The physical attributes of the Swan Coastal Plain, our love of the Coast and the "freedom" of the motor vehicle strongly influenced the nature of the City and in many respects continue to do so today.

Perth's Foundations and Early Innovation

Perth was founded by Captain James Stirling on Whadjuk country as the capital of the Swan River Colony in 1829. It was the first free-settler colony in Australia established by private capital, however from 1850, convicts began to arrive at the colony in large numbers to build roads and other public infrastructure.

The settlement was comprised of three towns along the Swan River, being Fremantle as the Port, Perth as the administrative and defence centre, and Guildford as the agricultural hub. By the 1880s these towns were connected by the railways and associated settlements established along these lines (noting the colony was still struggling with fewer than 20,000 residents). It was around this point where the State saw the first of its resource booms with the Gold Rush of the 1890s and an influx of residents to the Goldfields and Perth. In some ways this set the foundations of linking Perth's suburbs to transport and resource booms.

In addition to the rail, the suburban development of Perth at the turn of the century was supported by the development of tram lines. In some instances, these extensions of the system were organised, paid for, or even operated, by land developers. Trams helped in this way to sell blocks of land in Mount Lawley Estate, the Maylands subdivision, Nedlands Park and Osborne Park.

Despite a constant fear of being left behind by the "major" cities, Perth has been at the forefront of urban development concepts from early in the 20th century. W E Bold, Town Clerk of the City of Perth for four decades undertook a study tour of UK and USA in 1914 and upon his return he refined his "Greater Perth" concept to embrace satellite garden and seaside suburbs, a redeveloped civic centre like Chicago's, and an overall plan on "City Beautiful" lines.

Bold was able to convince the City to purchase the 1,300-acre (526 ha) Limekilns Estate, adjacent to western seaside endowment lands already owned by the City. These areas were developed from the 1920s in line with City Beautiful principles resulting in the now prestigious suburbs of Floreat Park, Wembley Park and City Beach. Bold was also central in the advocacy of Town Planning legislation, resulting in the 1928 Town Planning and Development Act. Bold is widely considered the founder of Town Planning in Western Australia. Interestingly Bold was widely criticised at the time by the State Government that his interest in this new suburban development resulted in the neglect of the inner city. Perhaps a sign of things to come in terms of focus.

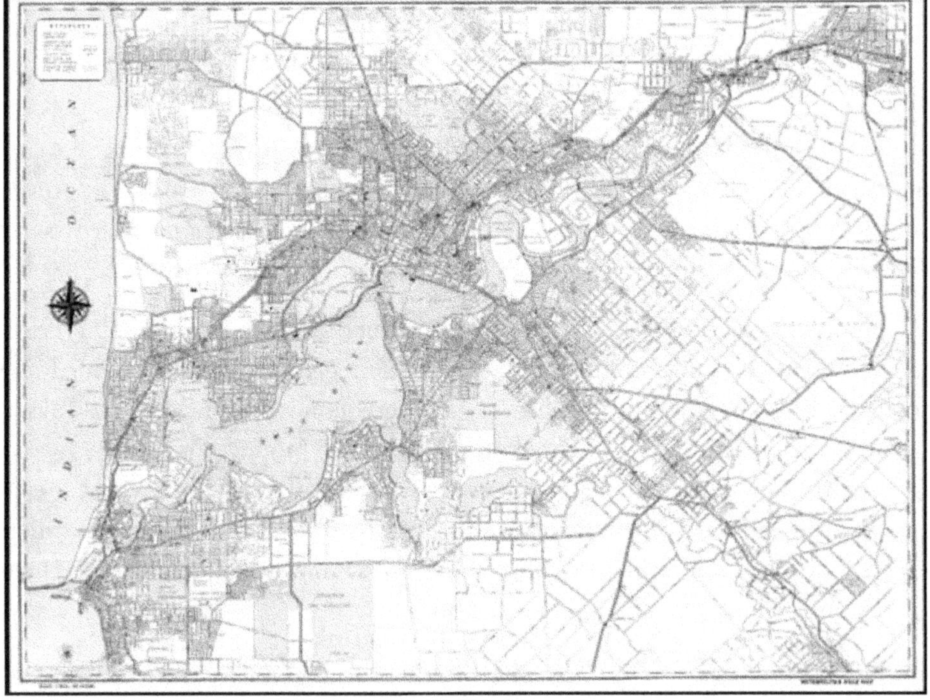

Figure 12.1: Early suburban development of Perth and Fremantle centres of the rail and trams, until the rise of the motor car

The Suburban Carpet Roll Out

By 1950 greater Perth had a population of some 400,000 and was at a pivotal point post World War 2. Driven by continued growth through post war immigration and the still strong British influence, the Town Planning Board sought to prepare a regional plan for Perth and Fremantle in the style of Abercrombie's Greater London Plan.

The Town Planning Board advocated for the creation of an Honorary Royal Commission of the Legislative Council which was formed in 1951. The commission first reported in 1952, and as a result, English Professor G. Stephenson, and the Commissioner of Town Planning, Mr. J.A. Hepburn, released the Stephenson-Hepburn Report in 1955 which informed the creation of the Metropolitan Region Planning Scheme (1959).

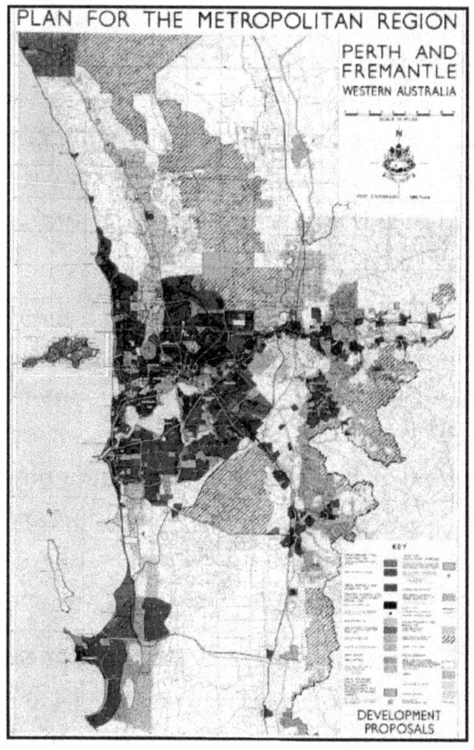

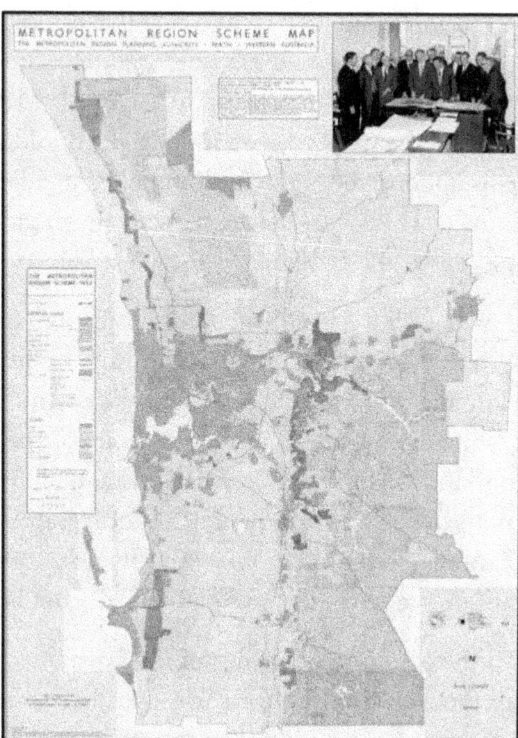

Figure 12.2: The Stephenson and Hepburn Plan for Perth and Fremantle and first Metropolitan Region Scheme; DPLH

The Plan for the Metropolitan Region introduced key elements, principles and ideas of contemporary planning of the time. The Plan and associated report was a highly technical document which sought to create a "modern" city and these principles have informed and shaped the Metropolitan Perth to this day:

1. The separation of land uses and creation of dormitory residential areas, connected by highways and freeways.
2. The notion of suburbs taking advantage of the amenity of the river, hills and coast.
3. Distributed suburban hubs for commercial and civic activities (shopping centres).
4. Reservation of key amenity, along Swan and Canning River and Darling Range.
5. The creation of an industrial and manufacturing hub, port and associated "New Town" at Kwinana.

To be fair to the authors, the original plan did envisage an expanded rail network; however, by the translation to the Perth Metropolitan Region Scheme this had been lost and the car was seen as king. It should also be noted that although a number of assumptions about the future may have fallen short, the population growth estimates proved to be very accurate with the region hitting 1 million by the 1980s and 2 million by the 2000s.

It was at this point that Perth truly embraced its suburban future. A centralised system through the State Government controlled all subdivision enabling structure planning and facilitated through large landholdings acquired by land development companies of the time. The rollout of the north coastal suburbs was enabled by the land being virgin coastal bushland – noting that this is before the community truly valued environmental or Indigenous heritage. Embracing the contemporary planning of the time, the result was the swaths of spaghetti subdivisions – a sea of culs-de-sac along the spine of the Mitchel Freeway.

To the south, the delivery of the Kwinana Freeway via the Narrows Bridge opened up the southern suburbs, while further south the new heavy industrial area of (and freeway namesake) Kwinana was developed and supported by its "new town". I should confess at this point to being a Kwinana boy, representative of the time. I was born at Kwinana Maternity Hospital shortly after the arrival of my parents from the Netherlands seeking new opportunities. A blue-collar multicultural enclave, ultimately becoming known more for its social challenges, unemployment and social housing dominance as the industrial landscape changed in the 1970s.

Figure 12.3: Artist's Impression of the Narrows Bridge Interchange Kwinana Freeway – Main Roads WA

This was an era where the government was actively and directly involved in creating suburbs dominated by public housing. This is perhaps particularly notable in our current environment of housing shortage, both in relation to solutions and lessons to be remembered. Mirrabooka/Balga/Girrawheen in the north, Hilton/Willagee in the south and Kwinana are all examples of this approach. They were all subject to renewal and privatisation programs in later years (see next section).

Representing the change in planning from design process to a science, corridor planning principles were identified as the preferred approach in the late 1960s culminating in the Perth Corridor Plan in 1970. The Corridor Plan, recognising characteristics of the Perth region, and the underlaying nature of suburban growth, proposed corridors of expansion to extend Northwest, Southwest, East and Southeast of the City. This was complemented by sub-regional centres to be developed in each corridor at the nearby towns of Rockingham, Midland,

and Armadale (Bycroft 1974). A completely new centre was proposed to the north at Lake Joondalup. These sub-regional centres were intended to act as countermagnets to the attraction of the Perth central business district (CBD).

America's Cup and the Rise of the Estate

The 1980s were an interesting period for Perth, not just in terms of fashion, hair and music (I thought my acid wash, fluro fingerless gloves and bleached blond was iconic). Suburban life was the established norm for the vast majority of the population. The inner suburbs were only for the gays, Vietnamese migrants and ageing southern Europeans in Fremantle (a generalisation I know).

The notion of density had been tainted forever by the cheap and uniform blocks of flats. Density was the poor option, with aspirations being a four-bedroom two-bathroom, double brick home on 800+ square metres – preferably somewhere near the beach.

A combination of Planning Controls (i.e., no residential lots allowed to front roads over 3,000 vpd), market shifts and social change saw the rise of the "Estate" or "Private Estate" within Perth. Walled enclaves with design and building controls to provide a (false) sense of security and quality, such that one can build a house with peace of mind that only "quality" houses and neighbours will surround them. Examples include Beaumaris Beach, Sanctuary Waters, Settlers Hill all of whom do not mention the actual suburb name (Iluka, Canning Vale and Baldivis).

The evolution of the estate suburban form also saw the inclusion of an increasing focus on amenity through provision of packages including front landscaping, developed parklands (often including a lake or water feature) and street trees.

Rather than new residential areas being a sand pit slowly converting over time, a significant focus was on creating a sense of establishment in a curated setting. Roll on lawn, transplanted palm trees and faux heritage styles creating an impression of an established suburb and this clearly achieved a market response (perhaps in line with societal appetite for instant gratification). In a change of approach from previous periods, rather than developers creating tensions with Local Governments for not making suitable contributions to local amenity it became necessary to limit these works. During my time at the City of Gosnells, there was a need to establish special area rates to cover the cost of maintaining the water bodies and landscaping being developed at the core of the various estates that had sprung up in Canning Vale.

Figure 12.4: High Quality Open Space, Canning Vale

While suburban utopia evolved, other changes were also afoot in the West. The America's Cup win by Alan Bond's Australia 2 in the 1980s was seen as putting Perth on the map as we approached the first million residents. This also spurred a rejuvenation of Fremantle, which underwent a metamorphosis with new appreciation of the heritage buildings (now painted in pastels) and going from bogan working port to alfresco dining, coffee culture and the rise of the yuppie. The first signs of urban regeneration and popularity of urban living started to be seen.

From a planning perspective there was a shift too with regional planning looking to start containing the sprawl through urban consolidation as reflected in Metroplan. East Perth and Subiaco (through Federal Government funding support) saw the establishment of Redevelopment Authorities to enable urban regeneration and facilitating the delivery of new development into the inner locations. Highly acclaimed projects, it is notable that the greatest criticism directed to these projects is that they failed to deliver sufficient density. I do consider this to be unfair in the context of the time. These projects had to entice people back into the inner-city and the notion of 200m2 lots and 6 storey apartments was high density in the suburban landscape of Perth in that era.

Figure 12.5: Claisebrook Cove East Perth, East Perth Redevelopment Authority

Figure 12.6: Claisebrook Cove East Perth, East Perth Redevelopment Authority

Although Subiaco and East Perth projects demonstrated excellence in design and creation of amenity as part of comprehensive redevelopment projects, this was not representative of the delivery of density in Perth more broadly. The most prolific form of housing outside the urban fringe was the delivery of triplex and villa development through the middle suburbs.

My first post graduate planning job in the early 90s was for the City of Stirling, assisting on the density review which was seeking to respond to the community backlash on the redevelopment in areas including Dianella, Doubleview and Yokine. These suburbs had been zoned medium density and the traditional houses on quarter acre (1,000m2) lots were being demolished and replaced with 3 or 4 single story villa units affecting streetscapes, parking and local amenity. This was representative of what was being seen in many of the middle suburbs of the time, although notably a number of affluent areas had managed to include density limits or heritage restrictions to limit or prevent infill.

Despite the reaction of some, this form of development was popular based on a few elements. The scale of development saw many individuals (or family trusts) undertake the development, therefore being an accessible form of wealth creation. The conversion of the family home into units created numerous developers, who would seek to extract maximum value. The developments were in the known and safe form of double brick and seen as a safe investment (safe as houses). This tension became highly apparent when I attended community consultation and forums on the proposed down coding of areas as part of Stirling's density review.

The emerging conflict was centred on the desire to retain the character and amenity of areas, however people also wanted to retain the opportunity for the family home to provide an investment base for their retirement. This remains an issue in Perth's suburbs and I expect most of Australia's major cities. Although redevelopment and densification is a challenge in these settings, it should be considered that the pre-war urban form (grid streets and large lots) is robust enough to adapt. The areas developed since the 1970s, with curvilinear and cul-de-sac streets present more of a challenge.

Perth's love for Trains and FIFO Commuting

Since the turn of the millennium Perth's suburbs have been impacted by some key changes politically, economically, and socially. From a Planning policy perspective, WA were early adopters of New Urbanist principles. The WA Planning Commission's "Liveable Neighbourhoods" framework was highly acclaimed in applying a different approach to neighbourhood design which drew upon traditional community design (grid road network, walkability, etc). This significant policy shift required significant leadership to bring to delivery but the pivot away from culs-de-sac and estate walls has been to the benefit of the more recent suburban landscape. The Ellenbrook Joint Venture's new master planned community in north-east Perth was a notable early adopter of the approach and received numerous awards in acknowledgement of its design and delivery.

From the 1990s Perth also bucked the trend, being the first Australian City to expand (and electrify) its suburban rail network in decade. The success of the Joondalup rail line in providing a passenger rail service to the northwestern corridor, set the scene for the ongoing passion for rail up until the present day. The ever-expanding northern suburbs were previously completely reliant on the Mitchel Freeway with commuters embracing the new option. The use of the Mitchel Freeway central median for the rail line was a notable innovation in delivery, however this has also resulted in stations delivered in highly suburban settings which have limited density and a "park and ride" emphasis, with the notable exception of Joondalup CBD (as seen in Warwick Station below).

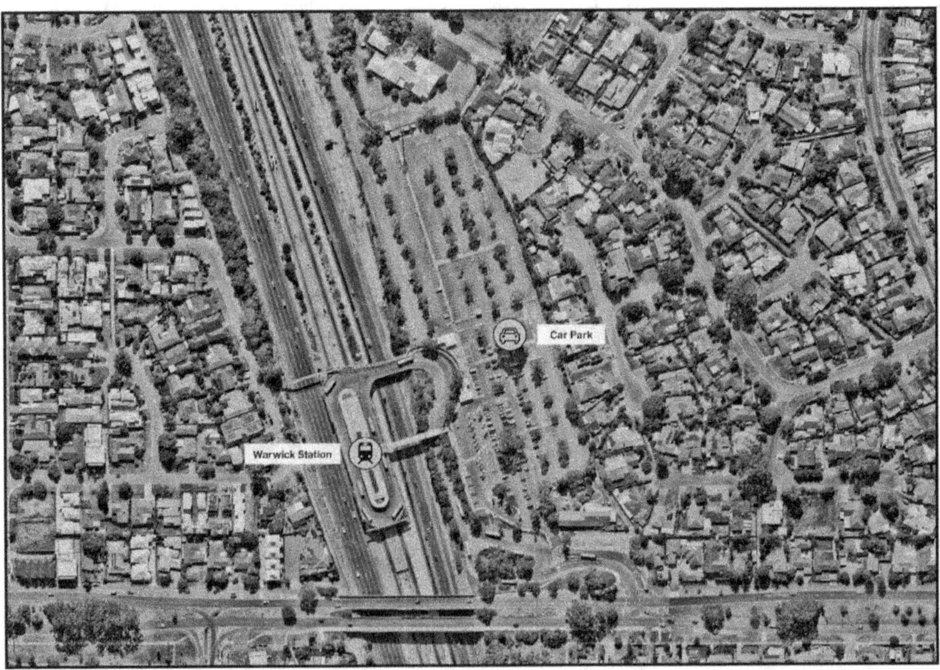

Figure 12.7: Warwick Station suburban setting with large carpark (Near map)

Following the success of the Joondalup line (and perhaps reflecting the constant north south rivalry in Perth), the conservative Richard Court Government announced the Perth to Mandurah rail line. The project was ultimately delivered (and reworked) by the Gallop Government and spurred significant growth of the southern suburbs and effectively bringing Mandurah (74 kilometres to the south of the CBD) into the Perth suburbs. Like the Joondalup line, this project utilised the Freeway median to accommodate the rail line through the existing suburbs. Some strategic locations were able to be developed with some level of integration (Murdoch, Cockburn Central and Wellard), however the line is similarly reliant on park and ride within a suburban setting.

This delivery of rail was so popular it became a foundation platform for the 2017 election campaign by Mark McGowan. The METRONET project proposes a network of rail lines through the suburbs with construction underway for the Yanchep extension, Thornlie to Cockburn line and Ellenbrook.

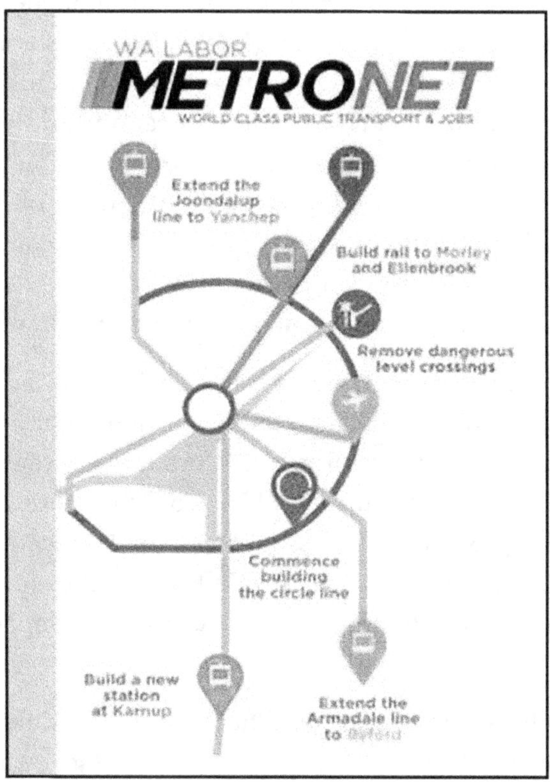

Figure 12.8: Metronet

The investment in the delivery of this new transport is over $10 billion, being significant in any context. A remaining challenge for the project is the ability to deliver density as part of the project. It has been cited as not just a transport project, with the integration of transport and land use being at the core of its objectives.

Although there has been some more urban development in Cockburn and Murdoch it has relied upon strong government intervention rather than being market driven. In recent times this can be placed at issues around construction costs, with the Perth market apparently reluctant to embrace apartment living, particularly in a suburban context. Applecross/Canning Bridge being a high amenity riverside location is perhaps the only site to see significant private investment, however this has seen significant controversy beyond what I could cover in this chapter.

In the last two decades the WA Economy has seen significant growth of the back of the resource sector, which has also been an influence on our suburban lifestyle. Driven by major Oil & Gas and Iron Ore projects in the Pilbara, the resources boom had two key impacts on the suburban landscape. Many of the projects in this sector were located in remote locations and were serviced by a Fly-in Fly-out (FIFO) workforce. The rotations were variable depending on the sector and the company, however 2 weeks on and 1 week off was the prevailing cycle. These roles changed the dynamics of lifestyle and commuting. The local lingo began to reflect these changes, with FIFO, High-Viz clothing and CUB (Cashed-Up-Bogan) becoming synonymous with the growth of Perth.

FIFO workers were not new in WA, with the offshore oil and gas sector using this method since the 1970s. The change was in the quantum, with some 60,000 estimated in 2018 (Centre of Transformative Work Design) representing some 60% of all those in the mining sector in WA. This would be considered conservative given the significant growth in the resource sector in recent years. There are continued debate around the impacts of FIFO on families, people and regional communities, however I would argue that it has also had impacts on the suburbs of Perth.

Increased household income and modified work schedules have inevitably changed the preferred form and location of housing. A need emerged to accommodate a new style of suburban housing, with house and land packages advertising dual-living homes and extra-large garages for "boy toys" (4WD cars, jet skis and dirt bikes). The change in the commute dynamic saw the increased focus on lifestyle and amenity rather than distance to Perth employment nodes. Anecdotally an increasing portion of FIFO workers spend their down time in the likes of Bali, however it is apparent that many also choose high amenity locations away from the CBD based on cost and lifestyle. A hobby farm in the southwest becomes a more appealing prospect when the drive to work is weeks apart.

Current Issues and Trends

In a post COVID world many of the issues raised remain true and current while others have changed in priority and relevance. The number one issue now is simply the availability and affordability of housing. Although Perth remains the second most affordable capital after Darwin, increased demand and supply constraints are taking effect on house prices and rental housing stock (vacancy rate of sub 1%). This is a national challenge, however as we seek solutions a core question emerges whether this could represent a change in the form of growth to a more urban and infill focus. Given our suburban heritage and construction constraints this seems unlikely.

The battles and conflict around infill and density remain real, with community resistance to density remaining a significant item for debate. Although planning processes and frameworks have become more accommodating to density, it remains a highly sensitive issue, particularly in the most affluent areas of Perth where more centralised processes have seen new developments proceed.

This said, the outer suburban environment is changing in density and form with shrinking lot sizes, driven by affordability and planning policy. Perth now has the smallest average lot size of any capital in the country, with sub 400m2 being the average since 2020. Although house size has decreased, this has been not as significant, with the average house size currently circa 215m2. This is particularly challenging given the retained focus on double brick and thereby single storey housing. The loss of yard space and the associated issues around tree canopy and urban heat islands are key themes in the debate around residential development in Perth.

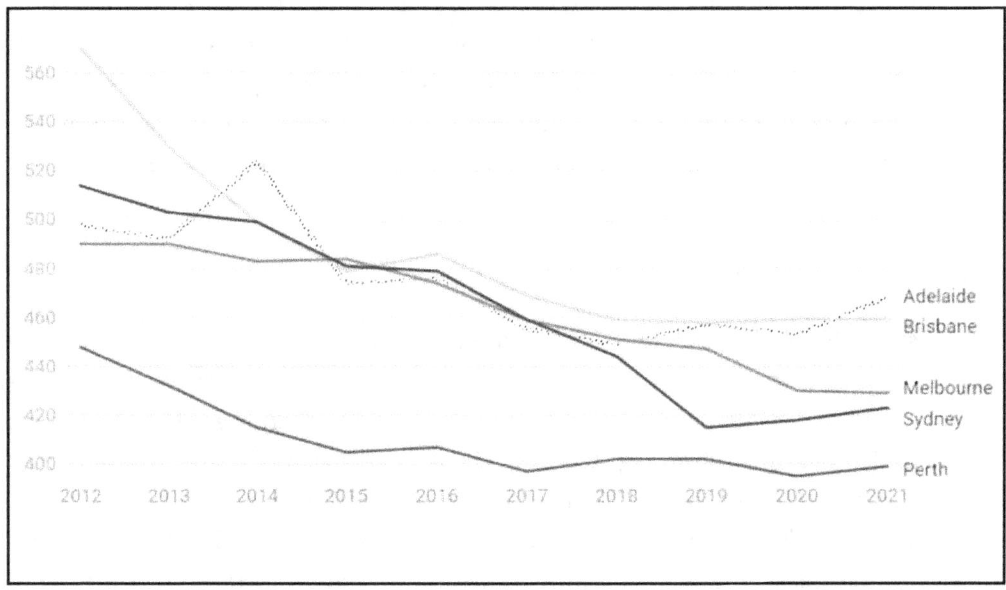

Figure 12.9: Average Site Area of House Approvals in Australian Capital Cities(m2), 2012-2021

(Source: ABS)

A more compact urban form and density strategically located in transport nodes will continue to be a key objective at the metropolitan level, with decarbonisation, affordability and land availability increasing the pressure for change. The likely reality, however, is that Perth's love of the single residential home suburb will dominate for some time to come.

There is no doubting the appeal of the suburban setting, however we will need to ensure that amenity is suitably distributed and not just the realm of expensive middle suburbs. We need to ensure that outer suburbs do not become a series of heat islands, with a tree canopy being fostered through both physical planning and community education. Without suitable consideration the suburbs of Perth in the future may just be partially pregnant – not offering an urban density and activity nor suburban lifestyle and amenity.

The Future of Perth

The evolution of the suburbs of Perth has reflected the changing trends and considerations around development more broadly. An increasing awareness of the environmental impacts, financial cost and social implications of an ever-increasing spread of suburbs is influencing the extent and form of suburban development. Despite a drive for increased density and sustainability, we have not seen a true translation through infill and apartment development within the existing urban footprint, despite significant focus and incentives. Rather we have seen the lots on the fringe decrease in size.

Social and financial factors will see a continued demand for suburban product on the fringe. The cost of apartment development has increased markedly post COVID and is unviable in all but the most prestigious locations. Residents of Perth are apparently also rather fond of the suburban lifestyle, however as the distances increase and lot sizes decrease it will be interesting to see the extent to which this will continue. Housing availability and affordability are expected to be a hot topic for the next decade as population growth returns to peak levels.

I would like to think that the planning community with the development sector will be able to lift the bar in the quality and liveability of our city through both the delivery of balanced and considered fringe development and strategic and targeted infill and density based on amenity, employment and infrastructure.

Providing genuine access to a choice in housing based on lifestyle and lifecycle is the goal. This goal rolls off the tongue so easily, however delivering this will require great fortitude and strategic direction by many. I hope we are up for the challenge.

References

Hedgecock, David; Yiftachel, Oren (1989). "The Planning of Perth's Changing Form-Invention or Convention?", *Australian Planner*. 27 (1): 6–11. doi:10.1080/07293682.1989.9657405.

Perth Tramways - Perth electric tramway society. (https://www.pets.org.au/pets10p.html)

R. E. Robertson (1970). *W. E. Bold* M.A. thesis, University of Western Australia

Seddon, G; Ravine, D (1986). *A City and its Setting: Images of Perth, Western Australia*. Fremantle: Fremantle Arts Centre Press.

Stephenson, Gordon; Hepburn, J. A. (1955). *Plan for the Metropolitan Region, Perth and Fremantle*. Western Australia: Government of Western Australia.

Transforming Perth (2013). *Regenerating Transport Corridors as a Network of High Street Precincts*. The Property Council of Australia, The Greens and AUDC

M. Webb (1968). *Planning and development in metropolitan Perth to 1953*, Perth City and Region, Australian Planning Institute Congress Perth.

13

Suburban South Australia

John Stimson

Since the turn of the century suburban Adelaide has changed substantially in some locations and hardly at all in others. This chapter does not go into much detail regarding regional towns as little has changed there.

Demography

The Estimated Resident Population (ERP) for SA increased from 1,496,828 in March 2000 to 1,844,600 in March 2023[1] which is an 23.2% increase, or just over 15,000 extra persons per annum. Greater Adelaide is 77.8% of the State's population. The average population increase for Greater Adelaide between 2015-2020 was 0.96% per annum.

Following the release of the 2021 Census a revised ERP[2] was issued by the ABS. The SA figure was revised upwards from 1,772,787 to 1,781,516 persons. This meant that there had been an extra increase from 2016-2021 of almost 2,000 persons pa. While this is a reasonably small number it represents almost 15% more growth than was thought.

Natural increase (births - deaths) in population in South Australia has remained reasonably steady over the past two decades with the annual 2000 figure being 4,778; this rose to be more than 7,000 pa in the late 2000 and early 2010 decade.[3] The number dropped back to being around 5,000 in the latter half of the 2010 decade and the 2021 figure being 5,377 persons.

On a quarterly basis South Australia has typically lost between 500 and 1000 persons in net interstate migration (NIM)[4] during the 2000-2015 period. The losses increased during the 2015-17 period with the biggest quarterly loss being in March 2017 at almost 2,500 persons. This loss of persons had been occurring since the State Bank disaster in the early 1990s. However, since 2017 the trend has been to lower losses and during the COVID era there has been minor gains in NIM with the September 2022 quarterly figure being a gain of 1,438 persons.

In terms of net overseas migration (NOM) South Australia had a very low number in the 1990s (typically around 2-3,000 persons pa).[5] By 2004/05 the number had grown to 8,700pa and peaked at 16,200pa in 2008/09 before settling in the 12,000 - 14,000 range until 2017. Then the number increased with a peak of 18,029 in the year ending March 2020. Covid dramatically reduced NOM to a negative number until December 2021. By March 2022 NOM had increased to 7,053 for the quarter. In the year to end of March 2023 the NOM in South Australia was 25,657.[6] The increase in NOM over the past decade has in part been attributed to university student numbers increasing as well as a variety of different visa categories.

Dwellings

Whilst there have been more high rise apartments and townhouses built in the past decade than was previously the case however, the overall breakdown of house type has not changed much since 1991.[7] Detached dwellings have increased from 77.8% to 78.0% of all dwellings between 1991 and 2021. Semi-detached, row/terrace and town-houses have increased from 13.4% to 14.6%, but flats or apartments have decreased from 7.2% to 6.8% of all dwellings over the same period.

The average number of people per household has not changed much in the past couple of decades with the 2000 figure being 2.44 which dropped to 2.36 in 2006 then peaked at 2.44 in 2014 and in 2020 is at 2.40.[8]

Planning Policy

In 2001 the key planning strategy document in use was the 2020 Vision which had been produced by the State Government in 1991.

The 30 Year Plan for Greater Adelaide was produced in 2010 by the State Government. A key principle was to have 70% of urban development being classified as infill. This led to planning policy change in some locations to enable infill development to occur. For instance, parts of arterial roads in inner suburban locations such as Churchill Rd, Prospect Rd, Unley Rd, Anzac Hwy, Greenhill Rd, North Tce, Fullarton Rd and Port Rd were rezoned to various types of Urban Corridor Zone which enable multi storey residential and mixed use development in 2012. Further sites were similarly rezoned in 2017. The development of these Urban Corridors has been mixed in terms of outcome with large parts of the corridors yet to be redeveloped.

An update to the 30 Year Plan was produced in 2017. The State has recently embarked on preparing seven regional plans including the Greater Adelaide Regional Plan (to replace the 30 Year Plan for Greater Adelaide). These plans are expected to be completed in late 2024.

From a legislative perspective the Development Act 1993 was in force in 2001. Following a multi-year expert panel review the Planning Development and Infrastructure (PDI) Act was passed by Parliament in 2016. It came into full effect in March 2021 with the Planning and Design Code and a new e-planning system being implemented.

The PDI Act has Infrastructure Schemes sections incorporated in it, however there are a number of issues in the negotiation of the Act in Parliament which means no Scheme has been prepared or implemented yet. This has left the private sector to negotiate Deeds and Land Management Agreements with local and State authorities to try to deliver infrastructure. Such deeds typically deal with roads, stormwater and some Council related social infrastructure, but the timeliness of delivery of the infrastructure is generally poor-average except where developers are building it on an in-kind basis. Typically there are some transparency issues with regard to the use of collected funds. While the private sector is generally at ease with paying for infrastructure that is usually provided by the State/Council as development proceeds, an ongoing issue is the need for an injection of funds up front to get certain infrastructure in place before land can be developed and dwellings built. To date neither Councils nor the State Government seem overly keen to provide this injection. In early 2023 the SA Government announced the formation of the Housing Infrastructure Planning and Development Unit (HIPDU) with the Department of Trade and Investment which has the aim of planning and coordinating the provision of infrastructure for urban development.

An expert panel appointed by the Minister for Planning (Nick Champion) completed a review of the implementation of the new planning system in April 2023. The report is expected to be released along with the Government's response in early 2024. Some of the key issues being considered include infill development and its impact on character and heritage areas as well as carparking and the loss of trees.

Development in the Past Two Decades

In 2001 the growth of Adelaide could be characterised, like most other capital cities in Australia, as almost exclusively occurring in outer suburban locations. Unlike most other capital cities Adelaide has, for most of the last 50 years, had the State Government through its main land development agency controlled the release of the majority of land that could be used for urban purposes. By way of background, originally the Land Commission (formed in 1973) created the land bank largely using Commonwealth grants. They also developed around 25% of all residential lots at a price that undercut the privately developed estates and thus controlled pricing of land. Following a change in government the South Australian Urban Land Trust was formed in 1982 and concentrated on land banking and release of broad hectare parcels of land for development by the private sector. In 1995 the SA Urban Projects Authority took over. Then it became the Land Management Corporation (LMC) in 1997 and more recently Renewal SA in March 2012.

Typically, in 2001 the LMC either partnered with a developer or sold land outright for its subsequent development. The main estates being developed in 2001 included the final parts of Golden Grove, Mawson Lakes and Seaford Rise. The main land developments on privately owned land were at Blackwood Park and Sheidow Park. LMC were also developing industrial land at Seaford.

The regeneration project known as Westwood of the suburbs of Mansfield Park, Angle Park, Athol Park, Ferryden Park and Woodville Gardens, which were predominantly SA Housing Trust (public housing) owned dwellings that was being undertaken by Urban Pacific was well underway in the 2000s. Other regeneration projects involving SAHT land included Hawksbury Park at Salisbury North and Mitchell Park.

At the time both the greenfield and regeneration projects being undertaken were often seen as best practice in Australia.

A key factor in the ability for planning and coordination of urban development to be undertaken in a well considered and timely manner changed in the late 1990s and that was the corporatisation and privatisation of key infrastructure agencies (electricity and water/sewer). Prior to this occurring it was a relatively simple exercise for the relevant Minister to get the then heads of ETSA (Electricity Trust of SA) and E&WS (Engineering and Water Supply) to plan and deliver the necessary infrastructure for a new development front as these entities were government owned. The effects of this change were not really felt for a number of years as the various players (government and private) in urban development sector continued to operate in a similar manner as before. Maximising the utility of assets was an economic mantra that came into effect, which meant that any spare capacity was used to a much greater extent than previously was the case before undertaking expenditure on new assets and expenditure of capital for new infrastructure had to pass more stringent tests.

During the decade of the 2000s additional master planned estates were begun to be delivered at Aldinga, Seaford Meadows, Golden Grove, Blakeview and Cheltenham. These estates can be characterised as greenfield however, some are infill locations.

Regeneration continued to occur in the suburbs of Woodville West and Salisbury North.

In the 2010s major estates were begun to be delivered at Lightsview, Seaford Heights, West Lakes, Playford Alive and Eyre. The substantial urban growth area in southern Mt Barker has resulted in over 14 estates by different developers so far and will ultimately result in around an additional 10,000 dwellings being constructed. Renewal SA took on more of development focus with it becoming the land developer for the redevelopment of the former Clipsal site at Bowden, and purchasing strategic infill sites such as the former Mitsubishi site at Tonsley, the former Caroma site in Norwood and the Le Cornu site at Keswick. They also released the second stage of Seaford Meadows to the private sector.

Regeneration of older public housing areas took a new direction in the latter part of the decade with the transfer of around 5,000 SAHT dwellings to not for profit community housing groups such as Anglicare, Community Housing Ltd, Common Ground Ltd, Junction Australia and Unity Housing Company. They are tasked with building new affordable, social and market housing.

Infill development has occurred in two main forms and has produced 72,200[9] new dwellings in the period 2010-2019, although there were 20,000 dwellings[10] demolished to make way for these new dwellings:

- strategic sites, CBD and Corridor development which include projects like Bowden, West, Lightsview and Oaklands Park. Between 2010 and 2019 this has contributed 30% of new dwellings.

- general infill which is typically one house being subdivided into two or three with new houses. Between 2010 and 2019 this has contributed 37% of new dwellings.

The top two suburbs in each of the six regions of Adelaide in terms of infill development are shown in the table[11] below. Most of these suburbs were mainly developed in the 1950s and 1960s.

SUBURB (Region)	Gross Number of Dwellings Built	% of Current Stock Built Since 2010	Estimated Net Dwelling Increase (minus demolitions)	Average Annual Demolitions 2014-2020
Warradale (Inner South)	644	29%	314	33
Seacombe Gardens (Inner South)	486	42%	296	19
Christies Beach (Outer South)	656	29%	436	22
Morphett Vale (Outer South)	649	6%	489	16
Campbelltown (Inner Metro)	1,002	23%	552	45
Magill (Inner Metro)	695	16%	375	32
Seaton (Adelaide West)	828	14%	478	35
Henley Beach (Adelaide West)	478	16%	228	25
Ingle Farm (Inner North)	551	13%	241	31
Northfield (Inner North)	524	21%	294	23
Elizabeth East (Outer North)	112	5%	62	5
Elizabeth Downs (Outer North)	106	5%	66	4

Table 13.1: Urban Infill in Adelaide

In the three major growth areas of Greater Adelaide the three figures[12] below show which suburbs have had the most dwellings constructed between 2010 and 2019.

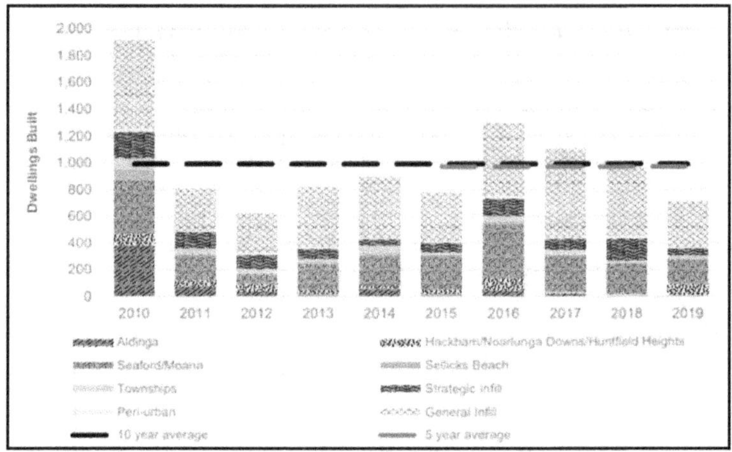

Figure 13.1: Outer South

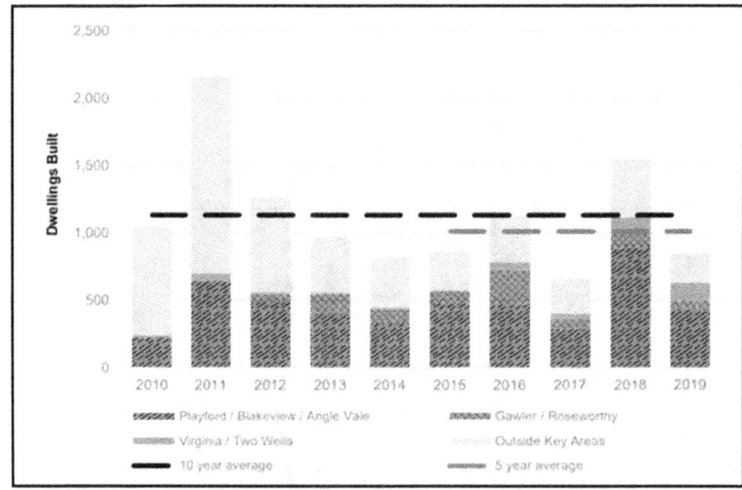

Figure 13.2: Outer North

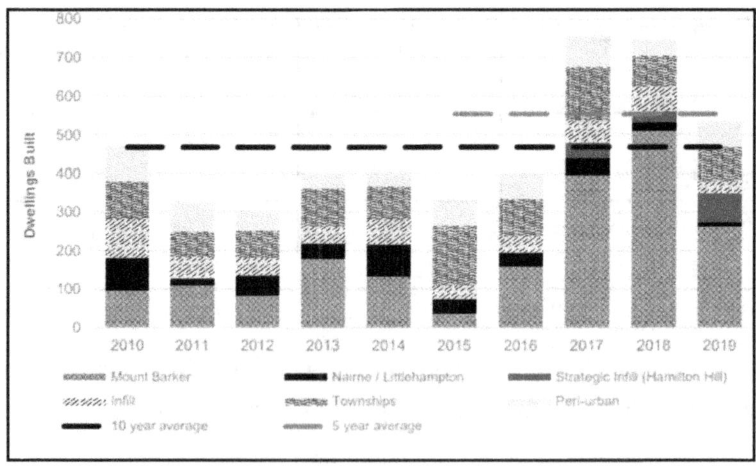

Figure 13.3: Hills

The general housing market in Adelaide has increased in price, but part of the reason is that supply of houses for sale has been decreasing for the past decade as shown in the figure below from Matusik.

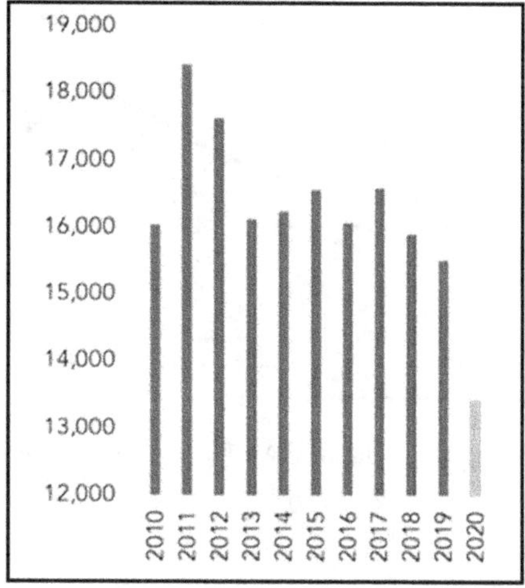

Figure 13.4: Dwellings for Sale

(Source: Matusik Price Finder + Matusik estimates. Calendar years.)

Affordability

Affordability has significantly reduced over the past two decades. In the figure below from Demographia[13], Adelaide went from 4 in 2001 to 9 in 2021 - measured by household income to median dwelling price ratio. It should be noted that during this time the variable housing interest rates declined from 8.07% in January 2001 to 4.52% in March 2021 which gives the borrower about 70% more capacity in repayments in 2021 in comparison with two decades previous. With twelve interest rate increases in the past year the amount house purchasers are able to borrow has decreased, and along with a 35% increase in building costs in the past two years affordability has taken a serious hit.

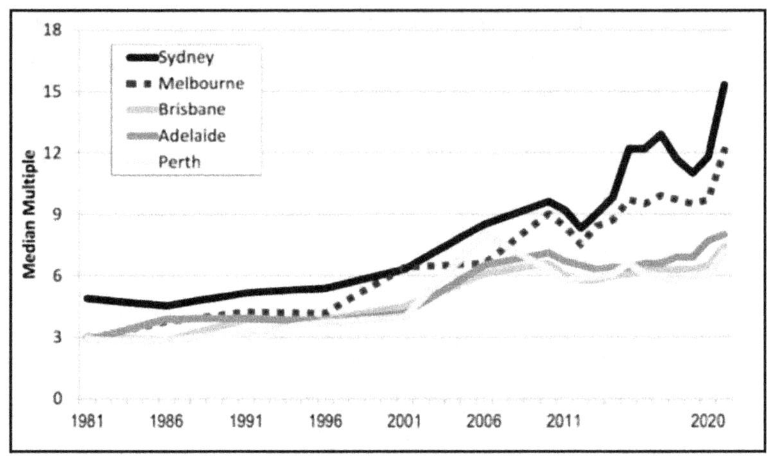

Figure 13.5: Middle-Income Housing Affordability Australia: Capital City Housing Markets: 1981-2021

(Source: Demographia)

The median house price in metropolitan Adelaide has grown from just under $150,000 in 2001 and as of September 2023 is $712,000[14] with the two periods of largest growth being 2006-2008 and 2020-2023 as shown on the following figure.

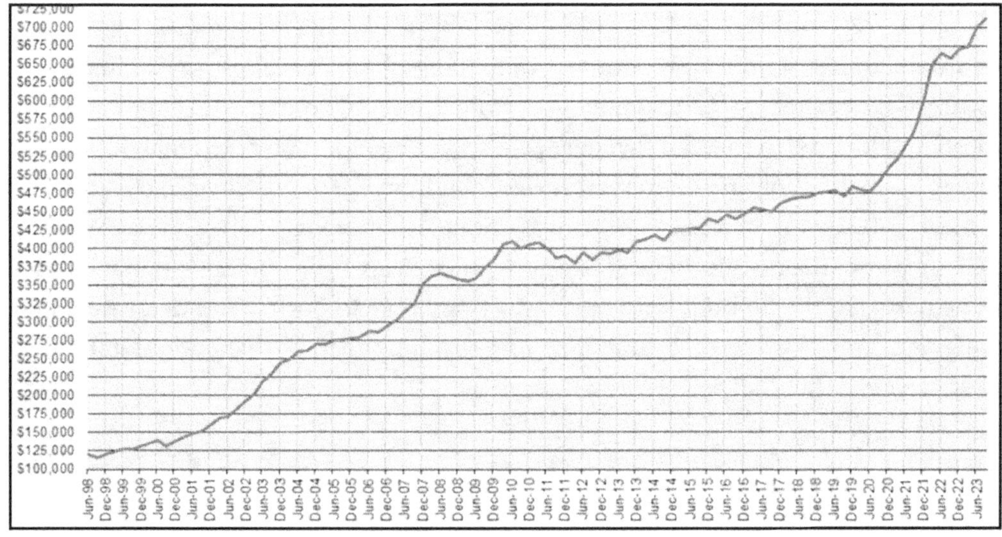

Figure 13.6: Adelaide Metropolitan Area - Median House Price by Quarter

(Source: SA Valuer-General)

The median lot price in 2002 was \$90,513.[15] The average lot size decreased from 525sqm in 2002 to 468sqm in 2011. The price per square metre was \$172/sqm in 2002. During the 2000s decade price per square metre increased, in part due a lack of releases of broadhectare land in the mid 2000s, particularly in the northern suburbs, coupled with declining interest rates. Essentially supply did not keep up with demand.

This led to some private sector developers acquiring or optioning rural land at the edges of zoned residential land with the aim of getting the land rezoned. Significant rezonings to enable residential development occurred in the first half of the 2010s at Mt Barker (1170ha), Buckland Park (892ha), Evanston South/Evanston Gardens (259ha), Angle Vale (560ha), Virginia (120ha), Playford North Extension (580ha), Two Wells (365ha), and Roseworthy (334ha). The majority of these areas were in private ownership. This privately owned development pipeline of developable land is in stark contrast to the previous four decades where the State land agency had released most of the land for residential development. There are some planning and governance issues associated with this that are yet to be resolved.

While these rezonings have provided a zoned land supply, mainly in the Outer North, that should last more well more than 15 years in total, the lack of infrastructure planning and delivery means much of the land is not actually development ready.

This substantial increase in residentially zoned land had the effect of the median lot price stagnating somewhat during the 2010s decade as shown in the table below.[16]The median allotment size varied a little over the decade 2011-2021 but did not change much overall. The median allotment price did increase from \$337/sqm in 2011 to \$416/sqm in 2021 which is a 23% increase, but is much less than the 95% increase between 2001 and 2011.

	Annual Net Land Sales	Average Number of Active Estates Per Quarter	Median Lot Size (SQM)	Annual Median Lot Price	Annual Median Land Price ($/SQM)
2011	1,467	45	468	$158K	$337
2012	1,613	53	489	$156K	$324
2013	2,544	67	463	$164K	$353
2014	1,944	66	443	$163K	$368
2015	2,162	62	419	$158K	$379
2016	1,739	57	413	$167K	$404
2017	1,851	58	450	$167K	$371
2018	2,223	71	422	$175K	$415
2019	2,054	75	449	$179K	$400
2020	3,917	84	458	$183K	$400
2021	5,488	67	450	$187K	$416

Table 13.2: Greater Adelaide Greenfield Market Performance Summary Table

(Source: UDIA, Research4)

Rental affordability has worsened over the past decade and in particular over the past three years. Rental vacancies and vacancy rates in Adelaide have been below 1% since mid 2020 whereas they are typically around 1.5-2.5% over the past decade[17] as shown on the figure on the following page. The more affordable suburbs for rental are shown on the map[18] below – they are typically located in the outer northern suburbs and along a corridor along South Rd where there are a lot of industrial and commercial properties so the amenity of those locations is not as high as other nearby suburbs.

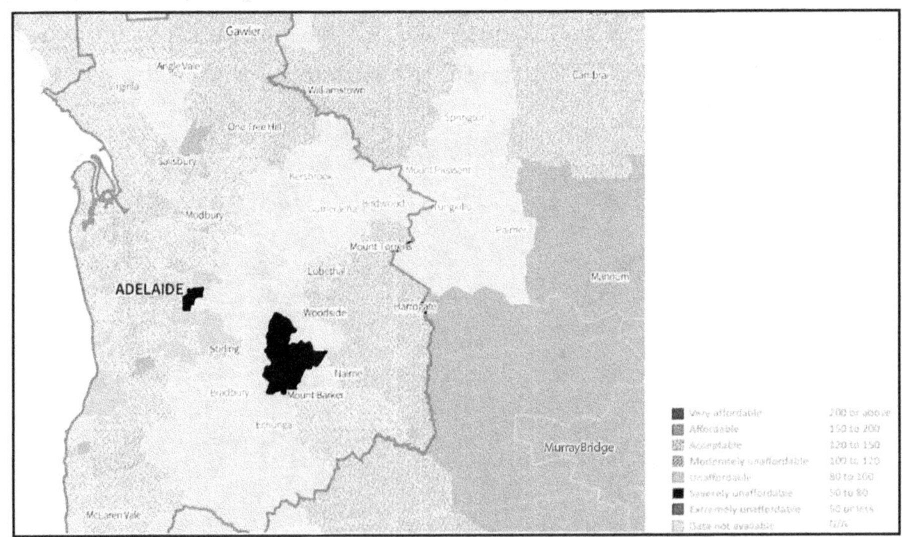

Figure 13.7: Greater Adelaide, June Quarter, 2022
(Source SGS Economics and Planning, 2022)

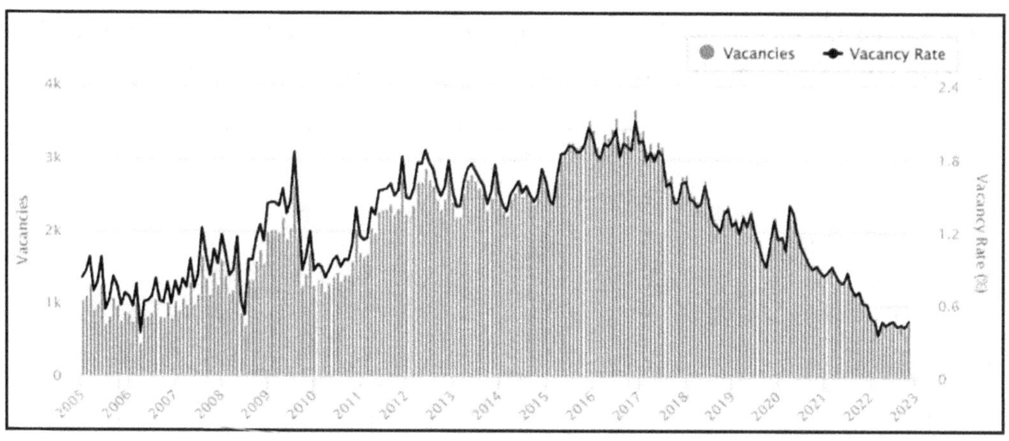

Figure 13.8: Residential Vacancy Rates
(Source: SQM Research, Highcharts.com)

The amount of land tax raised in SA has increased 289% from $140M in 2000-01 to $545M in 2020-21.[19] The rates have not increased substantially, however the exempt threshold levels have not moved much either. The rebate scheme that was in place in the mid-late 1990s for developers, so that the first 12 months of a new allotment's existence did not attract land tax no longer applies. Many developers have made changes to the way they operate as a result. Many developers now form joint ventures with the land owners, so that the developer does not ever own the land or the allotments that are created. This saves on holding costs and land tax. As part of these business operation changes developers have moved to a more just in time approach. That is, producing allotments only when they are ready for settlement. This has significant implications for the market and the pricing of allotments when periods of increased demand occur.

Impacts of Covid

In the first few months of COVID in 2020 the market for new residential allotments fell, but once the Homebuyer stimulus package was announced in June 2020 a substantial boom in activity occurred which the development industry was still trying to recover from in late 2023 due to material and labour shortages. New allotment sales in Greater Adelaide increased from 2,054 in 2019 to 3,914 in 2020 and to 5,488 in 2021 before dropping to 3,488 in 2022.[20] By early 2021 almost all the stock of new allotments had been sold and since then many developers have been selling allotments that have settlement periods that are much longer than usual as civil construction times have increased due to supply and labour shortages. Pricing of allotments in metropolitan

Adelaide has been very steady for almost a decade as shown on the figure below[21] at around \$180,000 and in 2022 the median lot price has increased by 25%.

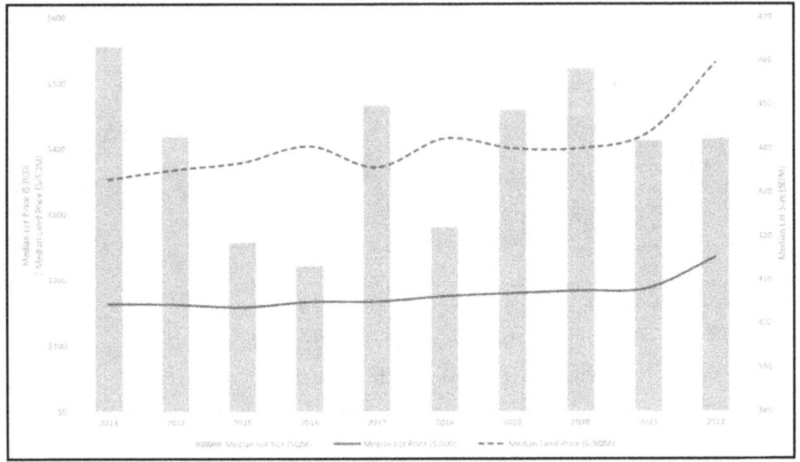

Figure 13.9: Median Lot Price, Land Price (\$/sqm) and Median Lot Size

(Source: UDIA, Research4)

COVID saw the loss of international students which had underpinned much of the development of apartments in the CBD and nearby suburbs in the previous decade. With the desire for more space in houses as a result of working from home (i.e., need for a home office) and a decrease in commuting larger homes in outer suburban locations have become more popular (greenfield developments have been supplying over 40% of new dwellings in the past couple of years up from the mid 30% in the previous decade). With net overseas migration for Australia hitting a record 500,000 in the twelve months to September 2023[22] as shown in the figure below there is substantial addition to the demand side of the housing equation.

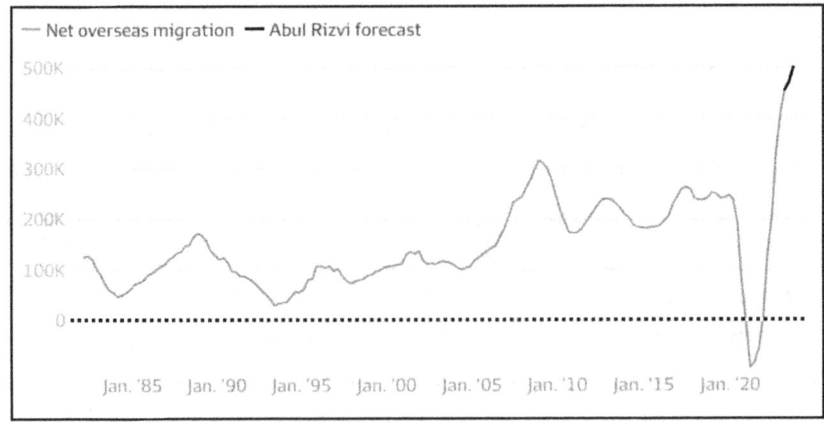

Figure 13.10: Net Overseas Migration - Annual Growth

(Chart by Michael Read, AFR, source: ABS; Abul Rizvi)

The Future

So what is likely to occur in the remainder of the 2020s in South Australia?

The following two tables from Matusik, which were prepared prior to COVID, show what the underlying demographics are expected to produce in South Australia for the first half of the decade. While COVID and the subsequent rebound in migration may have amended the numbers the trend is not expected to be fundamentally different. If net overseas migration occurs at the rate now being experienced with South Australia attracting around 6% and the NIM for South Australia remaining positive the increase in population might be closer to 20,000 persons pa. This would be 30% higher than the Matusik estimates below.

Table 13.3: South Australia – Resident Population by Lifecycle Segmentation

Lifestyle Segment	As June 2020		Forecast June 2025	
	Population	Distribution	Population	Distribution
Children living at home	370,000	21%	387,250	21%
Young renters	156,250	9%	159,000	9%
First home buyers	236,500	13%	235,000	13%
Families	445,500	25%	450,500	24%
Downsizers	321,250	18%	326,000	18%
Retirees	194,250	11%	229,500	12%
Aged	46,000	3%	50,250	3%
Total	1,769,250	100%	1,838,000	100%

(Source: Matusik + ABS. Population Projections, 2017 edition (medium series) including Matusik estimates based on last five years rate of annual population growth.)

Table 13.4: South Australia – Forecast Housing Demand by Lifecycle Segmentation

Lifestyle Segment	Annual Growth Next Five Years	Average House-hold Size	Annual Housing Demand	
			Number	Distribution
Young renters	550	2.35	250	5%
First home buyers	-175	2.71	-60	-1%
Families	1,200	3.25	370	7%
Downsizers	950	2.26	420	8%
Retirees	7,075	1.88	3,780	70%
Aged	850	1.57	540	10%
Total	10,450		5,300	100%

(Source: Matusik + ABS. Population Projections, 2017 edition (medium series) including Matusik estimates based on last five years rate of annual population growth. Average household size as of June 2019. Next five year period between 2020 and 2025 financial years.)

Key issues (excluding macro issues such as interest rates, inflation, climate change, immigration) include:

. affordability

. provision of physical and social infrastructure

. reducing supply of strategic infill sites

. dissatisfaction with many of the outcomes of general infill development

. suburbs developed in the 1960s will become the key locations for demolition and redevelopment

. working from home

. mobility.

Privately owned land will continue to be the main source of land for urban development in the next decade.

Enhancing the offerings in suburban activity centres and having more of them will better serve suburbanites, more of whom are working from home than in the past.

It is considered there is a need for more integrated planning over privately held lands in two ways. First, in greenfield locations so that the resulting population has good access to services and facilities that communities desire and require. Secondly, in regeneration areas so that upgrades to infrastructure (physical and social) are provided in a more equitable and timely manner.

The tension, that is seemingly a constant across all western cities, remains between redeveloping existing low density areas into medium density locales versus keeping the existing character of existing suburbs. One of the widely held objectives, and one that does not seem to get much opposition, is for places we live in to be walkable. Seemingly the necessary ingredients to achieve a walkable suburb are not well understood. Being walkable means not having to walk for more than about 10-15mins (which is an 800-1000m distance) to get to daily and some weekly activities. This requires an area of between 200-300ha. Within a fully functioning suburb around 50% of the land will be taken up with roads, parks, retail, commercial, civic and educational and other non-residential uses. The economics of having uses such as a small-medium sized supermarket or a primary school depends on having around 5,000-7,500 people. With a household ratio of 2.5 persons you need to build around 2,000-3,000 dwellings. The actual number will depend on the wealth (household income levels) of the neighbourhood. As such, the average density needs to be between 20-30 dwellings per hectare. Typically to get public transport to be supportable (not financially viable) dwelling density needs to be at least 35 dwellings/ha. The average allotment size at 20 dw/ha is 500sqm and for 30dw/ha is 333sqm. Functioning communities have dwelling types and sizes for a wide range of household types and different stages of life. This means there should be both small and large houses and sizes of allotments in a suburb. With an average desired density of around 30dwellings/ha this means for every lot that is larger than 333sqm there needs to be one that is equally under that size. The challenge is in designing and building dwellings that harmoniously fit in with each other, particularly when introducing a wider array of dwelling types in an area that has a consistent type/size/style. While much of the infill development in recent decades has not blended in well there are plenty of examples of good infill development to learn from.

In greenfield master planned communities allotment sizes often range from under 150sqm-over 600sqm with the average size currently being around 450sqm. However, with all the other uses that are required in a functioning suburb the density is typically around 15-20dw/ha. In strategic regeneration projects such as Lightsview the density is closer to 25dw/ha. This development is as close to walkable as you will find in newer parts of Adelaide.

In many existing suburbs dwelling density is typically 8-12dw/ha with allotment sizes being at least 600sqm on average. This means the regenerated suburb needs to have around three times as many dwellings as is currently the case. In metropolitan Adelaide the replacement ratio averaged 1.7 in the 6 years prior to 2011[23] and was 1.85 dwellings[24] in 2012-2018 and there are only five LGAs where the ratio is just over 2.0 dwellings for each dwelling demolished.

Current planning policy for most of the residential zones in existing middle ring suburbs enables minimum allotment sizes of 300sqm for most dwelling types. This means these suburbs will never be able to be walkable. Thus, it is considered planning policy needs to change so that greater density is achieved in the areas where regeneration is desired. However, the politics of regeneration of existing suburbs, particularly where they are in middle to upper socioeconomic areas can at best be described as challenging.

Renewal SA has been active in the past couple of years in acquiring sites for future development, including the former West End brewery site at Thebarton, the army barracks at Keswick and the defence land at Smithfield.

During 2023 the State Government has announced the fast tracking of release of land that will ultimately accommodate 25,000 dwellings at Concordia, Golden Grove,

Dry Creek, Hackham, Aldinga, Noarlunga Downs and Sellicks Beach.[25] Critical to making these developments occur will be the planning and delivery of infrastructure, which is struggling to keep up with existing development fronts in suburbs like Mt Barker, Angle Vale and Munno Para West. In mid 2023 the formation of the Housing Infrastructure Planning and Development Unit (HIPDU) within the Department of Trade and Investment to facilitate infrastructure provision in growth areas across the State should mean the early planning and coordination of infrastructure is undertaken with a whole of government approach in coordination with local government and industry. The role that HIPDU is to undertake is considered to be a missing element in planning for growth areas for the past couple of decades in South Australia.

Much of the next decade's worth of development can largely be determined by existing zoning and announcements that have already been made. One of the key yet to be determined factors is what policy settings might be adjusted that will influence what is termed general infill. That is, one dwelling into two or three dwellings. There has been community backlash in many suburbs about the form of this development and the politicians are very aware of the matter. Policy adjustments have been made to improve the design of such development through the "Raising the bar on infill development" document prepared by the State Planning Commission (SPC) in April 2022, but the number of completed developments that have been approved using these new policies is still quite small so the real impact of the policy is somewhat unknown at present. It is expected that there might be more policy amendments to be made dealing with infill redevelopment. A stronger focus on strategic infill development seems to be coming from State Government.

The public consultation period for the discussion paper with regard to the Greater Adelaide Regional Plan[26] (GARP), which is the upcoming replacement for the 30 Year Greater Adelaide Plan, about where and how will Greater Adelaide grow in the coming three decades recently concluded. The SPC through Planning and Land Use Services (PLUS) which are part of the Department for Trade and Investment are also undertaking regional planning in six regions across South Australia over the next couple of years. The SPC now has the task of reviewing the comments received, undertaking analyses of potential scenarios and drafting the GARP in 2024 before undertaking further consultation in the second half of 2024. The population projections that have been undertaken to inform the GARP process indicate that around 670,000 additional people might be living in Greater Adelaide by 2051. This is expected to be around 300,000 additional dwellings. This represents a more than 40% increase in total population.

How much of this growth will be infill redevelopment and how much will be greenfields will be subject to some serious debate in the coming year. The implications of such growth, in terms of education facilities, hospitals, recreational facilities, community facilities, retail, commercial and industrial land requirements as well as the physical infrastructure of roads, rail, water, sewer, etc are substantial. As are the potential impacts on the land, that will be required for this growth, that is currently being used for something else. How all of this is to be funded and financed will be one of the big issues to be resolved in the coming period.

These issues seem to be relevant to all growing cities and no-one seems to have found the idealised utopia. Each city is likely to find a slightly different path to their solution based on a mix of technical, ideological, political, financial and community influences.

Endnotes

1   ABS 3010.0 Table 4 - South Australia.

2   Rebasing of Australia's population estimates using the 2021 Census | Centre for Population

3   Population Change: Natural Increase: South Australia | Economic Indicators | CEIC (ceicdata.com)

4   ABS 3101.0 Australian Demographic Statistics.

5   Population Change: Net Overseas Migration: South Australia | Economic Indicators | CEIC (ceicdata.com).

6   National, state and territory population, March 2023 | Australian Bureau of Statistics (abs.gov.au).

7   ABS Catalogue 2710.4 *Census Characteristics of South Australia 1991*, pp.42-48.

8   South Australia: Average Persons Per Household | Economic Indicators | CEIC (ceicdata.com).

9   Department of Planning, Transport and Infrastructure, *Minor Infill Greater Adelaide reports 2008-2014, 2012-2018*.

10 Department of Planning, Transport and Infrastructure, *Residential demolition and resubdivision report 2004-2010*.

11 Government of South Australia - Attorney General's Department, *Land Supply Report for Greater Adelaide Part 2 Urban Infill* Table 4, p.13.

12 Government of South Australia - Attorney General's Department, *Land Supply Report for Greater Adelaide Part 1 Greenfield*, Figure 7, p. 9, Figure 28, p. 33, Figure 44, p. 53.

13 Demographia, *International Housing Affordability Report 2022*, Figure 4, p. 6.

14 Published Data and Statistics, Office of the Valuer-General (valuergeneral.sa.gov.au).

15 UDIA, *State of the Land Report 2013*.

16 UDIA/Colin Keane/Research4, *State of the Land Report 2022*.

17 The Property Tribune, Liam Wignell. 19 February 2021.

18 SGS Economics and Planning, National Shelter, Beyond Bank and Brotherhood of St Laurence, *Rental Affordability Index November 2023*. Figure 44 p. 73.

19 South Australian Treasury.

20 UDIA, Research4, *State of the Land 2023*, p. 82.

21 Ibid, p.81.

22 *The Financial Review,* Michael Read and Tom McIlroy, 24 October 2023.

23 Government of South Australia Department of Planning, Transport and Infrastructure, *Residential demolition and resubdivision report: 2008-2010*, p. 36.

24 Government of South Australia Department of Planning, Transport and Infrastructure, *Minor Infill Greater Adelaide – 2012-2018*, p. 4.

25 Plan SA, *Residential land release and rezoning,* https://plan.sa.gov.au/state_snapshot/better-housing-future/residential-land-release-and-rezoning

26 Plan SA, *Greater Adelaide Regional Plan*, Discussion Paper https://plan.sa.gov.au/__data/assets/pdf_file/0009/1259208/Greater-Adelaide-Regional-Plan-Discussion-Paper.pdf

14

Suburban Development in Hobart, Tasmania - Past, Present, and Future

Jason Byrne, Sebastian D. Rossi, Emma Riley

Introduction

Hobart, founded in 1804, is Australia's southernmost capital city and its second oldest. Before European invasion, Tasmanian Aboriginal people lived on and around the land and waters of what is now Hobart, for tens of thousands of years. The land occupied by the City of Hobart was home to the mouhenneener/muwinina[1] people. Greater Hobart occupies the lands of the South East, Oyster Bay, and Big River Aboriginal nations.[2] Traces of past Aboriginal occupation can still be found around Hobart and many Tasmanian Aboriginal people call the city home.

Urban scholar Graeme Davison has argued that from their inception, Australia's cities were suburban.[3] Unlike their European (and to some extent North American) counterparts, Davison says Australian cities did not experience intensive urban development. Instead, suburban development predominated early on, driven by a combination of evangelical and romantic values (order, purity, proximity to nature); medical science and the sanitation and moral reform movements (rationality, hygiene, wellbeing); the desires of comparatively wealthier settlers to own a parcel of land; weak local government systems with little responsibility for infrastructure provision; and real estate interests that sought to capitalise on an appetite for land.

Hobart's suburban growth partly exemplifies these characteristics, but also exhibits some differences. Patterns of suburban development in Hobart have been shaped by the city's geography, history, characteristics of the property development sector, and systems of governance, including planning.

Hobart's Suburban History

Hobart was founded as a penal colony with administrative functions supporting the convict settlement. A desire to enforce physical separation between convicts and settlers saw New Town, one of Australia's oldest suburbs, established at virtually the same time as the capital, Hobart. New Town embodied village ideals, with wooden cottages and brick houses on larger blocks, well-spaced from their neighbours.[4] Hobart's early suburban form was partly a response to concerns about convict morals and behaviours. Physical distance from docks, workshops and warehouses enforced social distance – insulating respectable society from the so-called rabble.[5] Notably, the 1826 town plan required that future expansion create allotments "for houses and gardens", locking in a suburban form for the city that persists to this day.[6] Hobart today has the highest ratio of detached housing of any Australian capital.

By 1842, Hobart had become a municipality. Within a decade it was Australia's third largest city.[7] Yet Hobart did not achieve the same model of municipal power as mainland (continental) capitals until 1861. The city was initially unable to raise its own taxes for infrastructure provision, such as reticulated water. Hobart's initial wealth was driven first by agricultural enterprises and later by mining and servicing the newly developing Port Phillip colony in Victoria. But this quickly stagnated as rich pastures and mineral deposits were found on the mainland.[8] Hobart grew slowly for much of its early history.

Hobart's pre-war suburban development occurred outside town planning processes as we now know them. Historian Stefan Petrow observes that Tasmania's cities have historically resisted town planning. Although in 1811 Governor Macquarie ordered a town plan for the fledgling settlement, which established a core grid pattern that survives to this day, the plan itself was not completed until 1826. Tasmania's first planning legislation, the Town and Country Planning Act, was only gazetted in 1944, following decades of sporadic action and lacklustre public support.[9] The arguments that eventually persuaded sceptics to support that legislation still strongly resonate with today's suburban aspirations. They included public health and safety, pleasant environments in which to live, and play, high quality housing, access to open space, the needs of the family, and wellbeing.

Physical geography

Hobart's present suburban form is partly dictated by its physical geography, but also is partly due to past advances in transport and industrial development. In 1967, Geographer R.J. Solomon carefully documented the spatial extent of Hobart.[10] In his survey of the city's growth since 1805, Solomon observed how much of the city's urban expansion had been confined to the western shore of the River Derwent, spreading northwards to Claremont and Brighton, and south to Kingston and Blackman's Bay (see Figure 14:1). kunanyi/Mount Wellington (elev. 1,271 metres) still presents a formidable physical barrier to westward expansion (with suburbs like Ferntree below 470m elev.) and the River Derwent constrained eastern expansion prior to the development of a modern bridge.

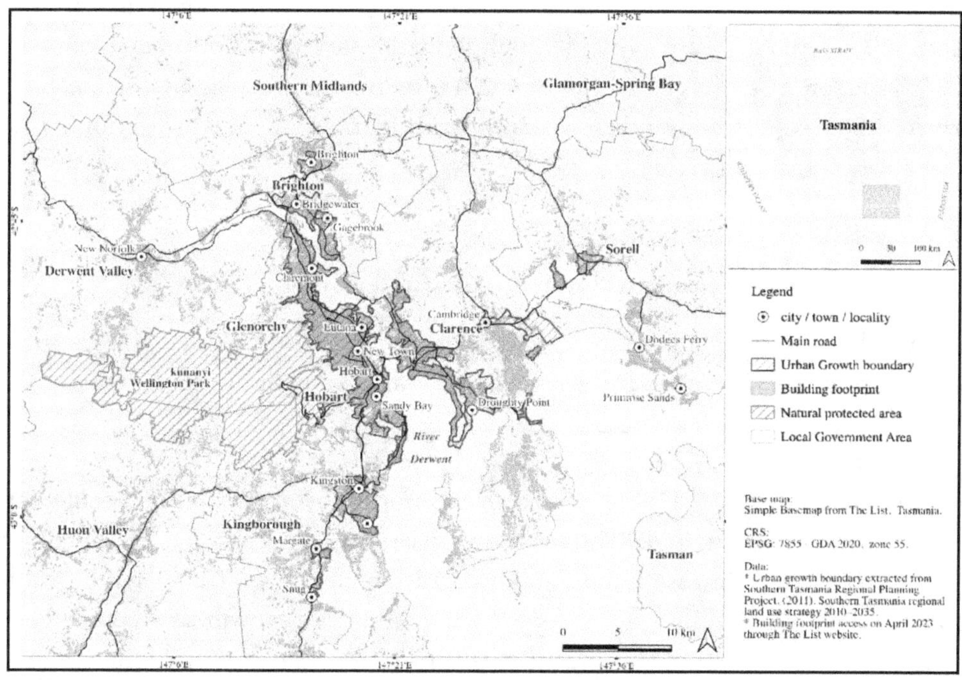

Figure 14.1: Greater Hobart urban morphology

Transport and industry

Hobart was the first city in the southern hemisphere with an electric tram system, developed in 1893, which enabled residents to live in suburbs further away from the city centre.[11] At its peak, the tram network handled two-fifths of suburban passenger traffic. In the early twentieth century, from 1910 to 1929, Tasmania developed a comprehensive hydroelectric power grid, which enabled large-scale industrialisation; new jobs enticed international migrants, especially following the Second World War.[12] The Zinc works at Lutana and Cadbury's chocolate factory in Claremont served as employment hubs but also provided model workers housing, based on templates such as Bourneville in the UK. These industries contributed to suburban growth; until the mid-1970s, they were connected to downtown Hobart by a railway line.

From the 1950s, with increasing wealth and upward mobility, residents could afford private automobiles, accelerating post-war suburban expansion. Indeed the post-war population boom saw an increase of nearly 20,000 residents within a seven-year window from 1947-1954[13], an unprecedented period of growth in the city's history. The automobile enabled rapid infill development of land that had once separated smaller townships, much like suburban expansion in the southern corridor of Perth, Western Australia (see Chapter 12). Suburban development grew especially rapidly in the northern suburbs around Glenorchy following the construction of the Brooker Highway (1954-1966). It also expanded rapidly to the east, in Clarence, first following the construction of the Hobart bridge in 1943, then a new bridge across the River Derwent in 1964 (notwithstanding a shipping accident in 1975, which crippled the bridge for two and half years).

Contemporary Suburban Development Characteristics

Hobart today is a markedly different city to its 19th and 20th century precursors, in spatial form, population characteristics, and to some extent land use planning.

Spatial form

The metropolitan area of Hobart now extends north-west to the historic settlement of New Norfolk, north to Brighton, west - past Dodges Ferry, to the southern beaches, including Primrose Sands, south past Margate to Snug, and south-west to Huonville – an agricultural centre experiencing suburban growth (see Figure 14.2). The area of metropolitan Hobart (as defined by the Australian Bureau of Statistics) is approximately 1,695 km^2, with a population of 247,086 (2021 census).[14] There are 106,298 dwellings within the metropolitan area, with an average of 2.4 people per dwelling. Separate detached houses comprise 85.1% of the building stock (80,846 dwellings), flats or apartments 8.2% (7,759 dwellings), and semi-detached dwellings (row, terrace, or townhouse) comprise 6.1% (5,768 dwellings). Nearly half of the dwellings (47.9%) have 3 bedrooms and almost a quarter (24%) have 4 bedrooms. Population densities range from a high of 4,330 persons per square kilometre in older suburbs in the urban core such as Battery Point, to a low of 177 persons per square kilometre in suburban areas on the metropolitan periphery, such as Primrose Sands.

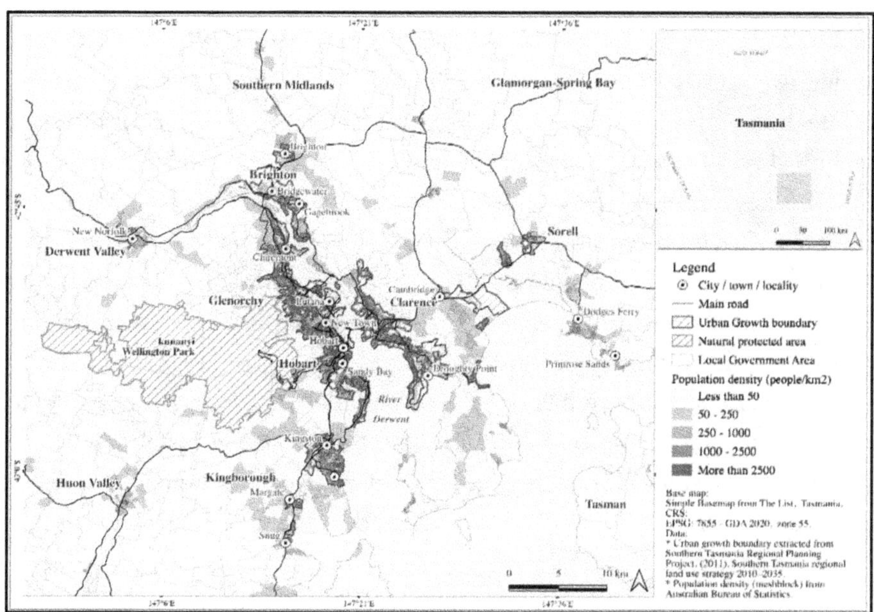

Figure 14.2: Greater Hobart population density

Population and dwelling characteristics

Across the metropolitan area the sex ratio is roughly evenly split (51.2% female), and the median age is 39 years of age. Just under a fifth (18.8%) of residents are aged over 65 years of age and just over a fifth (22.2%) are younger than 19 years of age. Aboriginal people comprise 4.5% of the population. Just over three quarters (76.6%) of residents were born in Australia, with China (2.2%), Nepal (1.7%), and India (1.6%) the next most common birthplaces. Other than English (82.6%), the next most common languages spoken at home are Mandarin (2.6%), Nepali (1.8%), and Punjabi (0.7%). The median weekly household income is $1,542 p/w, though there is considerable variation across the city. Families comprise most households (68.1%), typically families with children (38.8% couples with children; 18% single parents). Just over two thirds (68.3%) of residents either own their home outright (33.9%) or have a mortgage (34.4%) with just under a third (28.8%) renting. Most residents travel to work as either a driver or passenger (67.3%) in a private automobile with just 5.4% using public transport for commuting. A total of 8.1% of residents work from home. Car ownership averages 1.9 vehicles per household, with 55.8% of households having 2 or more vehicles. Just under half (43.2%) of the population have a long-term health condition, including mental health (11.6%). These characteristics are highly variable across the Greater Hobart area. For example, multicultural diversity is pronounced in the northern suburbs (e.g., Moonah).

Employment

Just under two thirds (61.6%) of metropolitan Hobart residents are in the labour force. The main employment sectors are professional (24%), community service (14), technical and trades (13.2), clerical and administrative (12.9%), and managerial (12.3%). The key employment industries are healthcare, social and administrative services, State Government, the hospitality sector, and retail, recognising that small businesses comprise 97% of businesses in Tasmania, among the highest per capita in Australia. The industries with the biggest economic impact, however, are the visitor economy, the education sector and agriculture and primary production support services. In recent years there has been substantial economic growth associated with the logistics and transport hub in Brighton (a 60% increase in jobs over what existed previously). The Greater Hobart region accounts for nearly all jobs (92%) in Southern Tasmania. Nearly half of these (47%) are located in the City of Hobart, followed by Glenorchy and Clarence (31%).[15]

Planning

The Greater Hobart Plan covers the local government areas of Clarence, Hobart, Glenorchy, and Kingborough. This area is smaller in extent than metropolitan Hobart (1,297 km^2) with a smaller population (210,528) and a slightly higher median age (40). According to the Greater Hobart Plan, the area's population has increased nearly 15% over the past decade. By 2050, the plan forecasts that an additional 60,000 people will call the area home, requiring 30,000 additional dwellings.[16] Much of the development across Greater Hobart presently occurs on greenfield sites. Projected land supply for new residential development is 695 hectares, which the Greater Hobart Plan suggests can be accommodated within the urban growth boundary identified in the Southern Tasmania Regional Land Use Strategy.[17] The Greater Hobart Plan anticipates a development ratio of 70% infill (21,000 dwellings) and 30% greenfield (9,000 dwellings) to accommodate population growth. In other words, a pattern of development consistent with urban consolidation.

Since the 2006 census, however, the mix of residential development in the four municipalities comprising Greater Hobart has favoured detached housing. In 2006, the ratio of detached (single house) versus multi-unit housing was 81.3% detached and 18.7% multi-unit, versus a 2021 ratio of 83% detached and 17% multi-unit. The overall housing stock has grown from 68,586 dwellings in 2006 to 80,672 dwellings in in 2021. What this data does not capture is population growth outside the Greater Hobart Plan. This is occurring in the Sorell and Brighton components of the urban growth boundary and in separate towns such as New Norfolk, Huonville, and Cygnet and nearby rural and rural residential areas.

An additional 35,558 metropolitan residents live outside the jurisdiction of the Greater Hobart Plan. The local governments of Sorell, Huon Valley, Derwent Valley, and Brighton are all approving new suburban development. This new housing stock is popular because of its comparative affordability and proximity to beaches, rural lifestyles, and Tasmania's natural areas. This trend points to challenges that lie ahead in achieving the intent of the Greater Hobart Plan specifically, and regional planning more generally.

Discussion

Over the past decade, Hobart has developed a reputation for cutting edge art, food and music festivals, fine dining, and bespoke, artisanal design, although these sectors evolved somewhat organically and were unplanned. Less well known are the planning innovations that occurred in the past. Scholars have observed how the city has flirted with suburban planning innovations throughout its history.[18] These include the partial implementation of city beautiful ideals, several partially implemented garden suburbs, and ideas for affordable housing. Unfortunately, those initiatives were partly thwarted by vested interests, conflict between local and state government, resident opposition, bureaucratic apathy, and a lack of skilled staff and resources.[19] Such problems are not unique to Hobart. Despite these obstacles, the city is considered by many to be very liveable, in part because past growth has been slow. This view of liveability has been challenged more recently due to higher than expected, unplanned population growth, a trend likely to continue.

Contemporary planning in many ways threatens to see history repeat. Tasmania has no ongoing system of strategic planning at the metropolitan and regional scale. Strategic planning is seen by government as a one-off project with no regular monitoring and evaluation. The few updates made to the STRLUS are ad-hoc and in response to political pressures. Stalled strategic projects include a long-proposed rapid transit link to the northern suburbs to replace the defunct commuter rail corridor. Many feasibility studies have been produced but not much else. Efforts to establish park and ride facilities in outer suburban locations have had mixed success. A cross-river ferry trial has been extended, but without state government commitment to a larger ferry network. The failure to deploy an integrated ticketing system is holding back advances in public transportation, such as on-demand travel and real-time bus information. And attempts to enforce the urban growth boundary to facilitate a more compact city are repeatedly undermined by the approval of subdivisions by outer metropolitan councils. Many planning issues stem from the city's high levels of car dependence, which can be traced to the collapse of public transport following a post-war boom in suburban construction - fuelled by immigration and growing levels of automobile ownership. They also stem from a history of competition and division among councils.

Most jobs in the metropolitan area are concentrated in Hobart's Central Business District. Hobart is still contending with an urban form that has entrenched a "hub and spoke" pattern of transport and employment. Despite efforts of the now decade-old Southern Tasmanian Regional Land Use Strategy to foster employment in key metropolitan activity centres, little has progressed on the ground. While there are some suburban employment centres, such as a retail mall in the City of Clarence (Eastlands Shopping Centre), a transport and logistics hub at Brighton, and a growing air-freight and logistics hub at Cambridge, near the airport, these are not yet substantial.

Contrasting with other capital cities in Australia, Hobart has a limited number of master planned communities and no large-scale developers (e.g., Lendlease, Peet and Co). Smaller scale developers who build to code often produce mediocre subdivisions that lack the type of amenity now taken for granted on the mainland (see Figure 14.3). While these developments are heralded as affordable, they tend to reinforce car-dependence and to some extent entrench the primacy of central Hobart as an employment node. Their dormitory character also generates traffic congestion in the morning and evening peak hours. And large expanses of concrete with little greenspace make them hot in summer and increase stormwater runoff.

Figure 14.3: New affordable housing in Sorell, outer metropolitan Hobart

There are signs of innovation that show alternative futures are possible. Brighton Council, for example, engaged design firm Holmes Dyer to prepare a masterplan to revitalise Bridgewater/Gagebrook – a traditionally lower socio-economic area. New social housing developed under this model by Centacare Evolve (see Figure 14.4), has achieved very high levels of amenity – although few facilities exist in walking distance from these dwellings. Kingborough Council is taking a different approach, at the other end of the price spectrum. Working with mainland developer Traders in Purple, a degraded town centre is being revitalised. A former high school site has been redeveloped for higher-end townhouses, apartment buildings, a civic centre (complete with an architect-designed award-winning community hub) and an aged-care and medical precinct (see Figure 14.4).

Glenorchy Council, while slow to take advantage of economic opportunities, is now experimenting with bespoke manufacturing and an emerging multi-cultural food scene in its ageing suburban light industrial areas. However, changes to the planning scheme are progressing to allow for residential development along the infill corridor. Many southern European migrants made a home in Glenorchy during Hobart's post-war boom, and the local government is now comparatively diverse, with around 26% of residents born overseas, including people from Poland, Greece, Germany, Italy, and Spain as well as Nepal, China, India, Vietnam, and the Philippines. Glenorchy Council has recently advertised a proposed planning scheme amendment to encourage apartment building along its main street commercial spine. This will allow medium to high density apartments above and behind shopfronts, capitalising on the density that developed around the old tram routes, much like the Rob Adams densification plan for suburban inner-Melbourne.[20]

Clarence Council is also regenerating its town centre but is grappling with a larger scale proposed master-planned, "new urbanism" inspired development at Droughty Point, which has faced considerable community opposition.

And Hobart City Council has embarked on a series of precinct-planning exercises. The first seeks to rejuvenate the city's core, with a focus on laneways, medium density apartments, and a health and knowledge hub. Architect-designed social housing (Cumulus Studios) is already emerging in the precinct, on Goulburn Street. These initiatives are not without controversy. Some community members are concerned with changes to the urban fabric (sometimes portrayed as NIMBYism). Business leaders question changes to traditional commercial land uses and restrictions on building heights. And a pro-car lobby worries about increased traffic congestion and finding parking directly outside shops.

Figure 14.4: New social housing in Brighton (left) by Centacare Evolve and up-market townhouses in Kingborough (right), by Traders In Purple

Conclusions

Once perceived as a sleepy backwater, the metropolitan area of Hobart is currently experiencing increased rates of growth. Some of the above-described changes are particularly striking. For example, during the past 10 years the location of social/community housing has begun shifting to the inner core, in contrast to the segregated "public housing" suburbs of the 1950s to 1980s (e.g., Risdon and Bridgewater). Even in established community and social housing suburbs, the non-profit sector is reliably delivering higher quality design outcomes than many private sector providers in the newer suburban estates, such as those on the Clarence Plains and around Sorell.

Most private sector developments are characterised by complete vegetation removal, large footprints, small blocks, dark roofs, and large areas of impermeable surfaces. While some Councils are working hard to retain green belts through subdivisions, guided by their biodiversity policies (i.e., Kingborough) or open space policies (i.e., Brighton), it is effectively assumed that most suburban lots will be fully cleared. In part, this is a result of managing bushfire risk but also because it is easier to sell an unconstrained lot. The economies of scale for suburban development are also different in Tasmania. A 500-lot land release in Hobart is a big deal. Tasmanian suburban development is not characterised by house and land package releases. People typically buy a vacant lot and go to their own designer/builder for house construction. Subdivision standards are very engineering driven, with little consideration of Water Sensitive Urban Design, community planning, and sustainability, redolent of 1980s style development on the mainland.

Suburban growth has leapfrogged the urban growth boundary. Some forms of rural living, such as those around Acton Park and Sandford, with large lots, hobby farm lifestyles, and equestrian activities are, for all intents and purposes, suburban. Large, expensive houses characterise these areas, and occupants often travel to the urban core in Hobart for work. Moreover, while reticulated water and sewerage may not yet be available in these localities, their relatively proximity to established suburban areas means that this is a grossly inefficient use of land.

Now that Hobart is starting to experience growth pains that accompany an increased pace of change, there is growing community opposition to development, especially in more affluent areas. This manifests mostly at the development assessment stage (and increasingly when planning scheme changes are proposed). While there are commendable efforts to accommodate a more diverse mix of housing styles within the existing urban footprint, and to provide more social housing as infill development, it is not uncommon for residents to push back - usually on grounds such as perceptions of increased traffic, overshadowing, loss of privacy, changing amenity and increased noise. These issues can be valid in some situations, but in others they are euphemisms for not wanting so-called "undesirable" people in a neighbourhood. Developers are also increasingly having to push yields and the scale of development to respond to financial challenges. In Tasmania it is much harder to get development to "stack up", unless developers push the envelope, due to higher construction costs.

Many of the problems exhibited in new suburban developments are environmental. Few local governments embrace water sensitive urban design and there is a growing problem with stormwater management and flood risk. Retrofitting the so called "greyfield suburbs" presents other challenges, with ageing infrastructure reaching the end of its life. The lack of decentralised employment and high levels of car-dependence in dormitory suburbs are worsening traffic congestion and increasing greenhouse gas emissions. Climate change has only limited integration into development assessment. Finally, high levels of car-dependence and substandard public transport infrastructure, which fails to meet national disability standards, combined with the high percentage of Hobart residents with a long-term medical condition or disability, means many suburban residents face transport disadvantage. Unless addressed through infrastructure provision and supportive government policy, car dependence will entrench and exacerbate long term health impacts such as overweight, obesity, anxiety, and depression, worsening the state's reputation for health inequalities.

Endnotes

1   In palawakani, Tasmania's Aboriginal language, there are no capitals for proper nouns.

2   J.B. Kirkpatrick, T. Lefroy, and A. Harwood, "Turning place into space–Place motivations and place spaces in Tasmania", *Landscape and Urban Planning*, 2018. 178: p. 112-121.

3   G. Davison, "The past and future of the Australian suburb", in *Urban Research Program Working Paper*, 1993, Australian National University: Canberra, ACT. p. 1-20.

4   P. Scott, "Hobart: an emergent city", *Australian Geographer*, 1955. 6(4): p. 19-31.

5   G. Davison, "Urbanisation", in *The Companion to Tasmanian History*, A. Alexander, Editor. 2006, Centre for Tasmanian Historical Studies: Hobart, Tasmania.

6   C. Craig, *Early town planning in Hobart.* Papers and Proceedings of the Royal Society of Tasmania, 1944: p. 99-109.

7   A. Alexander, and S. Petrow. *Hobart.* Companion to Tasmanian History 2017   [cited 2019 14/01/2019]; Available from: http://www.utas.edu.au/tasmanian-companion/biogs/E000482b.htm.

8   Alexander and Petrow (2017)

9   S. Petrow, "Against the spirit of local government: the making of Tasmanian town and country planning legislation", *Australian Journal of Public Administration*, 1995. 54(2): p. 205-218.

10 R.J. Solomon, "Sprent's Hobart, circa 1845", *Papers and Proceedings of the Royal Society of Tasmania*, 1967. 101: p. 49-67.

11   Davidson (2006)

12 Scott (1955)

13 ibid

14 Australian Bureau of Statistics. *Hobart (2021 Census all person quickstats).* 2023   April 12, 2023]; Available from: https://abs.gov.au/census/find-census-data/quickstats/2021/601.

15 B.S. Ragaini, et al., "Is greater public transport use associated with higher levels of physical activity in a regional setting? Findings from a pilot study", *Pilot and Feasibility Studies*, 2021. 7(1): p. 1-9.

16 Government of Tasmania, *30-year Greater Hobart Plan.* 2022, Department of State Growth: Hobart, Tasmania.

17 Southern Tasmania Councils Authority, *Southern Tasmania Regional Land Use Strategy, 2010-2035.* 2013: Hobart, Tasmania.

18 Petrow (1995) and D. Nichols, and R. Freestone, "Small green swards: Ideals and realities in town planning reform", *Tasmanian Historical Studies*, 2003. 8(2): p. 89-108.

19 S. Petrow, "Making the city beautiful: Town planning Hobart: c. 1915 to 1926", *Papers and Proceedings of the Royal Society of Tasmania*, 1989. 36(3): p. 99-112.

20 R. Adams, "Transforming Australian cities for a more financially viable and sustainable future: Transportation and urban design", *Australian economic review*, 2009. 42(2): p. 209-216.

15

Planning and Development in Canberra

Malcolm Smith, Mike Quirk and David Wright

In the Beginning

Canberra as the national capital, and a thriving, growing, city has largely been established in one person's lifetime. In the 1920s the site was occupied mainly by sheep stations. Today Canberra has a population of some 465,000 people, and is internationally recognised as a modern exemplar of planned, sub centralised, sustainable, metropolitan development. Canberra's legacy from the Griffins, Sulman, Butters, and the National Capital Development Commission is profound, as is the need to understand how the development of the city has evolved over time.

In 1901 the Commonwealth of Australia was created through an Act of Federation, and a Constitution drawn up, providing for a new national capital to be established in a Federal Territory, in the State of New South Wales, but no closer than 100 miles from Sydney. Forty possible sites were considered by the Commonwealth Parliament, and 23 were visited and evaluated in detail. In 1908 Parliament determined that the new capital city should be established in the Yass-Canberra district, and an area of not less than 900 square miles should be ceded to the Commonwealth for this purpose. This land is legally defined as the Australian Capital Territory. It was determined that the Commonwealth Government would maintain ownership of all land, with construction and development being facilitated through a leasehold system of land tenure. An important reason this site was preferred was its capacity for abundant water storage and supply, an important factor for an inland site in an arid continent.

In 1911 an international competition was launched for the design of the national capital. A target population of 25,000 was nominated in the competition brief. 137 entries were received from Australia and around the world. The competition was won by Walter Burley Griffin (WBG), an American landscape architect from Chicago, in association with his wife, Marion Mahoney Griffin, also a talented designer and illustrator.

The new national capital was formally named Canberra, at the laying of the city foundation stone, on 12 March 1913. Later that year the Griffins arrived in Canberra for WBG to take up the position of Federal Capital Director of Design and Construction. He replaced an interim government board which had been established to advance planning and design in his absence. Little progress was made after his arrival however, due largely to issues created by Australia's participation in the First World War, a downturn in the economy, and the numerous running disputes he had with various Ministers and bureaucrats about his plan.

The Griffins used their time wisely however, amending their winning plan to produce a revised plan in 1918. An increased target population of 75,000 was planned, while retaining the integrity of the original plan. Frustrated however by the lack of government support for the implementation of his plan, WBG left his position as Federal Capital Director of Design and Construction in 1920, and departed Canberra a disillusioned man.

Although there were various attempts by Government to tinker with his plan after the Griffins left Canberra, in 1925, Parliament, through the *Seat of Government (Administration) Act*, formally gazetted the *Plan of Layout of the City of Canberra and Environs* (the 1925 Plan), which included the key components of Griffins 1918 Plan. Only with the approval of Parliament could this plan be changed. Although basically a road layout plan it has ensured that Griffin's proposals were effectively enshrined in a legal framework.

Griffin

Griffin's plans integrated the landscape, proposed built environment, and broader setting, into an exemplary composition which took full advantage of the natural features of the site. He laid out formal avenues, structural landscaping, and grand buildings to correspond with a series of visual axes based on important topographical features such as Capital Hill and City Hill. Together with Russell Hill these apexes, joined by major avenues, formed his National Triangle within which important national buildings and functions would be located.

He proposed a central ornamental lake as a major unifying feature, and lined the foreshores with promenades, parklands, and public facilities such as galleries, theatres, cafes and the like. The lake was also envisaged as an excellent setting for major national buildings and works. Griffin also proposed that the hills and ridges surrounding the site of the new capital be retained in their natural state and kept free from development.

Griffin was influenced by the garden city concepts of Ebenezer Howard in developing planning principles to underpin the design of the residential areas. Griffin believed that these principles, with the emphasis on people participating in society, having good access to parks and to the workplace were fundamental to an emerging democratic nation. Griffin's plan had merit but proved inconsistent with the population's overwhelming preferences for low density dwellings and the car.

Griffin's 1918 plan, based on a population target of 75,000, introduced the concept of new neighbourhoods, topographically located along the axial lines generated from Capital Hill and City Hill. Griffin stated at the time that "it would seem desirable to extend the lines of extension as far as possible, in order to prevent an ultimate obstruction of orderly growth through land speculation or misdirected improvements".

Although there have been inevitable departures over the years, reflecting ever changing influences in town planning and urban design, the enduring qualities of Griffin's plans have stood the test of time, and generally been safeguarded by successive governments. Today for instance, the National Triangle is basically complete, Parliament House stands on Capital Hill, the avenues and land axis are established, the inner hills remain in their natural state, and the lake, acting as a centrepiece of his great design, is not only in place, but fittingly bears his name. Other major national institutions have been established in Griffin's National Triangle including the National Library, High Court of Australia, National Gallery of Australia, National Science Centre, National Archives, National Portrait Gallery, and Museum of Democracy (housed in the Provisional Parliament House).

There have been reviews of Griffin's plans over the years, including in 2004 the publication of the "Griffin Legacy" by the National Capital Authority (NCA). This examined the progress on the implementation of Griffins plans, and identified actions necessary and desirable to protect, extend, and enhance the important elements of his plan. The National Capital Plan, the current overriding statutory plan administered by the NCA, recognises the importance of Griffin's Plans, by identifying the Central National Area and other important Griffin elements such as the hills and ridges and major avenues and approach roads, as Designated Areas, i.e., areas having the special characteristics of the National Capital, for which NCA has sole responsibility for forward planning and development control.

Sulman (Federal Capital Advisory Committee 1920-1925)

Following Griffin's departure in 1920, the Government established a Federal Capital Advisory Committee with John (later Sir John) Sulman as its chairman. It was charged with the responsibility of accelerating the planning and development of the National Capital.

Sulman modified Griffin's subdivision pattern, preferring individual cottages on generous blocks of land, rather than terrace housing. In his view, trees and gardens were to dominate and there should be no back lanes or front fences (his "no front fences" objective has largely continued to the present day). Through this process he developed a basic template for neighbourhoods, which endured until recent times.

His Committee achieved real progress in other areas, for example the completion of Canberra's first water, sewerage and electricity systems, extensive tree plantings, construction of hotels, hostels, shopping areas, the first school and the first industrial area. Erection of the Provisional Parliament House was started during his tenure, and eventually completed in 1927.

Sulman also recognised that effective administration was as important as town planning in the ongoing construction of the city, particularly by establishing building standards and a system of urban leasehold. *The City Area Leases Ordinance 1924* was established during his term of office, setting the framework for the issue of crown leases for individual sites for specified land uses. The system of leasehold land tenure, and the covenants in crown leases, has been a valuable planning tool, used in conjunction with other planning instruments.

Federal Capital Commission 1924-1930

Ironically the success of Sulman's Committee, in achieving so much, particularly in administration and construction, in such a short period of time, led to its demise. It was seen necessary to replace it with a Statutory Authority, with greater powers. The Federal Capital Commission, was set up under the *Seat of Government (Administration) Act 1924.* Its extensive corporate powers were complemented by the experience and skills of the Commissioners, particularly its Chairman, John (later Sir John) Butters.

Under the FCC housing development proceeded apace, and between 1924 and 1926 the population more than doubled, from 3,000 to 6,500, driven largely by construction workers working on the Provisional Parliament House. The transfer of public servants from Melbourne to Canberra was also facilitated by the FCC, with more than 1,000 families accommodated in less than 20 months.

The Commission's tenure was productive but short. Its existence came to an end in 1930, a victim of both the Depression and the inflationary effects of rampant speculation at government land auctions. It did last long enough however to demonstrate that the integration of planning, administration, design, and development, within a competent technical authority, could meet the needs of a rapidly growing national capital. This was a model that again served the national capital well in the 1950s with the formation of the National Capital Development Commission (NCDC) with a similar brief and structure, but much larger budget and program.

The Mid Years (1930-1954)

The 27 years following the demise of the Federal Capital Commission saw responsibility for managing continuing growth of Canberra revert to various government departments, with little co-ordination between them. Political commitment to the new national capital disappeared and responsibility became divided and confused. The Depression and Second World War exacerbated this situation.

As a result, Canberra's growth basically stagnated leading to a growing backlog of unsatisfied requirements for offices, housing and basic community services. In this period development was restricted to a few national buildings such as the War Memorial, limited government offices, retail precincts at Civic, Kingston and Manuka, and the start of development, albeit slowly, of inner suburbs, such as Reid, Turner, Braddon, Griffith and Forrest. These suburban developments generally followed the principles of neighbourhood planning instigated by Sulman, although not all had primary schools or local centres. Neighbourhood design also had to be adapted to meet Griffin's geometry.

In the early 1950s the Commonwealth Parliament, under Prime Minister Robert Menzies, decided that mismanagement and the failure to implement an effective planning and development programmes could no longer be ignored. In 1954 a Senate Select Committee was charged with investigating the successes and failures of the previous 40 years, and recommending a way forward for the accelerated establishment of a National Capital which Australians could be proud of, and which would be regarded as one of the world's great new cities. An important recommendation of the Committee was that the system of divided departmental control of development be terminated and replaced by a single authority, responsible to a Minister holding a specific portfolio for the Australian Capital Territory.

Parliament accepted the Committee's recommendations, and subsequently commissioned eminent British town planner, Sir William (later Lord) Holford to advise on a suitable model for the proposed new authority. In 1957, based on the Committees recommendations and Holford's advice, Government introduced the *National Capital Development Commission Bill*. The Bill was enacted in September 1957. The Commission was duly established with John Overall (later Sir John) as the inaugural Commissioner, and commenced operation in 1958.

The National Capital Development Commission (1958-1989)

The National Capital Development Commission's (NCDC) role was to plan, develop and construct Canberra as Australia's National Capital. It had strong powers and relatively generous budgets. Canberra's population in 1958 was 39,000, which had taken 40 years to achieve. The transfer of government departments from Melbourne to Canberra was recommenced, and the need to develop residential areas to accommodate the influx of new residents was becoming critical. As a stop gap measure several Commonwealth hostels to house transferred public servants and their families were established to help deal with this demand.

NCDC had taken the view that the national capital significance of Canberra was not just confined to the inner areas designed by Griffin, but should be all pervasive, therefore requiring high standards of contemporary town planning, urban design, engineering, landscaping and amenity in the new areas. NCDC maintained only small staff numbers in the early years, albeit experienced and highly skilled personnel, but complemented this by engaging accomplished professional consultants in a range of disciplines, from Australia and overseas.

An early priority of NCDC was to identify *Areas of Special National Concern,* giving particular focus on the major elements of Griffin's plans, and gave them extended expression as Areas of Special National Significance, to which specific policies and proposals applied. These later formed the basis for the definition of Designated Areas in the National Capital Plan.

NCDC also moved quickly to tackle the housing backlog. New suburbs were developed including Dickson, Watson, Downer and Lyneham in the north, and Deakin and Curtin to the south. Each was developed in accordance with the neighbourhood planning principles espoused by Sulman, but planned to a higher level of sophistication.

By the early 1960s NCDC had confirmed it needed to adopt a new strategy of accommodating metropolitan growth, up to a population of 250,000 (well beyond Griffin's 75,000). The strategy it produced in 1965 (as published in the *Future Canberra*) proposed development in the form of new towns, each with a town centre, and residential areas in the form of discrete but connected neighbourhoods. Woden and Belconnen were identified as the first two new towns. The strategy of new towns was refined and expanded in 1969 in *Tomorrow's Canberra* (The General Plan Concept or Y-Plan as it became known) to cope with Canberra's revised long-term growth, up to a population of 1 million. Canberra was experiencing rapid growth at this time, with the population increasing by 9% to 10% per annum, i.e., doubling every seven years.

The sub centralised approach inherent in the Y-Plan option had to a large extent responded to a major transport study undertaken by Voorhees and Associates which had looked at the transport and traffic impacts of various growth scenarios for the developing city. The Y-Plan was considered to best meet the needs to protect the Central National area from undesirable traffic congestion, while seeking a good balance between residential and employment location. It also sought to achieve efficient inter town and intra town traffic movements including public transport, and to minimise the need for extraneous traffic to enter residential areas.

The Y-Plan

The 1969 Y-Plan was based on a model of sub centralisation, and comprised eight new towns, three of which would be in New South Wales. The new towns were grouped into three corridors emanating from Central Canberra, thereby forming a 'Y' shape (see Figure 15.1). Other important principles of the Y-Plan were:

- A centres hierarchy with Civic to serve as the prime centre for commercial, retail, employment, entertainment, and other facilities and services requiring a metropolitan catchment. The next level of the hierarchy would be Town Centres of 10,000-15,000 workers providing employment, retailing, community and entertainment services and facilities to meet the needs of each town. The centres hierarchy lower levels were defined as "regional centres" and "other centres", later to be redefined as group centres and local centres;

- Each town to have a residential population of 100,000 to 120,000, with a self containment level of 70 per cent to be achieved when the population of each town reached 75,000;
- The Central National Area to have 25 per cent of the city's workforce at a population of one million, consistent with the policy of sub centralisation and employment dispersal;
- Hills, ridges and buffer spaces would provide a clear boundary between the respective towns and link to a more extensive open space system outside the urban areas, to be defined later as the National Capital Open Space System. These areas provided a landscaped open space setting for the towns, and accessible recreation opportunities for the community;
- The transport system was to comprise a system of peripheral parkways, and an express public transport route connecting the town centres and running through the built-up spine of each town. At the town centres the express buses would interchange with local buses serving the neighbourhoods

A major function of the Y-Plan was to guide land development programming and housing supply in a period of rapid growth. The neighbourhood model was endorsed by the Y-Plan as the main residential unit. A metropolitan land development sequence was established, facilitating more detailed planning and construction, which was effective in ensuring residential development and housing completions largely met program targets. Integrated programs flowing down from disaggregated population projections and housing demand forecasts saw major earthworks and land development, provision of utility services and other physical infrastructure, land sales and housing construction delivered in a highly co-ordinated process. The timing of other neighbourhood facilities such as shops, primary schools, and open spaces and playgrounds, were also able to be integrated through this process.

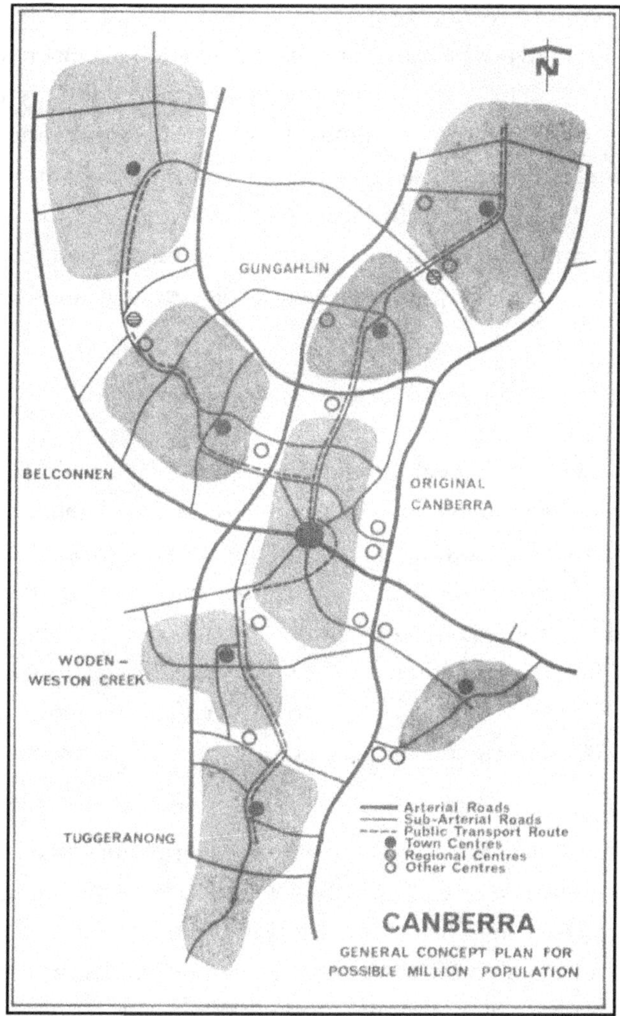

Figure 15.1: General Plan Concept (Y-Plan) (NCDC)

The Y-Plan had critics, including commercial and business interests, and large property developers, who, from time to time have contended that the dispersal of employment and major retailing to the new towns and other areas has prevented the City Centre (Civic) from reaching its full potential as a strong and dominant CBD. Some of the same interests have also lobbied for a freehold system of land tenure to replace leasehold. None of these alleged weaknesses seem to have deterred major private investment in Civic and the town centres however.

Other critics of the Y-Plan point to its predominant low density structure and car dependency. At the time of Y-Plan preparation the dominant family unit was the nuclear family, and their overwhelming preference was for a detached house and generous, private, garden. The Y-Plan dealt with these preferences by ensuring low density neighbourhoods had close proximity to places of employment (the town centres), and were well served by safe and efficient road linkages, public transport and pathway systems. The Y-Plan didn't foresee new towns, such as Gungahlin, or major new, non conforming urban districts such as Molonglo, being without major employment, resulting in onerous journey to work trips for most of their work force.

The New Towns

The Y-Plan guided Canberra's development between the 1960s and the early 2000s with the completion of the new towns of Woden-Weston, Belconnen, Tuggeranong, and part of Gungahlin. The intention to continue linear growth along the two northern arms of the Y-Plan into NSW has not been achieved however mainly because of the failure of the NSW and Commonwealth Governments to agree on the necessary institutional arrangements for cross border development. Since then much of the areas in NSW identified for new towns have been subject of many rural subdivisions, and the task of assembling the land from multiple land owners would now be difficult.

In the absence of planned cross border development, private interests have taken the opportunity to establish large residential estates such as Googong to the south of Queanbeyan and Tralee close to the Hume Industrial estate. The ACT Government has also entered into a Joint Venture to develop a large urban district at Ginninderry, to the west of Belconnen, which straddles the NSW border. These developments cater largely for the Canberra market, rather than sub- regional demands. Otherwise, the continuing growth of Canberra will need to be contained within the Territory borders, although some demand may still decant to planned estates in the immediate sub region.

The legacy of the new towns has followed the principles of the Y-Plan, and includes town centres and a hierarchy of group and local centres, high schools and primary schools, extensive cycle and pedestrian networks, peripheral arterial roads and parkways, the inter-town transport spine linking the town centres with Central Canberra and the City Centre, and a highly valued open space system including parks and playing fields. The major residential unit has continued to be the neighbourhood.

Neighbourhood size has been determined by residential density, walking distances, traffic generation, topography, the road system, and the catchment of the primary school. Early neighbourhoods had a population of 3,500 to 4,000 with 90% of housing stock being in the form of standard detached dwellings. Each neighbourhood generally accommodated a primary school and pre-school, a local shopping centre, a service station, and neighbourhood park or playing field.

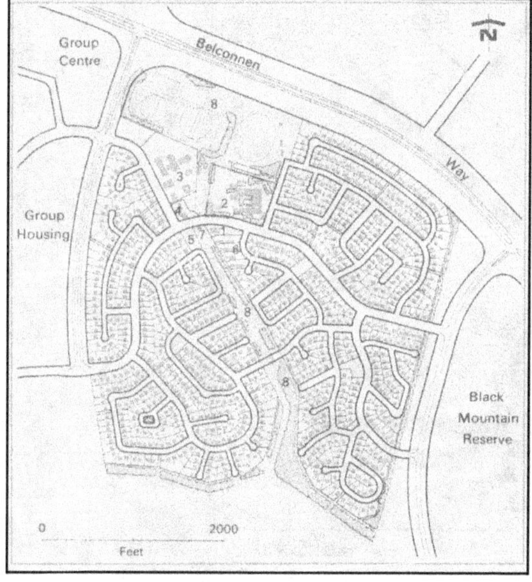

Neighbourhood of Aranda, Belconnen

Legend

1. Shops
2. Primary School
3. Parish Centre and School
4. Joint Church
5. Pre-School, Mothercraft Centre
6. Group Housing
7. Pedestrian Underpass
8. Recreation

Figure 15.2: Typical Neighbourhood (NCDC)

Efficient subdivision design and large blocks (generally above 700m2) ensured residents enjoyed high levels of privacy and amenity. The hierarchical road networks were designed to efficiently move traffic out of the neighbourhoods and on to the external major roads, and to discourage extraneous traffic in the residential areas. A system of pedestrian ways provide convenient walking and cycle access to schools, shops and bus stops. Local bus routes typically service all neighbourhoods, linking with the inter town services at a dedicated bus interchange in each town centre.

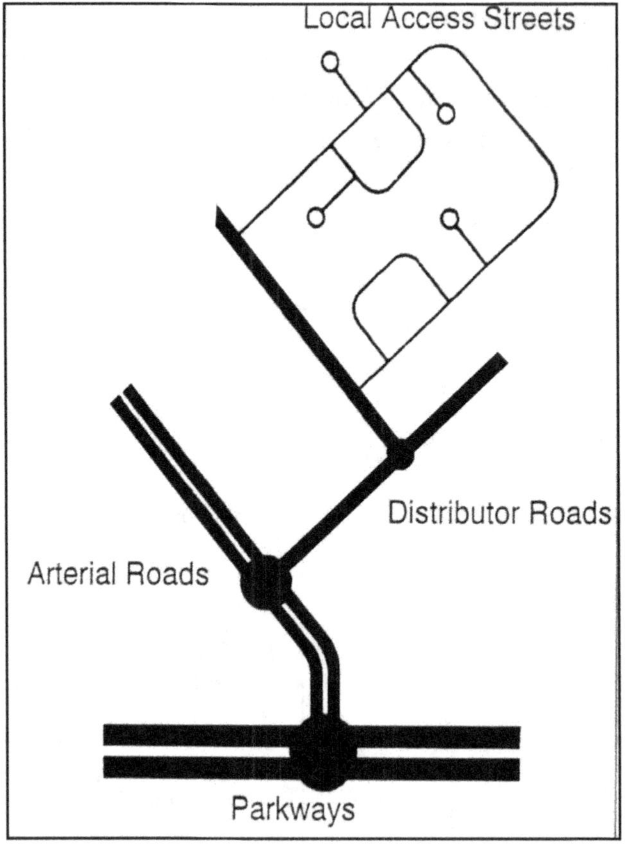

Figure 15.3: Road Hierarchy (NCDC)

The town centres generally contain major employment (except Gungahlin Town Centre), higher order convenience and comparison retailing, other services and businesses, social, leisure, entertainment, recreation and community facilities. Each town centre also accommodates a Year 11/12 college and a public transport interchange. Accessibility to each town centre, by public and private transport is good, as it is for cyclists and pedestrians. Adequate short stay parking is generally available, and limited commuter parking is provided on the site of most office developments.

Group centres, serving a "group" of 4 or 5 neighbourhoods were developed to primarily meet the needs of major convenience shopping, and the social and business needs of the community. They were often associated with a government high school and district playing fields. They fit a gap between the town centres and local centres, with the major magnet being one or two large national chain supermarkets.

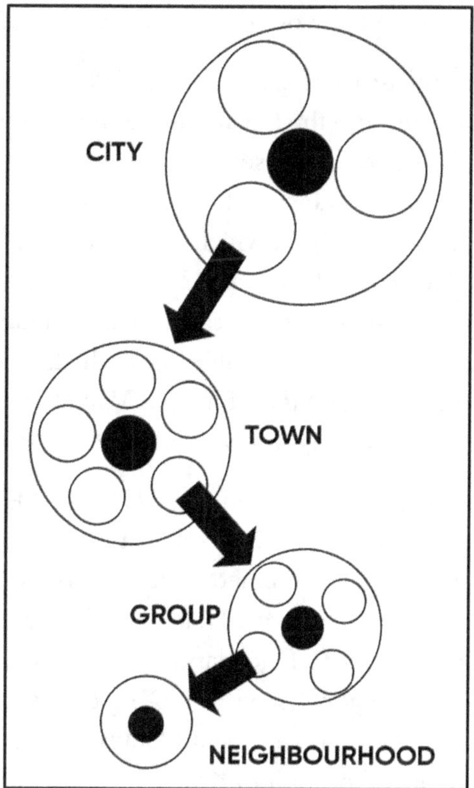

Figure 15.4: Centres Hierarchy (NCDC)

Little or no residential development was originally integrated into the early town centres, although medium density estates were established close to the centres, but generally not within reasonable walking distance. Only relatively recently have medium to high density residential developments occurred in the cores of the centres, through a process of vacant land being released to the market, or redevelopment. Gungahlin, being the most recent town centre was able to be planned with integrated residential development from the start.

All developments in the new towns were established in a landscape setting consistent with Griffin's plans for a garden city. Considerable effort was made to protect and incorporate existing trees in subdivision designs, which also took account of terrain and aspect. NCDC also undertook significant advance planting in neighbourhoods including street trees, so that they were established before building works started. The government also had a program of issuing 10 trees and 40 shrubs to each residential block owner, free of charge, from the government nursery. Many residents took advantage of this scheme, thereby further contributing to the attractive landscape character and environmental quality of the neighbourhoods of that time.

It was acknowledged that the urban structure of the Y-Plan would be defunct after the completion of Gungahlin, because the linear pattern of new towns across the border could no longer proceed. Growth to the south of Tuggeranong was also taken off the plans because of major environmental and heritage concerns, and unsuitable terrain. Land to the west of the Murrumbidgee, which was part of the original Tuggeranong Structure Plan was also declared to be unsuitable for urban development, because of its environmental sensitivity, numerous sub catchments draining directly to the river, steep terrain, and the high cost of the several bridges which would be required. ACT Government consequently identified the Molonglo Valley, to the west of Canberra's existing urban areas, as the next major, town scale, development area.

After Molonglo the only land remaining in the ACT suitable for large scale urban development is Kowen, an area currently used as a pine forest in the north east of the Territory. Access at present is confined to a rural road (Sutton Road) via the Federal Highway or through Queanbeyan. Neither is ideal. More direct access is not possible because of high security Defence land holdings, some of them apparently littered with UXO. This accessibility issue is yet to be resolved. However the recently released projections by the ACT Government identify a metropolitan population of 784,000 by 2060, without any allocation to Kowen.

Overlapping Neighbourhoods and Territorial Units

Surveys conducted in the early 1970s confirmed that neighbourhoods had worked well, with residents expressing a high degree of satisfaction with the residential environment. Local shops were well patronised, 70% of children walked to the primary school, and traffic on local streets was well within acceptable standards. Professor Hugh Stretton, in his 1970 book, *Ideas for Australian Cities,* gave strong endorsement to neighbourhood planning and subdivision design as being implemented by NCDC in Canberra during his era.

Later analysis of emerging contemporary educational, retail and social patterns together with changing household size and declining population growth, found that the neighbourhood unit was not sufficiently flexible or adaptable in the face of these challenges. As household size and neighbourhood populations declined a number of primary schools closed, and some local centres lost their key trader or closed down completely.

In the later development areas of North Belconnen the principle of overlapping catchments was introduced into neighbourhood planning, partly in response to these issues. Local centres were sited at the boundary between two neighbourhoods, adjacent to major roads, where visual prominence was much improved, and good accessibility directly from the major road network as well as local streets was facilitated. Schools remained at the centre of the neighbourhoods however, breaking the nexus between the two most important elements of neighbourhood planning. This allowed the development of a much larger retail-community centre serving 15,000-20,000 people in order to meet changing lifestyles.

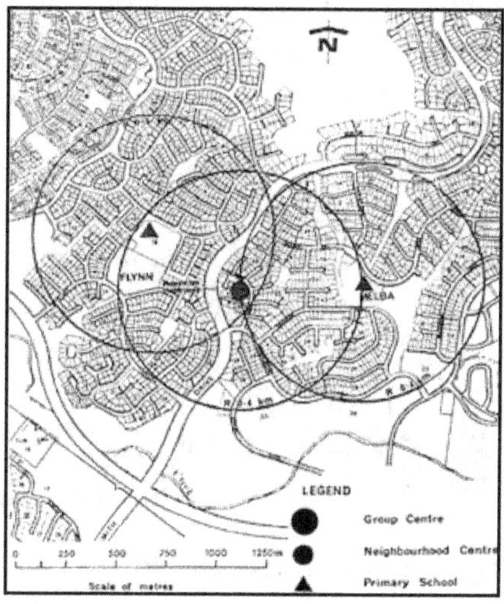

Figure 15.5: Overlapping Catchments - Belconnen (NCDC)

Before the establishment on the ground of the overlapping catchments in North Belconnen, structure planning for Canberra's third new town, Tuggeranong, was well under way. A fundamental question was whether Tuggeranong's development should be based on the neighbourhood planning unit as in Woden-Weston Creek and Belconnen, or on an alternative, more adaptable planning strategy. NCDC was constantly seeking new and innovative approaches in planning, and feedback, analysis, and consultation with community and business leaders at the time concluded that an alternative approach should be explored.

The concept of Territorial Units (TUs) was consequently established, with planned populations of 8,000 (Wanniassa) to 30,000 (Kambah). Boundaries of these units were related more to topography, trunk service lines, and road corridors, rather than population based per capita standards. A major feature of TUs was a central activity spine, a linear clustering of schools, group and intermediate centres and community uses, in an expansive open space setting which included playgrounds, playing fields, tennis clubs, and other open space and outdoor recreation uses.

The central activity spine was linked to surrounding residential areas by a system of pedestrian routes, cycle ways and a local network of loop roads and culs de sac. Within the residential areas Local Activity Centres (LACs) were established instead of traditional neighbourhood centres, taking on the role of an integrated corner shop, owner's residence, and community meeting hall. These were located at the confluence of major pedestrian routes and local roads, including distributor roads, and were sited to be within easy walking distance of the majority of the population. However the nexus between the local shop(s) and the primary school and pre- school was in some cases broken.

The intention of providing community spaces within the LACs was not successful however and in most cases the total LAC building was used for retail and commercial services. Instead individual government houses were converted to community use and some still exist today. More recently cafes and coffee shops have located in some LACs, partly fulfilling their original intended purpose as community meeting places. The flexibility in the LAC concept has allowed change to occur over time in line with community preferences.

Locating schools and larger shopping centres in the activity spine has allowed growth and change to occur without disruption to other spine uses or surrounding residential areas. For instance, within the Kambah-Wanniassa spine, a new "super" school (for years 1 to 10) has replaced a former primary school, while another has been redeveloped as a retirement village. The original plan for a Kambah Group Centre within the spine was abandoned when a general retail over supply was apparent, and the site has instead provided the opportunity for a number of small scale commercial and community services, plus a small local retail centre. The flexibility of the Territorial Unit and central spine concept has allowed these changes to occur without major disruption.

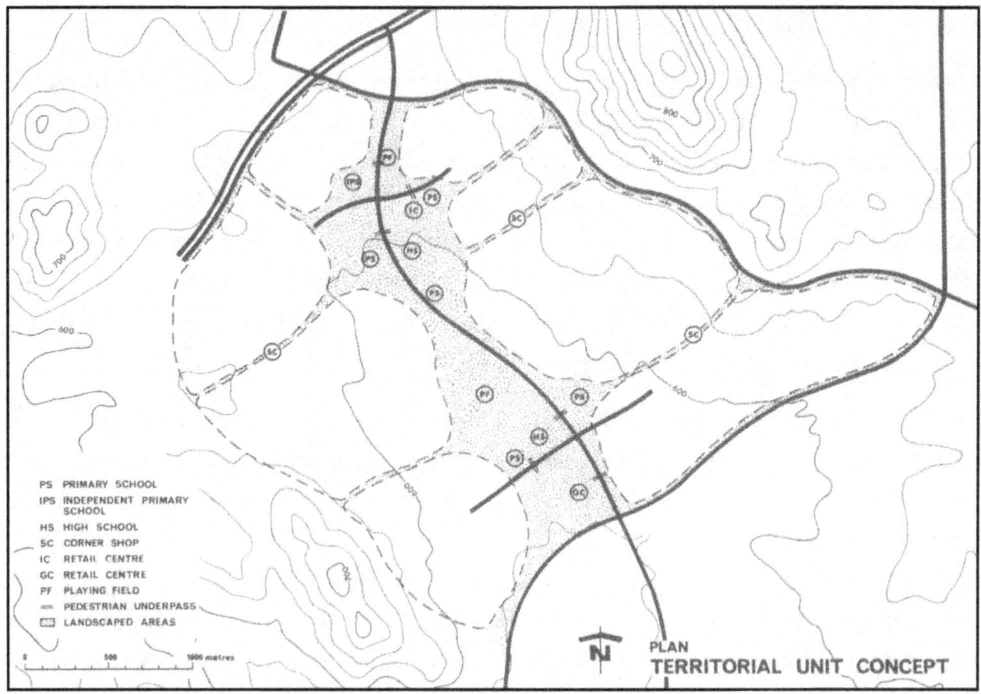

Figure 15.6: Territorial Unit - Kambah (NCDC)

A flaw in the TU concept was that residents in neighbourhoods developed a strong sense of community identity, through the neighbourhood schools, neighbourhood centres, and open spaces, even the suburb name, whereas it was more difficult for this same level of identity to be achieved in what some saw as a fairly amorphous Territorial Unit.

NCDC Initiatives and Innovation in Residential Planning

During its tenure, NCDC was frequently looking for opportunities to innovate in its response to residential planning. Professor Pat Troy of the Australian National University observed that the development of Canberra contains examples of almost every credible planning idea and implicit ideology of the 20th century.[1] Many ideas were implemented on the basis that the particular initiative was used as a test bed to demonstrate the performance of different approaches, with the aim of improving housing choice and residential area quality. Some of these include:

JVMAH (Joint Venture for More Affordable Housing)

During the 1980s and 1990s development of new suburbs focused on sustainable use of land and energy with focus being given to issues of orientation and solar access. The JVMAH was a national program which aimed to formulate approaches to reduce land development costs and improve housing affordability. Measures included smaller blocks, narrower roads, swale drains, single line utility services rather than loops, etc. Two large demonstration estates were developed in Canberra based on JVMAH principles, both in Tuggeranong (Calwell and Isabella Plains). These were at the forefront of the national roll out of JVMAH estates.

Empirical feedback suggested that house prices achieved in these two estates were below the average at the time. The extent to which this was the result of smaller houses and blocks and more efficient land development and servicing was not determined. Over time however successive governments have moved to progressively reduce block size but with little control over house size. This has coincided with a growing market preference for larger houses, with the result in the newer areas of Gungahlin, and Molonglo, of large houses on small blocks, with consequent amenity issues.

The JVMAH was later rebadged as "Green Street" and the responsible Commonwealth department marketed the concept around Australia with the aid of information packages. The overall framework was provided by AMCORD (Australian Model Code for Residential Development).

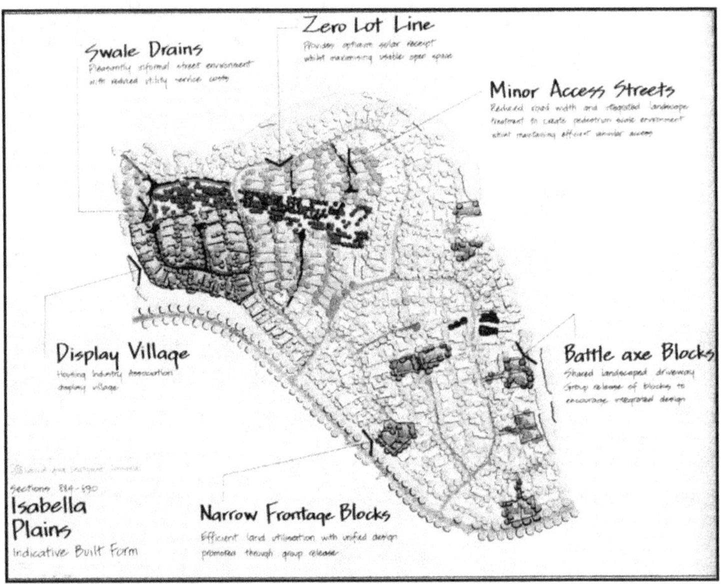

Figure 15.7: JVMAH - Isabella Plains (NCDC)

Small Lot Housing

In the 1970s the NCDC introduced the concept of small lot housing, defined as Courtyard Blocks, Cottage Blocks, and Town House Blocks. These were considerably smaller than the standard blocks of the day, and were capable of being released separately or in groups. Specific design and siting policies were introduced for each of these block types, to ensure house design and size was consistent with the block size and character. Elements such as zero setbacks and single aspect houses were introduced and high levels of amenity were achieved through careful site planning. Many of these blocks were released onto the market in the early days of Tuggeranong's development.

Radburn Housing

The concept of Radburn housing, first introduced in Radburn New Jersey in 1928 by Clarence Stein and Henry Wright, was adopted by NCDC in a number of locations. The main principle was that houses fronted pedestrian systems and open spaces instead of a road. A rear lane provided vehicle access. A precinct of 140 blocks in Curtin (Woden) was developed on these principles, and two smaller Radburn estates were subsequently developed in Fisher and Rivett (Weston Creek). These developments were seen as successful and later a whole suburb - Charnwood (Belconnen), was developed in accordance with Radburn principles. In this case much of the housing was public housing or poor quality private housing, and maintenance of blocks and open spaces has been inadequate. Consequently Charnwood has inherited a stigma, unfairly blamed on Radburn planning rather than poor design interpretation, unauthorised and unsympathetic modifications, and the inappropriate social housing mix, where in reality all contribute.

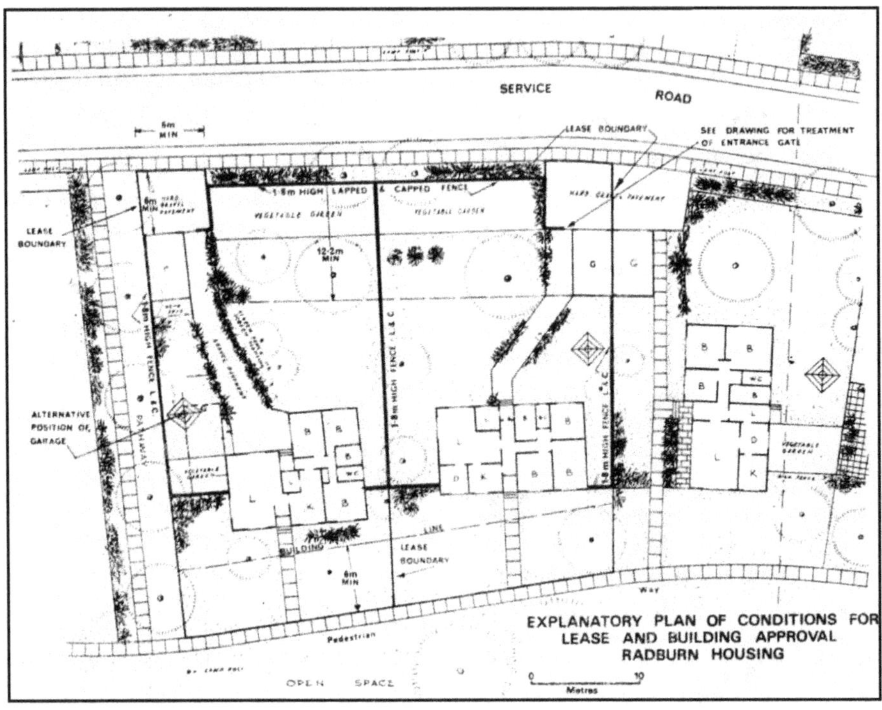

Figure 15.8: Radburn Housing (NCDC)

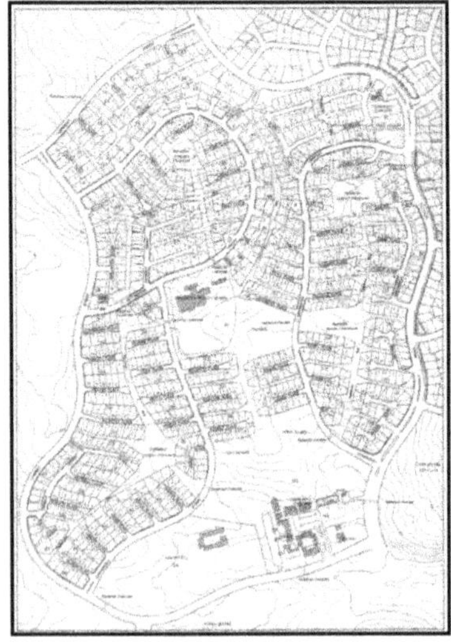

Figure 15.9: Charnwood (NCDC)

Preserved Environment Housing (PEH)

This concept was introduced as a way of developing steep or sensitive land which in most cases had an existing mature landscape. The intent was to introduce a less formal type of subdivision which consciously aimed at minimising impact on the natural environment and was sympathetic to the terrain. Under this concept, carefully sited cluster housing was seen as a better solution than standard or medium density subdivisions. A small demonstration development was successfully undertaken in Wanniassa but a later proposal to develop a 150 block PEH estate near the village of Hall was not proceeded with.

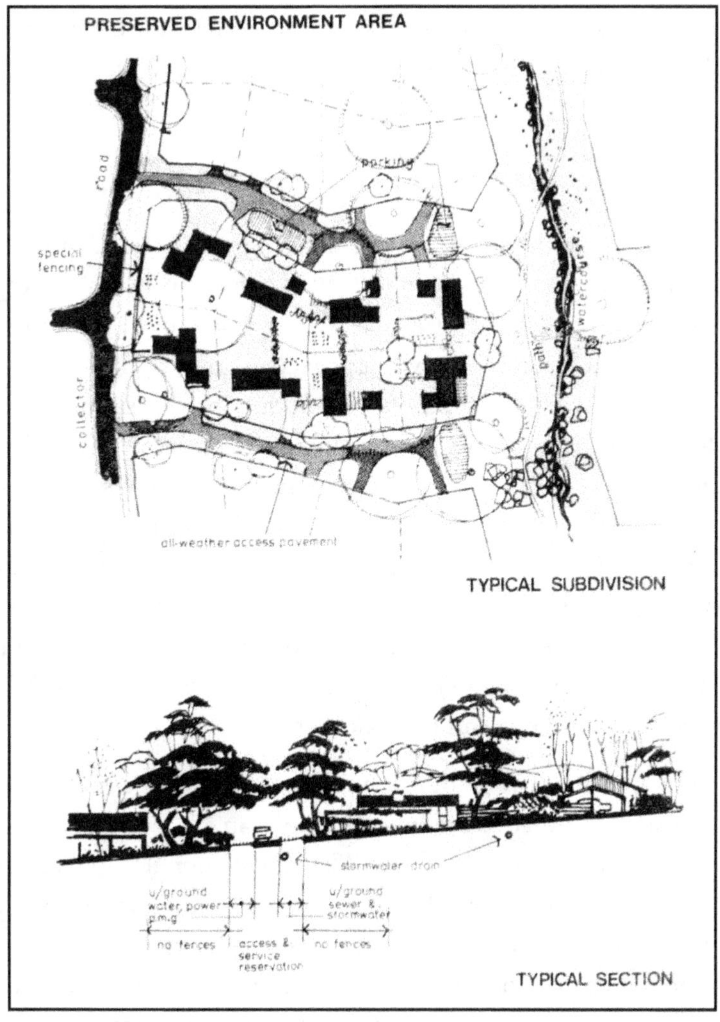

Figure 15.10: Preserved Environment Housing (NCDC)

Co-operative Housing

Two substantial residential developments were undertaken by housing co-operatives, one in Kambah (Urambi Village), the other in Cook (Wybalena Grove) in the 1970s. The members of each co-operative secured the land from government as a direct sale at an agreed market price, and managed the development of the two sites. Both engaged an eminent architect and landscape architect to master plan each development. The developments are of high quality and much admired for their sensitive housing design and siting, attractive natural environments, sustainability and energy efficiency. Because of its self build nature, the costs of the development were borne entirely by the respective co-operatives and their members. Despite its acknowledged success the co-operative housing model has not been repeated until 2023, when a smaller co-operative venture has been announced for Watson.

Urban Change and Redevelopment

By the 1960s and 70s some of the older housing stock in Canberra was 50 years old and many owners were faced with the choice of extensive repairs and maintenance, demolition and rebuild at higher densities, or selling to developers. To test the benefits of a comprehensive approach to redevelopment, the NCDC in 1970 developed special redevelopment conditions for the suburb of Kingston, one of the earliest suburbs to be built in Canberra. These identified rules for both single block and multiple block redevelopment, including bonus GFA allowances for amalgamated blocks. A zone around the edge of Kingston was identified for high rise development, otherwise building heights of 2 or 3 storeys were mandated. There were no compulsory processes imposed on house owners and it was left to individuals to decide whether they wanted to participate in redevelopment or not. Over time, the low density, detached housing character of Kingston has been largely replaced by apartment buildings and town houses.

The concept of comprehensive redevelopment policies for a particular suburb has not been repeated. Instead planning provisions in NCDC's Policy Plans and Development plans, and later in the Territory Plan and National Capital Plan, provide the framework and criteria against which redevelopment proposals are assessed. Much of the redevelopment activity has concentrated on single block redevelopments in the inner suburbs, including dual occupancy or small-scale redevelopment depending on land size and location. Higher density redevelopment has occurred along major transport routes such as Northbourne Avenue and Canberra Avenue, and the City

Centre, e.g., New Acton (a former Commonwealth hostel site), or by redevelopment of redundant former government sites such as Realm in Barton (another former Commonwealth hostel site).

Master Planned Medium Density Estates

Swinger Hill in Woden, Emu Ridge in Belconnen, and the Melrose Drive corridor in Woden are examples of NCDC instigating planned medium density estates as a demonstration of the benefits of master planning on a large scale combined with best practice urban design, landscape design, engineering, energy efficiency and sustainability. The first stage on each estate was delivered as public housing so the private developers who followed had a tangible example of the planning and design standards to be achieved.

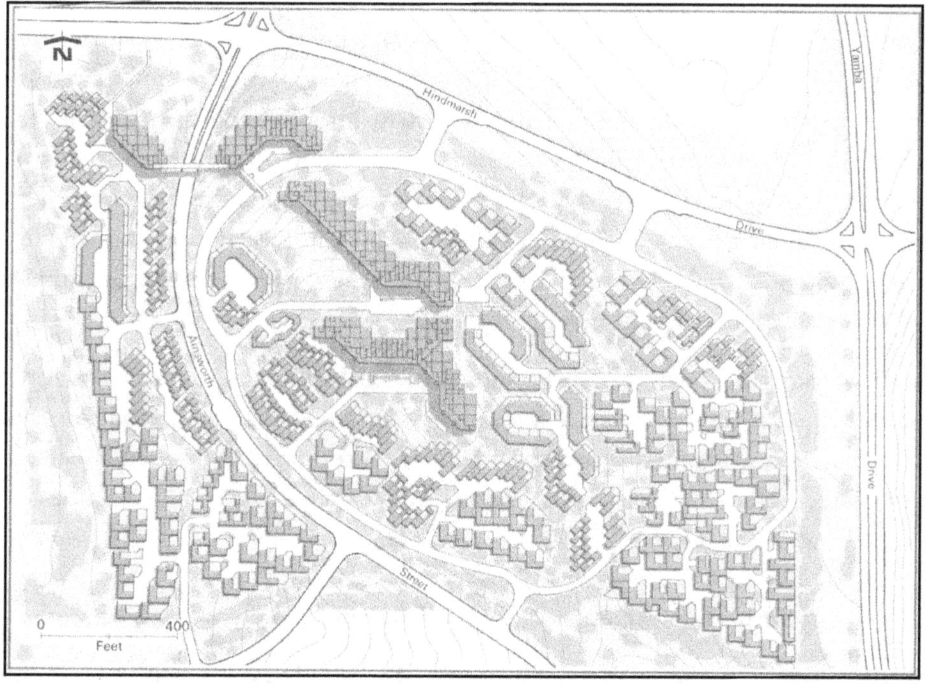

Figure 15.11: Swinger Hill Estate - Woden (NCDC)

Public Housing Failures

Not all NCDC residential development innovations were successful, and in response to a large public housing waiting list, three large public housing complexes were developed; at Conley Drive in Melba, Burnie Court in Lyons, and Fraser Court in Kingston. The main reason was to be able to build about 400 dwellings in each complex quickly. It was also thought that the economies of scale of comprehensively designed large complexes would best meet the needs of the socially disadvantaged, homeless, and welfare recipients. These well-intentioned ideals were not met, with each complex experiencing crime, domestic violence, threats, property vandalism, and anti social behaviour. Residents adjoining these complexes were adversely affected and many complaints were received by politicians and government agencies. Each complex was eventually closed and demolished well before the economic life of the buildings expired. Since then public housing agencies have adopted a "salt and pepper" approach to distribution of public housing.

Changed Planning Arrangements

In 1989 the ACT was granted self government, and the new ACT Government was given responsibility for management, planning and development of municipal areas, while the Commonwealth retained its interest in areas of special national capital significance, and national land. For the first time Canberra was subject to a two-tier planning system. The NCA, a statutory authority, represents the Commonwealth's interest in Canberra as the National Capital. There is no specific or single authority representing the ACT Government's planning interests, with the main planning unit absorbed into a larger, multi function Directorate.

Each administers its own statutory plan, i.e., the National Capital Plan and the Territory Plan. Both are dynamic, evolutionary plans, and subject to public processes of Amendment and Variation respectively. The Territory Plan is not allowed to be inconsistent with the National Capital Plan.

Development Implementation – Pre Self Government

The sub-centralisation model of separate towns which guided Canberra's development during the NCDC era can be characterised as a "jobs to the people" strategy. The strategy provided the opportunity for residents to minimise the length of trips to work by living in a location close to their place of employment.

Until the late 1980s the implementation of the strategy was facilitated by NCDC's ability to locate Commonwealth offices in the town centres in Woden, Belconnen and Tuggeranong. Consequently, each town achieved fairly high levels of self containment. Neither Commonwealth nor ACT Governments, in the post NCDC era, have managed to locate a major government office building in Gungahlin Town Centre, requiring most of the Gungahlin work force to commute to other employment locations each day. The new Gungahlin tram to the City Centre meets part of this travel demand but journey to work congestion remains an issue.

The NCDC planning framework delivered a low density city that provided high amenity to residents. Along with the leasehold system of land tenure, high population growth and effective management by the NCDC, the framework facilitated the timely and efficient delivery of housing and the related social and physical infrastructure. It avoided the "sprawl" that characterised the fringe development of other Australian cities.

The NCDC was keen to achieve good urban design and visual quality throughout the urban areas and did this mainly by maintaining tight control of development. Standard detached housing was subject to Design and Siting Policies, which contained quantitative and qualitative measures. This gave NCDC the ability to negotiate mutually beneficial outcomes. The NCDC for many years also ran a free Homes Advisory Service, staffed by Commission architects. This service provided energy planning and house design advice to new housing block owners.

Many other sites, e.g., for medium density housing, local and group shopping centres, trades and services, and other commercial developments etc, were subject to "control drawings" attached to the sale conditions. These drawings were generally in the form of architectural standard final sketch plans, and apart from illustrating the three dimensional development form and architectural detail required, also specified site planning, colours and materials, GFA, height and setbacks, landscaping, vehicle access and parking, etc. Lessees and smaller developers generally welcomed this approach as it often meant they didn't need to engage their own architects, only a basic drafting service. NCDC was satisfied it was achieving good planning and design outcomes through this process. The control drawing process lasted for many years but was eventually replaced by simpler development conditions, sometimes including a basic development intentions sketch.

Development Implementation - Post Self Government

Development proposals are assessed against the Territory Plan (except those in Designated Areas), including the various development codes. Developers, builders, and other applicants are encouraged to discuss proposals with ACT Government planners before lodging development applications, and neighbour consultation is in many cases mandatory. Development applications for all development, except standard housing in new areas, are publicly notified.

Up to 1990s, Canberra was an exemplar of how to manage city growth. Since the Y-Plan was formulated there has been extensive social, environmental and economic change which have influenced the planning and development task. The changes have included:

- Labour force participation, particularly of women, has increased;
- The population has become older;
- The community is more affluent with increased car ownership and consumption of housing, household goods and services;
- The proportion of the population in government housing has decreased;
- Housing affordability has decreased reflected in the increase in the ratio of housing prices to income;
- Fertility rates have declined considerably and households are smaller requiring larger catchments for schools;
- Shopping patterns have changed resulting in a decline in trade at local centres and an increase in the demand for extensive low rent retail space;
- An increased awareness of the environmental impacts of development, particularly on biodiversity and the atmosphere;
- A weakening in the means to implement the strategy particularly the ability to influence the location of Commonwealth government office employment;
- The development of major office and retail precincts at Canberra Airport, which have not been subject to any effective control or direction by NCA or the ACT Government. Canberra Airport only has to comply with their own master plan, as approved by the Commonwealth Department of Transport. Some of the major office developments at the airport may have been more ideally located in Gungahlin Town Centre and other areas such as Molonglo, where they would have been supported by a large population base and other town centre scale infrastructure. The airport office precinct, in contrast, is remote from the nearest township. The large-scale retail uses at Majura Park, adjacent to the airport, are not supported by local residential catchments or by adequate physical, social and transport infrastructure. The land use linkages which are critical for a successful

town centre are not in place at Majura Park. The airport owners claim such development was essential for Canberra Airport to remain competitive with other Australian airports, and to ensure an upgraded Canberra Airport terminal and precinct is an attractive and welcoming gateway to the national capital.

- COVID has had a major impact on the relationship between home and work, with working from home still continuing in some parts of the public and private sectors. Depending on the level of work from home arrangements, this could become a critical factor which could influence both house design, and the demand for traditional town centre land uses.

Building on the legacy of the Y-Plan, and in response to the changes listed above, the Territory Plan (1993) the Spatial Plan (2004) and the ACT Planning Strategy (2012) progressively recalibrated Canberra's growth strategy. The major direction is the facilitation of redevelopment and intensification within the existing towns, especially North and South Canberra, in response to demographic changes and a reduced ability to influence the location of employment, particularly Commonwealth office employment The supply of green fields land would continue to be met predominately by Gungahlin and Molonglo Valley, and potentially Kowen in the future. A green fields/ infill share of about 50/50 was adopted in these strategies as a target.

An increase in the multi unit development and redevelopment share in both new and existing areas is a strategy designed to help reduce the amount of travel and car use and associated greenhouse gas emissions by placing additional population close to existing employment and major public transport routes. The aim is to encourage increased public transport usage, walking and cycling and make better use of existing social and physical infrastructure. Other expected benefits include easing infrastructure demands on the urban fringe, widening housing choice and contributing to a more diverse, vibrant, urban environment.

The reduced ability to determine the location of employment i.e., the "people to the jobs" strategy inherent in the Y-Plan, has been balanced in demand terms by the unplanned emergence of a major employment node at the Airport, and increased residential development in surrounding NSW. However, there are significant issues relating to these locations including increased travel, car dependency and the need for proportionally greater infrastructure expenditure.

The 2018 Planning Strategy

This involved a review of previous land settlement and housing strategies but did not include a basis to guide long term metropolitan growth. Nor did it generate or evaluate alternative residential and employment strategies or provide justification for a proposed increase in the infill (non greenfield) share from 50% to 70%. In summary, the 2018 Planning Strategy, while promoting an increase in infill development, did not:

- Analyse the comparative costs and benefits of green field and infill development including the extent of available spare green field capacity compared to the cost of augmenting infrastructure in established areas;
- Demonstrate what the optimal level of redevelopment and intensification should be and its locational priorities;
- Demonstrate Kowen has significantly higher infrastructure and environmental costs, as alleged, than the preferred western areas;
- Develop strategies to increase employment in the new towns and Molonglo;
- Provide a costed infrastructure plan indicating when and where development is to occur;
- Investigate housing choice options and the extent to which a reduced detached housing supply in the Territory would fail to meet community preferences, and result in increased car-dependent development in surrounding NSW;
- Analyse the water and energy use of alternative dwelling types and housing locations;
- Evaluate implications for housing affordability including whether the increase in demand for higher density housing is a response to higher housing costs;
- Demonstrate light rail is more cost effective, efficient and flexible than alternatives such as bus rapid transport.

The acceleration of multi unit developments, including high rise apartment buildings, as promoted by the 2018 and earlier strategies has led to community concern over perceived poor design and construction of some new infill developments. Issues which concern the local communities are that many have inadequate green space and landscaping, poor solar access, little protection from overlooking and noise, cause overshadowing, diminish the quality of residential streetscapes, and lead to congestion and parking blight in the wider areas.

Future Residential Growth in Canberra.

Gungahlin represents the last new town of the Y-Plan. Development is proceeding apace, generally consistent with the new towns strategy, with a structure based mainly on greenfield neighbourhoods, but at increased densities generally due to smaller residential block sizes.

The Molonglo Valley was determined to be the most suitable area for the next town scale major development, despite its environmental sensitivity, difficult terrain and poor accessibility. The ACT Government however saw these challenges as an opportunity to establish major urban areas and continuing greenfield developments in the Molonglo Valley in a way that demonstrates best practice in ecological conservation, bushfire management, provision of recreational facilities, and incorporation of distinctive landscape design features. The environmental attributes of the Molonglo River Corridor have been recognised and protected under the Commonwealth Government's *Environmental Protection and Biodiversity Conservation Act 1999* (EPBC Act).

The Structure Plan for Molonglo and North Weston (ACT Government 2008) was released in December 2008. Planning proposals were influenced by "New Urbanism", aimed at improving urban sustainability. Principles included walkable, mixed use neighbourhoods, inter connected street systems, centres incorporating higher density housing, and a well defined, high quality public realm. An independent review undertaken by consulting company ARUP in 2019 found that many principles had been achieved or partly achieved. Others however, such as the provision of community infrastructure and services, and retention of existing vegetation, had not been achieved.

The design population target is 55,000, to be achieved within 30 years, while in 2022 the population was estimated to be 12,000. This is largely accommodated in single houses in Wright, Coombes, and Denman Prospect, and in multi unit development along Molonglo's major spine (John Gorton Drive) and adjoining areas. To achieve the population target of 55,000 for Molonglo will require an additional 22,000 dwellings by 2060, mainly in greenfield estates and multi unit developments at major centres.

Revised population projections recently released by the ACT Government forecast significant increases in many districts by 2066, although there is no information on where and how these new targets will be achieved (see Table 15.1). For instance, Belconnen is forecast to increase From 105,976 to 175,826 by 2060, Gungahlin from

90,383 to 146,799, and Molonglo from a design population of 55,000 to 86,148. These are major increases which most likely would require significant redevelopment, higher densities, peripheral growth into non urban land or a combination of all of these. If the increased population forecasts are ratified, then one of the two group centres planned for Molonglo would be expanded to a town centre, in association with substantial multi unit housing within walking distance.

Table 15.1: 2022-2060 Population Forecasts

District	2022	2031	2041	2051	2060
Belconnen	105,976	121,436	138,195	158,154	175,826
Canberra East	1,851	2,241	2,274	2,238	2,232
Gungahlin	90,383	106,723	11,6451	130,077	148,799
Molonglo	12,102	33,122	67,594	83,832	86,148
North Canberra	62,045	82,355	98,469	119,198	140,999
South Canberra	32,119	38,425	42,070	49,191	58,342
Tuggeranong	88,965	88,118	87,287	87,954	88,914
Urriarra - Namadgi	571	485	428	423	469
Weston Creek	24,315	24,489	24,634	24,969	25,671
Woden Valley	39,238	41,399	42,747	48,274	56,643
ACT Total	457,565	538,793	619,876	704,310	784,043

The Draft Molonglo District Planning Strategy (ACT Government 2022) proposed Sustainable Neighbourhoods as the main building block for Molonglo. They require residential development to be of a height and density appropriate to neighbourhood characteristics and amenities, provide a mix of housing types, and include enhanced walkability and better connections to centres. The spatial extent of the sustainable neighbourhoods is based mainly on the need to maintain an acceptable interface with the natural environment and to conserve sensitive areas. They generally do not follow the typology of traditional neighbourhoods, and even with the higher residential densities now being achieved in Molonglo it is difficult to locate convenient local shops and services. The Wright and Coombes centre is based on the overlapping catchment concept, while the remainder of Molonglo's structure is closer to the Territorial Unit concept than Neighbourhoods. There appears to be no single suburban typology evident in Molonglo's ongoing planning, which is still a work in progress.

The Draft Planning Strategy for Molonglo also introduces the concept of Change Areas i.e., areas which have future potential for change of use and/or intensification. Some areas identified as sustainable neighbourhoods are also defined as change areas. Detailed planning for later stages of Molonglo is still a work in progress and given new increased population projections and land shortages, change areas currently identified for greenfield estates could possibly be converted to medium density, multi unit, areas.

To accommodate the higher population projected of some 784,000 in 2060, about 150,000 additional dwellings could be required. The ACT Government's target for 70% infill means an additional 105,000 new dwellings are required in infill areas and 45,000 new dwellings in greenfield areas. Potential greenfield supply in Gungahlin, Molonglo (as defined in the Draft District Planning Strategy) and Belconnen, including 5,000 dwellings in the NSW component of Ginninderry, is 37,000 dwellings. There is conservatively capacity for an additional 2,500 dwellings on the CSIRO land at Ginninderra.

Concluding Comment

Canberra's development, from the early days of Griffin through to NCDC (except for the mid years) has benefited from the work of highly skilled and innovative professionals and administrators, a strong commitment from successive governments, the support of the Australian people for their national capital, a leasehold system of land tenure, and adequate funding to allow the development of Canberra. The single, multi disciplined, model which NCDC and the Sulman and Butters organisations conformed with, ensured a focus on the important job of planning and building an exemplary national capital. NCDC, while recognising the importance of protecting the important symbolic elements of the National Capital also established an effective urban structure to guide growth of the metropolitan city, i.e., the Y-Plan, where a series of largely self contained new towns were established, separated from each other by hills, ridges, and other "green" buffer spaces.

NCDC's brief was terminated in January 1989, to coincide with the introduction of self government in the ACT. It was replaced by a National Capital Planning Authority, and an Interim Territory Planning Authority, and coincided with a period of significant economic and social change. The ACT Government was faced with set of different challenges, including declining land for greenfield expansion, although it has continued with greenfield developments in Gungahlin largely consistent with original plans, and commenced the development of Molonglo, albeit with a lower proportion of greenfield estates. The focus has shifted to multi unit intensification and redevelopment, i.e., infill, in and adjacent to existing areas. As far as it is known the ACT Government has not yet made a final decision on the extent and location of greenfield developments after Gungahlin and Molonglo, although a 30/70% greenfield/infill split was proposed in the 2018 Planning Strategy. This proposed emphasis on infill suggests that most of Canberra's housing supply over coming years will be in the form of medium and high density apartment buildings.

Arguably there has been insufficient attention to the evaluation of alternative long term strategic growth options for Canberra, and a consequential over reliance on development facilitation. Planning responsibilities in the ACT Government are fragmented, and the main planning function, which sits in a large multi function Directorate, is mainly concerned with development facilitation, and not long term strategic planning.

Improved outcomes would benefit from the establishment of a well-resourced and specific planning and development authority, with skills and power to recommend and implement evidence-based and community-supported planning strategies. Current planning reforms in the ACT are targeted mainly at improving local planning and development processes and are highlighting concerns in the local community about alternative planning futures for Canberra.

Greater awareness and recognition within the ACT, NSW and Federal bureaucracies of the environmental consequences of location, and improved liaison within and between all levels of government are necessary to ensure an effective way forward. Sustainability would be improved if and when significant and appropriate employment opportunities arise they were directed to Gungahlin, and Molonglo.

There is little action to establish key priorities to provide for continuing urban growth while minimising damaging impacts on the social and physical environment, achieving the best use of limited public funds and responding to the preferences of the community. Such actions need the context of an authentic metropolitan assessment considering the pros and cons of alternative strategies. If, for example, the objective is to reduce car use then the relative merits of light rail improvements and bus based public transport need to be evaluated along with general travel demand management.

While increased density is desirable, consideration needs to be given to the preferences of those wanting a detached dwelling by ensuring new greenfield development opportunities are identified and that new suburban housing areas have acceptable access to employment and are well serviced by transport, retail and community infrastructure. This is especially important given that a significant part of new dwelling demand will be from family households seeking single family dwellings.

There has been a fundamental change in planning philosophy by the ACT Government, where the principle of a low congestion city espoused by Voorhees and incorporated into the Y-Plan is considered too difficult to achieve. Planners are now engaged in a process of normalisation where new residential development in Canberra is very similar to that being achieved in other Australian cities. Griffin's intention to create a *City like no Other* seems long forgotten and there has been very little development in Canberra since self government which could be regarded as innovative and successful, to the extent it could act as a model for other cities. There are exceptions including Kinston Foreshore and the mixed use precincts at New Acton in the City and Realm at Barton. The latter two have resulted from the enlightened visions and innovative thinking of the developers and their professional consultants rather than government policy or leadership, while Kinston Foreshore benefited from being master planned and managed through a single purpose government authority.

The ACT Government and its new metropolitan planning strategy is now beginning to impact on the image and functioning of Canberra as the National Capital. Whereas Northbourne Avenue was formerly a fitting approach to the National Capital, this is now questionable given the replacement of the attractive and symbolic avenue of mature eucalypts with a tram line and native grasses, flanked by new apartment buildings generally of average visual quality. Based on the Northbourne Avenue experience, the Canberra community are rightfully concerned about the potential impacts of the tram route being extended along Commonwealth Avenue, Adelaide Avenue, and Yarra Glen, to Woden Town Centre.

Urgent action is needed if Canberra is to avoid becoming *a City like any Other*, offering reduced amenity and a low liveability future. Instead, it once again needs to become an exemplar of world's best practice in city planning and development, and urban management.

Endnotes

1 Jago Dodson. (2023) 30 April. Available at https://twitter.com/urbanizationist/status/1652567484401319936? (Accessed: 17 May 2023).

References

ACT Government (2012) *ACT Planning Strategy*, Environment and Sustainable Planning Directorate, Canberra

—— *ACT Population Projections 2022-2060*

—— (1993) *ACT Territory Plan,* www.legislation.act.gov.au

—— (2022) *Draft Molonglo District Planning Strategy 2022*

—— *Structure Plan for Molonglo and North Weston 2008-2027*, www.legislation.act.gov.au

—— (2004) *The Canberra Spatial Plan*, ACT Planning and Land Authority

Arup (2019) *Independent Audit of the Molonglo Valley Strategic Plan*, Arups.com

Fischer, K.F. (1984) *Canberra: Myths and Models - Forces at work in the formation of the Australian capital* A Publication of the Institute of Asian Affairs, Hamburg

Fitzgerald, Alan (1976) *Historic Canberra (1825 to 1945)*

Moseley, G.E. (1974) "Residential Area Planning in Canberra" *New Zealand Surveyor,* vol.27 June, 474-494

National Capital Development Commission, Annual Reports 1958 to 1988

—— (1965) *The Future Canberra*, Angus and Robertson, Sydney

—— (1970) *Tomorrow's Canberra*, Australian National University Press, Canberra

—— (1972) *Development of the New Towns of Canberra*, A Case Study Prepared for the United Nations Conference on Human Environment, Stockholm, June 1972, NCDC, Canberra, October 1971

—— (1975) *Territorial Unit Concept*

—— (1982) *Review of Functional and Administrative Arrangements for Planning, Development and Construction in the ACT.* June 1982 (Submission 1 to Government Inquiry)

—— (1982) *To Plan, Develop and Construct - Review of Functions of NCDC* August 1982 (Submission 2 to Government Inquiry)

—— (1984) *Metropolitan Policy Plan Development Plan*

—— *The Way We Are*, NCDC annual review of major projects 1984 to 1988

Smith, Malcolm and Kece, Erkal (1992) *Canberra - A Model of 20th Century Urban Planning.* Paper presented to International Conference in Ankara Turkey, October 1992.

16

Healing Darwin in the Post-COVID Era

Michele Lobo

Healing Country comes from the past, it brings us to the present and take us into the future. We say here on Larrakia land when people are happy, country is happy. So, we strive, each and every one of us to not only make happy communities, but to heal country.

(Richard Fejo, Larrakia Nation Aboriginal Corporation Annual Report, 2021-2022, p. 10)

Among Larrakia people, traditional owners whose songlines run through the Arafura Sea, offshore reefs, suburban creeks, beaches, mangroves, urban Country is a place of love, loss, happiness and healing (Larrakia Nation Aboriginal Corporation, 2022). Greater Darwin (pop. 139, 902, 2021) that includes the capital city of the Northern Territory (pop. 85,397, area 111.8 sq kms), the satellite town of Palmerston (pop 39, 625, area 72 sq km) twenty kilometres south east built in 1982, and surrounding areas occupies the traditional lands of the Larrakia peoples. As Indigenous peoples Larrakia have been caring for Garramilla (original name for the place) for more than 60,000 years prior to white settlement in 1869. In comparison to large southern cities of Sydney and Melbourne, the tropical harbour city of Darwin has a polyethnic heritage, an outcome of intercultural relationships that began with the arrival of Asian traders and miners prior to white settlement. The suburbs of Darwin and Palmerston are home to First Nations peoples of diverse backgrounds, Anglo-Australians and ethnic minority migrants from countries in Asia, Africa and the Middle East. Filipinos, Malays, Chinese as well as more recent settlers from India, Myanmar, Iran and Sudan, for example, share space with Aboriginal peoples and white settlers in inner suburbs, expanding outer suburbs and new suburbs in Darwin and Palmerston.

The planning and coordination of suburban growth in Greater Darwin is situated within the broader federal policy economic agenda of Developing the North that focuses on growing the tourist economy, harnessing knowledge, building infrastructure, strengthening the energy export industry and mobilising investment (Commonwealth of Australia, 2015). The labour force participation of residents living in smaller town and cities in the Northern Territory such as Alice Springs (36,471, 2021) and Katherine (5, 980, 2021) where approximately 25% of the population are Indigenous and Torres Strait Islanders is more challenging. In addition, there was a temporary brake in economic growth from March 2019 when the COVID-19 pandemic led to international and interstate border closures which affected the "population churn" of tourists and fly-in fly-out workers in Darwin. Overseas travellers who did arrive, lived in the "gold star" quarantine accommodation at Howard Springs on the outskirts of Palmerston, which was a residential village from 2014 to 2018 for fly-in fly-out workers employed in the INPEX-operated Ichthys LNG Project.

As a strategic defence base in Northern Australia, Darwin is once again the destination for United States Marines who participate in an annual rotation program during the dry season and live in the Robertson Barracks in Holtze close to the Palmerston CBD. In the so-called post-COVID era, the suburban challenges are accelerating economic growth including the production/use of green energy, increasing labour force participation among Indigenous peoples as well as marginalised ethnic minorities, attracting overseas migrants, fly-in fly-out workers, international students, tourist and visitors (including from regional areas), the provision of affordable housing, sustainable infrastructure and accessible services. It is crucial that suburban policy agendas of place-making and economic development that focus on building a city that is smart, liveable, productive and sustainable (City of Darwin, 2022) is inclusive as well as diverse. Following the completion of construction of the Ichthys Liquid Natural Gas Project in 2018, the expansion of offshore and on-shore gas projects in the "last frontier" have been stalled following resistance by Indigenous/ climate change activists who use their sovereign rights to prioritise the health and wellbeing of country and flourishing green futures. Larrakia Energy, an initiative of the Larrakia Development Corporation with Korean power company KOMIPO will build a 300MW Solar Farm at Bladin Point south of Darwin from 2020.

Key Demographic Data - Greater Darwin

The following charts provide insights into employment, occupation and dwelling structure. The data source is the 2021 Census data available from the Australian Bureau of Statistics. State Government and Administration and Hospital and Defence account for more than 75% of employment (Figure 16.1). This is to be expected given Darwin is the capital city of the Northern Territory and a strategic defence base.

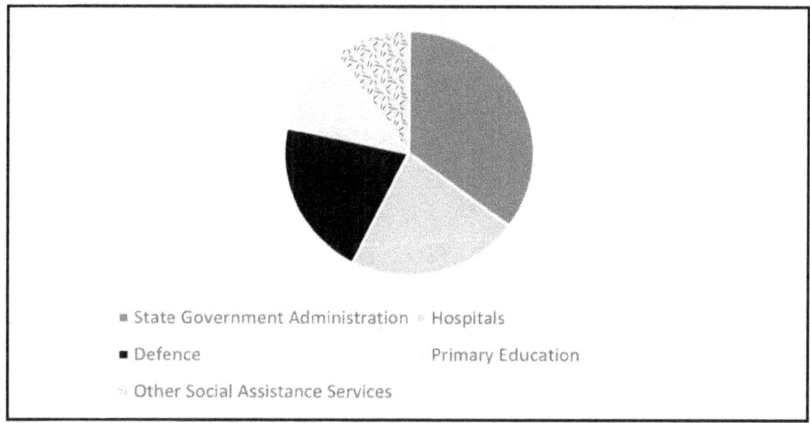

Figure 16.1: Industry of Employment, Greater Darwin

The highest rank occupations in Greater Darwin are Professionals, Community and Personal Service Workers and Technicians and Trade Workers (Figure 16.2). Many of these professionals are employed in Charles Darwin University which attracts students from Alice Springs, Katherine as well as smaller regional areas. Community workers are employed in government and non-governmental organisations and offer services to a culturally diverse population.

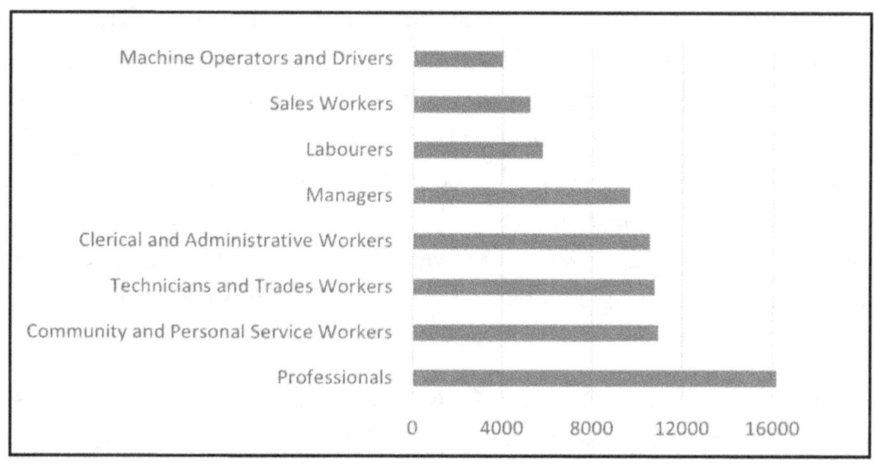

Figure 16.2: Occupation, Greater Darwin, 2021

In Greater Darwin, the main dwelling structure, particularly in the middle and outer suburbs is a separate house, but the number of flats and apartments is increasing particularly in the inner suburbs and waterfront suburbs.

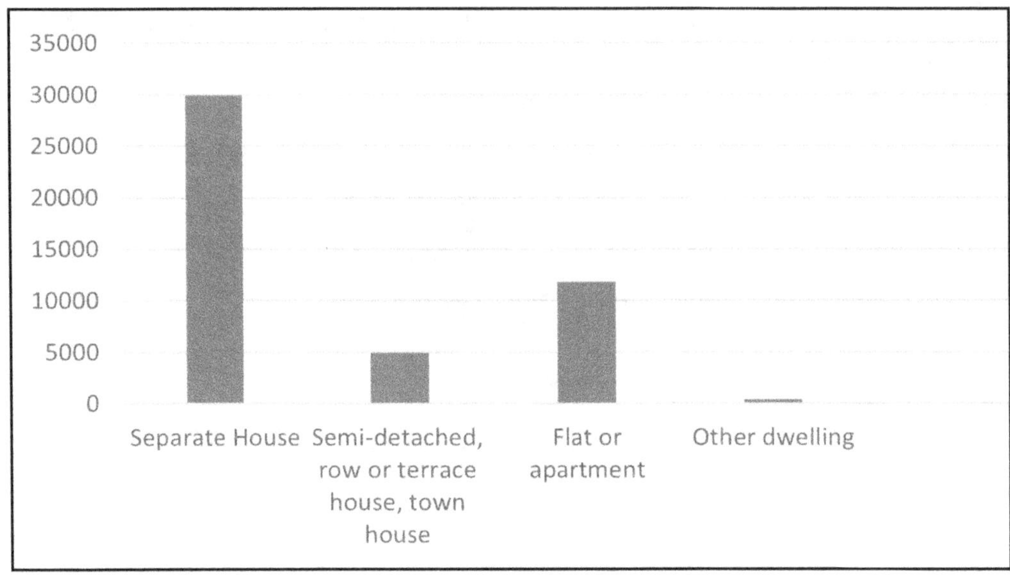

Figure 16.3: Dwelling Structure, Greater Darwin, 2021

Suburban Feelings: Better and Smart Suburbs!

Waterfront place-making projects in the inner city, gentrified inner suburbs (Fannie Bay, Nightcliff) and affluent ownership housing in the rapidly growing satellite city of Palmerston (Rosebery, Bakewell) strengthen Darwin's image as a glitzy global city that mobilises economic development as well as desirable place to live for young people, professionals and families. The median age of Palmerston City is 31 years and is celebrated as a "safe, family friendly place where everyone belongs". These "success" stories of suburban development are interrupted by images of run-down housing without power in inner suburban public housing as well as Aboriginal town camps (e.g., Bagot, One Mile Dam) that continue to be threatened by encroaching luxury-style multi-storeyed apartments and scattered clusters of disadvantage. The small community in One Mile Dam faces eviction, and I recall the long conversation with David Timber who fought to live on this culturally important place before he passed away.

Older suburbs of Palmerston including Gray, Driver and Moulden struggle to shake off popular stereotypical representations captured by "Palmoslum" or "single mum's capital of the world" that focus on crime and disadvantage. Loud conversations and scuffles at the Palmerston bus station are common among young people on Friday nights. I came to know many of these young people through conversations at the Casuarina Bus Station, "hanging out" at the Mindil Night Market and on Night patrols with Larrakia Nation Aboriginal Corporation. We often collected children and youth from the YMCA, a community hub and dropped them back home to suburban areas of Gray and Driver at midnight. When residents in Palmerston were asked by Council about important issues in the local area, more than half of respondents named crime, antisocial behaviour and safety issues (City of Palmerston, 2022). Other concerns were business and employability. Participation in surveys, however, inadvertently privileges voices that are loud and powerful rather than those who are most marginalised. The suburban image of a carceral place echoes in the hearts and minds of many new arrivals and Indigenous peoples who live in expanding prisons and once in four high-security asylum seeker detention centres including three that were purpose-built.

The 2023 Municipal Plans of Greater Darwin focus on building infrastructure that advances economic growth, supports environmental responsibility, cultural inclusion and reconciliation (City of Darwin, 2022; City of Palmerston, 2022). Residents, planners and stakeholders including Larrakia peoples aim to work together to strengthen Darwin 2030 vision as a capital city that is sustainable, clean, green, safe, smart inclusive, vibrant and creative (plan) city. The Council of Capital City Lord Mayors (CCCLM), The Northern Australia Capital City Committee (NACCC), The Top End Regional Organisation of Councils (TOPROC) and Local Government Association of the NT (LGANT) are stakeholders in a regional and national governance framework. "Better Suburbs" is one of the 7 key priorities to be progressed as part of the Darwin Municipal Plan, 2022-2023. Approximately 1.8 million of a total operating expenditure of 133.6 million is allocated for Better Suburbs and Enhancement Projects. The focus is on small projects that improve community infrastructures, invest in community and beautify streets. The projects driven by "wants" of the community in suburban areas include landscaping, upgrading of parks and playgrounds, improved traffic flow, footpaths and cycleways. The other 6 key priorities are a) Greening and beautification of the city b) Arterial road extensions c) A Safer Darwin d) Waste management e) Extension and maintenance of stormwater infrastructure and; f) Redevelopment of the Aquatic and Leisure Centre in Casuarina, a northern suburb of Darwin.

Suburban atmospheres of heat, sweat, convivial chatter and the buzz of mosquitoes can be felt on walks along streets of Darwin and at Asian-style open air markets (Nightcliff, Parap, Mindil, Rapid Creek, Palmerston), parks, ovals, beaches, shopping centres, bus stations, libraries and community centres. These public spaces are usually accessible to the most disadvantaged ethnic-minority migrants, refugees, asylum seekers and Indigenous peoples (including those who "live rough" in the "long grass"). In the post-COVID era, public spaces such as the Casuarina bus station and the Casuarina Square Shopping Centre continue to be meeting places that buzz with activity (Lobo, 2014). Malak Crescent in the affordable eastern suburbs of Malak and Karama is a social hub where the most marginalised are welcomed to participate in activities at the Community Centre, the Multicultural Council of the Northern Territory and the Northern Territory Stolen Generation Aboriginal Corporation. After dark, however, Darwin taxi-drivers and those who live in more affluent suburbs including Parap, Brinkin, Lyons, East Point and Fannie Bay rarely venture into this area perceived as very unsafe.

Older suburbs such as Nightcliff with multi-storeyed waterfront apartment show the impacts of urban consolidation and have become unaffordable for new migrants and Indigenous peoples who live in rental housing. As land is reclaimed for new housing along the foreshore, the local community call out "Save Our Mangroves". The new suburb of North Crest is planned in the northern outskirts of Darwin and new lots are being released in suburban Palmerston at Muirhead as well Durack Heights. In addition, a master planned estate is being built at Zuccoli in Palmerston. New housing is also planned for Holtze near Palmerston. Many residents also live in rural areas of Humpty Doo near Palmerston. Recent plans for the expansion of new defence housing at Binybara Lee Point in a northern suburb of Darwin led to collective resistance by Indigenous peoples, environmental groups and land defenders (Abbatangelo 2023a). Support by Traditional owners was withdrawn given the impacts on cultural heritage, biodiversity loss and the health of Larrakia Country (Morse 2023). In addition, the development of the Middle Arm Sustainable Development Precinct aims to boost economic development in suburbia but is fuelled by offshore/onshore gas projects and carbon capture projects by energy giants that fail to hear the Indigenous Voice (Abbatangelo, 2023b).

Conclusion

Fossil fuel energy futures, the migration of skilled workers (overseas and southern states) and increased foreign investment is perceived as crucial to Darwin's growth as a capital city. These strategic initiatives in the "last frontier", however, leads to an escalation in housing prices; the price of essential food supplies has always been much higher than southern states. The outcome is that socio-economically disadvantaged groups and Indigenous peoples (including migrants from the Tiwi Islands who live in the "long grass") who might be invisible in Census data struggle to survive. These "homeless" people live along the waterfront areas of Fannie Bay, Mindil beach and Casuarina beach and wander from place to place to enjoy the fresh air, collect "bush" food, fish and meet family members and friends. They participate in Indigenous as well as NGO-led weekly and bi-weekly social welfare and health programs that provide a cooked breakfast and medical care in open spaces.

This chapter has focused mainly on Darwin and Palmerston. Towns like Alice Springs and Katherine are places where I passed through or lived briefly. Tourist traffic is high in these areas because Uluru, Kakadu National Park and Katherine Gorge are popular destinations, particularly during the dry season (June-August). In these towns with a high Indigenous population, essential services are limited, food is very expensive and available jobs are often filled by settlers from southern Australian cities. There are many economic, environmental, political and cultural challenges in transforming regional towns and cities of the Northern Territory.

References

Abbatangelo, B. (2023a) "Actions speak louder than theVoice", *The Saturday Paper*, 10 June, 2023. Available at: Actions speak louder than the Voice | The Saturday Paper. Accessed 21 August 2023.

Abbatangelo, B. (2023b) "Binybara is not just home to the Gouldian finch. It's part of the Larrakia Nation. And it deserves protection", *The Guardian*, 12 July. Available at: Binybara is not just home to the Gouldian finch. It's part of the Larrakia nation. And it deserves protection | Ben Abbatangelo | The Guardian. Accessed 21 August 2023.

City of Darwin (2022) *City of Darwin Municipal Plan 2022-2023*. Darwin: City of Darwin. Available at: 2022/23 Municipal Plan | City of Darwin | Darwin Council, Northern Territory. Accessed 15 December 2022.

City of Palmerston (2022) *City of Palmerston Municipal Plan 2022-2023*. Palmerston: City of Palmerston. Available at: https://palmerston.nt.gov.au/sites/default/files/uploads/files/2022/Municipal%20 Plan_2022_23.pdf. Accessed 15 December 2022.

Commonwealth of Australia (2015) *Our North, our Future: White Paper on Developing Northern Australia.* Canberra: Commonwealth of Australia.

Larrakia Development Corporation (2022) Larrakia and Partner forging a renewable future. Media release, 16 November 2022Available at: Larrakia-Energy-Media-Release-20221116.pdf. Accessed 15 December 2022.

Larrakia Nation Aboriginal Corporation (2022) Larrakia Nation Annual Report, 2021-2022. Available at: LNAC_Annual-Report_2022_WEB.pdf (greerconsult.com.au). Accessed 10 December 2022.

Lobo, M. (2014) Everyday multiculturalism: "Catching the bus in Darwin, Australia", *Social & Cultural Geography,* 15(7), pp. 714-729.

Morse, C. (2023) *Larrakia Nation Aboriginal Corporation withdraws support for Binybara/Lee Point. National Indigenous Times,* July 24, 2023. Available at: Larrakia Nation Aboriginal Corporation withdraws su... | NIT. Accessed 21 August 2023.

Part Three: (Sub)Urban Futures

17

Autonomous Cars Are About To Transform The Suburbs*

Joel Kotkin and Alan M. Berger

The following chapter has been reprinted with the permission of Forbes magazine in which it originally appeared on February 21st, 2018.[1] Some edits have been made for clarity.

Suburbs have largely been dismissed by environmentalists and urban planners as bad for the planet, a form that needed to be eliminated to make way for a bright urban future. Yet, after a few years of demographic stultification amid the Great Recession, Americans are again heading to the suburbs in large numbers, particularly millennials.

So rather than fight the tide and treat suburbanisation as an evil to be squeezed out, perhaps a better approach would be to modify the suburban form in ways that address its most glaring environmental weakness: dependence on gas-powered automobiles. The rise of ride-sharing, electric cars and ultimately the self-driving automobile seem likely to alter this paradigm. In most other ways, suburbs are at the least no more damaging than dense cities, and they are superior in terms of air quality, maintaining biodiversity, carbon sequestration and stormwater management.

We may well be on the verge of evolving a new kind of highly sustainable, near-zero carbon form, one linked by technology, and economically (and increasingly culturally) self-sufficient. Autonomous cars will remotely park in solar-charged sheds off-site, to be called to the home through handheld devices, thus eliminating the need for garages and driveways. With safer vehicles that can see and react to situations better, roadways will be designed with much less paving to mitigate stormwater

---

runoff and flooding. Homes will have drone delivery ports built in, greatly reducing the number of daily household trips and congestion. With much less redundant paving and more undisturbed land, autonomous suburbs will expand parks, bike trails and farms, and reduce forest fragmentation. Some of the next generation of suburbs will be anchored by main street districts, some of them restored, while others will be built from scratch, as we have seen in places like the Woodlands outside Houston and Valencia north of Los Angeles.

Taming the car

The traditional urbanist view of suburbs is that, if they must exist, they should be linked by mass transit to the city core. But in the U.S., outside of a handful of older cities, transit ridership is stagnant or in decline despite billions in investment from federal and local sources. In Europe, where bullet trains efficiently link suburbs to cities, strict local and national land use policies and high tax subsidies block development of peripheral land, making compact city forms possible. The U.S. has no national land use policy and we highly doubt voters will agree to much higher taxes to protect peripheral lands from development. Our vast geography allows us to spread out: The U.S. is more than 2.5 times the size of the E.U.

Simply put, the advantages of private transportation are, for the most part, too compelling in a country dominated by long distances and dispersed development. Elon Musk recently shared a brutally honest critique of mass transit. "It's a pain in the ass," he said. "That's why everyone doesn't like it. And there's like a bunch of random strangers, one of who might be a serial killer, OK, great. And so that's why people like individualised transport, that goes where you want, when you want."

In fact, no regional rail system has managed to make any sort of dent in car use. Since 2000, the increase in workers driving alone has been 15 times the increase in those using transit. Even the Progressive Policy Institute, a research organisation affiliated with the Democratic Leadership Council, has noted, "The shortest distance between a poor person and a job is along a line driven in a car."

Los Angeles[2], **hailed by the amen crew in the media as the "next great transit city"**[3] has experienced a considerable decrease in overall transit ridership over the last few years. Transit's share of work trips has stalled in **such diverse markets**[4] as Houston, Dallas-Fort Worth, Atlanta and, remarkably, the transit mecca of Portland.

Meanwhile, instead of jumping on trains, **thirty-something**[5] millennials are **buying cars in huge numbers**[6], heading **toward the suburbs**[7] and starting families. Road travel this year hit **a record**[8], as it has the last five years. The increased popularity of ridesharing services like Uber and Lyft has been cited as a factor in the recent ridership declines in **Los Angeles**[9] and even on the **New York subway.**[10] It is also being cited as one reason why new **extensions of Boston's transit system**[11] may no longer be needed.

With the assumption that private transportation will prevail, we need to come up with different solutions to reduce greenhouse gases within the context of suburbia. Renewable technologies in the home and much more tree planting can greatly offset carbon consumption, but workforce behaviour also needs to change. One piece of the puzzle is the expansion of work at home. Demographer Wendell Cox has found that the share of the U.S. population that works from home has more than doubled since 1980 and now approximates the share that commute to work via mass transit, exceeding it easily outside of New York. The growth of home-based work, which requires no commute, may be the quickest solution to reducing greenhouse gases.

And how about the transit dependent? Ride-sharing technology for transit dependent populations could prove both more cost effective and less time consuming. For example, in **suburban San Francisco**[12] a transit operator has established a one-year pilot program to subsidise local ridesharing services and has cancelled a lightly patronised bus route, reducing costs. Ride-sharing could also **complement public transit** in the future, rather than replace it.

All these strategies could potentially reduce greenhouse gases far faster than the fanciful attempts of planners, notably in California, to reduce suburbanisation and impose forced densification. A recent Berkeley study suggests that 1.9 million new housing units be built only in infill locations, about 4 per cent of the state, saving about 1.8 million metric tons of California greenhouse gas emissions per year from reduced driving. This is less than 1 per cent of the new 2030 reductions mandated by the state, and statistically meaningless compared with current annual worldwide emissions of 49,000 million metric tons.

You ain't seen nothing yet

America's next suburban wave will be driven by technology, smart devices and Internet-of-things connectivity between cars, roads and homes, offering significant potential breakthroughs, particularly if shaped by the public need, not those of large tech firms. **Roy Amara,** the late president of the Institute for the Future has said, "We tend to overestimate the effect of a technology in the short run and underestimate the effect in the long run. Self-driving cars are as much of a paradigm shift as the invention of the telephone, and we all need to get prepared for the ride of our lives."

Americans continue to move, for the most part, to less congested, less dense areas with lower levels of transit service and away from the more tightly packed areas with better transit service, and autonomous vehicles will likely exacerbate this trend. By **one estimate**[13], as much as a trillion dollars of real estate value could swing to locations far from job centres that will become more attractive due to autonomous vehicles while reducing the "premium" now awarded to closer in neighbourhoods and inner-ring suburbs.

A recent **report**[14] by the global consulting firm Bain & Co. predicts that technological advances such as the autonomous car will help to create a "post-urban economy" that will be more localised and home-based. By 2025, its analysts write, fewer people could live in urban cores than in exurbs, which it defines as "beyond the traditional commuting belt."

Bill Gates' proposed new city[15] in Arizona, which will feature these new technologies, is located on the far fringes of the Phoenix area - to the **predictable horror**[16] of "smart growth" advocates.

Over time, the autonomous car could make even more revolutionary impacts on both the urban form and transit. Automated car proponents claim that the cost of operations will be considerably below that of today's cars. If that should be achieved, the autonomous car could be used to provide door-to-door mobility not only for the elderly and disabled, but also for people who currently cannot afford their own cars. Under any circumstances, this innovation seems certain to further weaken **conventional transit**[17] outside the cities with legacy cores. In the future, mass transit will be able to geographically refocus its resources on the most dense cores to provide better service, rather than spreading less dollars per square mile, and poorer service, everywhere.

There is considerable disagreement about how soon autonomous vehicles will become commonplace, but development activity is proceeding at a fast pace. There are currently 50 companies testing 387 autonomous vehicles in California alone, according to the state Department of Motor Vehicles.

The sunniest optimists suggest that by 2030 the conversion to autonomous vehicles will be nearly complete. Other researchers predict the roll out of autonomous cars is going to proceed at a **modest pace**[18], with total sales in 2035 equalling only one-quarter of present world production.

Despite these disagreements about the pace of change, our way of life, both in cities and suburbs, is being radically transformed. What we need to do now is envision how to design the fully autonomous, low-carbon suburb so that water, air and natural landscapes can be preserved in ways better than we have been capable of in the past.

Endnotes

1   Joel Kotkin and Alan M. Berger, "Autonomous Cars are About to Transform the Suburbs", 21 February 2018 https://www.forbes.com/sites/joelkotkin/2018/02/21/autonomous-cars-are-about-to-transform-the-suburbs/?sh=139a048c7e62

2   Wendell Cox, "Los Angeles Ridership Losses Lead National Decline", 15 November 2017 http://www.newgeography.com/content/005800-los-angeles-transit-ridership-losses-lead-national-decline

3   Matthew Yglesias, "L.A.'s Transit Revolution", 17 September 2012 https://slate.com/business/2012/09/l-a-metro-how-los-angeles-is-becoming-americas-next-great-mass-transit-city.html

4   Wendell Cox, "Evaluating Urban Rail", 4 December 2014 http://www.newgeography.com/content/004789-evaluating-urban-rail

5   Patrick George, "The Millennials Are Buying Cars Now That They're Having Babies", 22 August 2017 https://jalopnik.com/the-millennials-are-buying-cars-now-that-theyre-having-1798303521

6   Sarah O'Brien, "Millennials Like Buying Cars After All, Report Says", 31 August 2017 https://www.usatoday.com/story/money/personalfinance/2017/08/31/millennials-like-buying-cars-after-all-report-says/619626001/

7   Joel Kotkin, "The Screwed Millennial Generation Gets Smart", 27 January 2018 https://www.thedailybeast.com/the-screwed-millennial-generation-gets-smart

8   "Americans rolled up 3.2 trillion miles last year, DOT reports", 23 February 2017 https://www.fleetowner.com/for-the-driver/on-the-road/article/21184776/americans-rolled-up-32-trillion-miles-last-year-dot-reports

9   Laura J. Nelson, Dan Weikel, "Billions spent, but fewer people are using public transportation in Southern California", 27 January 2016 https://www.latimes.com/local/california/la-me-ridership-slump-20160127-story.html

10 Emma G. Fitzsimmons, "Subway Ridership Declines in New York. Is Uber to Blame?", 23 February 2017 https://www.nytimes.com/2017/02/23/nyregion/new-york-city-subway-ridership.html%20

11 Tom Keane, "Why self-driving cars will kill the T", 30 November 2017 https://www.bostonglobe.com/magazine/2017/11/30/why-self-driving-cars-will-kill/CBykcwHfDnqbft9VhL8i4K/story.html

12 Denis Cuff, "Dublin: Uber, Lyft to partner in public transit", 18 August 2018 https://www.eastbaytimes.com/2016/08/18/dublin-uber-lyft-to-partner-in-public-transit/

13 Phil Levin, "~$1 trillion of real estate is on the move...heres's why", 19 January 2018 https://medium.com/99-mph/1-trillion-of-real-estate-is-on-the-move-heres-why-94ee9233e5eb

14 Bain & Company, 2016 https://media.bain.com/Images/BAIN_REPORT_Spatial_economics.pdf

15 Fox News, "Bill Gates firm buys $80 million plot of land to create 'smart city'", 13 November 2017 https://nypost.com/2017/11/13/bill-gates-firm-buys-arizona-land-for-80-million-to-create-smart-city/

16 Henry Grabar, "Bill Gates' Smart City in Arizona Is Not Smart, Not a City, and Has Little to Do With Bill Gates", 14 November 2107 https://slate.com/business/2017/11/bill-gates-smart-city-in-arizona-is-not-smart-not-a-city-and-has-almost-nothing-to-do-with-bill-gates.html

17 Chris Martin and Joe Ryan, "Super-Cheap Driverless Cabs to Kick Mass Transit to the Curb", 25 October 2016 https://www.bloomberg.com/news/articles/2016-10-24/super-cheap-driverless-taxis-may-kick-mass-transit-to-the-curb

18 IHS Markit, www.ihs.com now at S&P Global www.spglobal.com

Technology and the Suburbs: Exploring the Multilevel Spatial Divide in the National Broadband Network

Tooran Alizadeh, Edward Helderop,
Tony Grubesic and Richard Ferrers

The recent global pandemic renewed the global push for telecommunication infrastructure, as many COVID responses (e.g., working from home, home-schooling, e-commerce) were challenged by the inequity of access to broadband services. This chapter examines the geospatial footprint of the National Broadband Network (NBN) in relation to Australia's cities, suburbs, and regions. Through data made available by the NBN, which describes the technologies used in its multi-technology mix (MTM) platform, and published data available via the Australian Bureau of Statistics (ABS), we explore the patterns of access to broadband technologies across the nation. The results show a persistent multilevel spatial divide in the NBN, showcasing the need to better understand the dynamic interplay between the NBN provision and the communities it serves.

Telecommunication Policy and Politics in in Australia

Reviewing the complex history of telecommunication infrastructure provision in Australia, is beyond the scope of this paper. However, it is fair to say it is closely linked to the political cycle in this country. The federal election in November 2007 saw the return of a Labor government – after 11 years of the Coalition ruling in Australia –

which promoted a policy platform promising a National Broadband Network (NBN). In 2009, the NBN Co. was formed to provide terrestrial fibre network coverage for 93% of Australian premises by 2020. Fixed wireless and satellite coverage would serve the remaining 7%. However, the early NBN rollout experienced substantial delays, and was criticised for being politically motivated (Alizadeh and Farid, 2017) and socioeconomically biased (Alizadeh, 2015) as the Coalition-held safe seats were the least likely to receive early NBN fibre access under the Labor government.

A turning point for the NBN was the 2013 federal election. The then-elected Coalition government suspended the first stage of the large-scale fibre to the premises (FTTP) rollout to reassess the scale of the national project. As a result, the multi-technology mix (MTM), also known as the Coalition's NBN, emerged. The MTM includes fibre to the premises (FTTP), fibre to the node (FTTN), fibre to the building (FTTB), hybrid fibre coaxial (HFC), wireless, and satellite broadband services. (NBN Co. Ltd., 2021b). However, a feature (and weakness) concerning households connected via HFC and FTTN technologies is that end-user speeds and ultimately quality of service depend on their distance from the node. The further a premise is from the node, the more opportunities for ambient environmental interference and slower speeds over longer copper lines. The use of loop extenders or similar technologies could potentially mitigate these challenges only if the copper lines are high quality and already have signal strength (e.g., 110%) capable of supporting the target/ promised rate for a household - a rarity for regional and remote customers (Grubesic and Mack, 2015). As a result, fibre to the curb (FTTC) was a late addition to the MTM, serving as a partial solution to the mounting complaints associated with the HFC network (Mason, 2017; Sas, 2018).

Politics of telecommunication is by no means a phenomenon exclusive to Australia and yet the evidence suggests that in the case of the NBN the supposed savings that prompted the Coalition's switch from FTTP to MTM never materialised (Gregory, 2019). The MTM took nearly as long as the predicted FTTP rollout (June 2021) – just one year quicker, despite the initial target for the Coalition's NBN to be complete by 2016 (Coalition, 2013). Further, multiple independent reports (ACCC, 2019a, 2019b, 2020) – featuring consumers' experiences – argue that despite the technological advances, internet pricing in Australia is not competitive, and the quality (speed and reliability) of access varies widely across the nation with severe implications for people's livelihoods.

Previous research has pointed out that the secrecy around the NBN made it challenging to assess the progress of the national infrastructure project and fully evaluate its equity and equality implications (Helderop et al., 2019). Indeed, repeated freedom of information requests to release a handful of NBN-relevant internal reports to the public were denied (Schram et al., 2018).The NBN Co. persistently fails to provide information concerning customer satisfaction by the NBN technologies (though they collect this information), performance and/or end-user speed information per NBN technology and location, nor do they provide detailed information concerning their locational plans for network upgrades.

In this chapter, we rely on the mixed-technology footprint of the NBN, officially released in July 2020 (Australian Government, 2020b). We acknowledge that these data may not represent a clear indication of final speed. That said, we are hopeful that the NBN's recent release of their technology footprint data will expand in the future to include data concerning the realised broadband speeds of end-users.

Data and Methods

Three datasets were used for our analysis. First, an Accessibility and Remoteness Index of Australia (ARIA) dataset that categorise all of Australia into one of five remoteness classes (major city, inner regional, outer regional, remote, and very remote) (ABS, 2016b). The divisions between classes are made based on relative service access. Second, as mentioned above, we employ the recently-released NBN technology footprint data. This is a shapefile dataset that details the spatial footprint of each of the NBN's technology types across Australia. Third, a shapefile of the Statistical Areas Level 1 (SA1) polygons, provided by the Australia Bureau of Statistics (ABS, 2016a).

These SA1 polygons are essential for our analysis, since the population density of Australia varies widely between urban and remote regions. SA1 polygon coverage of the country is complete (i.e., all of the land of Australia is contained within one and only one SA1 polygon), with each drawn to contain approximately 400 people (so, naturally, SA1 polygons in remote regions are much larger in terms of their spatial footprint than those in cities). Unfortunately, the NBN technology footprints are not perfectly aligned with SA1 polygon boundaries – so we cannot determine the precise number of people that have access to each technology type. However, by using the fact that SA1 polygons contain on average 400 people, we are able to estimate the population served by each technology type by examining the percent coverage of each polygon by NBN technology.

We run our analysis at two levels: 1) at the national level to assess the urban-regional divide across Australia; and 2) at the Greater Sydney level to represent the fine-grained patterns of the NBN within a metropolitan region. While the first level analysis is all-inclusive of the nation, the second level analysis is limited to the Sydney region only. This does not provide a comprehensive understanding of socio-spatial equity implications within metropolitan regions across the nation. Nevertheless, it sheds light on the multilevel spatial divide within the NBN (more on this follows).

Results: Multilevel Spatial Divide

Urban-Regional Divide in the NBN

Table 18.1 shows the NBN technology frequency for each of the ARIA's remoteness categories. It is important to note that the low total coverage rate for very remote and remote regions is due to the fact that large swathes of land categorised as such is entirely uninhabited. Unsurprisingly, for the same reason, the very remote regions that are inhabited rely primarily on satellite coverage. Meanwhile, the most common NBN technology type in remote regions of Australia is FTTN. This technology is also dominant in the outer and inner regions. These technology frequencies suggest a hierarchy of access to different types of telecommunication infrastructure based on a region's remoteness. This is in line with expectations and the reality of fibre deployment in practice, but does suggest that the original goals of the NBN – to transform regional Australia - remain incomplete (Parliament of Australia, 2011).

Table 18.1: NBN tech coverage by ARIA remoteness categories at SA1 level (%)

NBN Tech	Major Cities	Inner regional	Outer regional	Remote	Very remote
FTTP	10%	11%	9%	<1%	<1%
FTTB	1%	<1%	<1%	0%	0%
FTTC	17%	4%	3%	0%	0%
FTTN	28%	36%	24%	8%	2%
HFC	34%	<1%	<1%	0%	0%
Sat	2%	12%	20%	2%	7%
WL	1%	19%	16%	0%	0%
Total	93%	84%	74%	11%	10%

FTTP connections (representing the best NBN broadband technology type) have similar coverage in major cities, and in the inner and outer regional areas. This is the "best-in-class" broadband technology available from the NBN, and it is unfortunate that the coverage hovers around 10% for the most populated cities in Australia. However, this same figure of coverage for outer and inner regional areas does represent an improvement in broadband connectivity for at least a small portion of these more sparsely-populated areas of Australia.

Another clear indication of the urban-regional divide in the NBN footprint is the dominance of HFC in major cities only. This points to a bifurcated pattern of HFC versus FTTN at the core of the urban-regional divide in the NBN footprint across the nation. Indeed, earlier studies (Alizadeh et al., 2020) show that 50% of the total area in the three capital cities of Sydney, Melbourne, and Brisbane relies on HFC. Such an analysis, however, was conducted prior to the release of the July 2020 dataset. Below we share the fine-grained patterns identified within the Sydney metropolitan region, informed by the official data (NBN Co. Ltd., 2020).

The Fine-Grained Spatial Divide at the Metropolitan Level

Figure 18.1 displays the spatial distribution of the mixed-technology NBN across the Sydney metropolitan region. While satellite dominates the region (and more broadly the entire nation) from an areal perspective (see Table 18.2), we see significantly more variety in the NBN technology footprints present in urban areas (see Figure 18.2 for a close up).

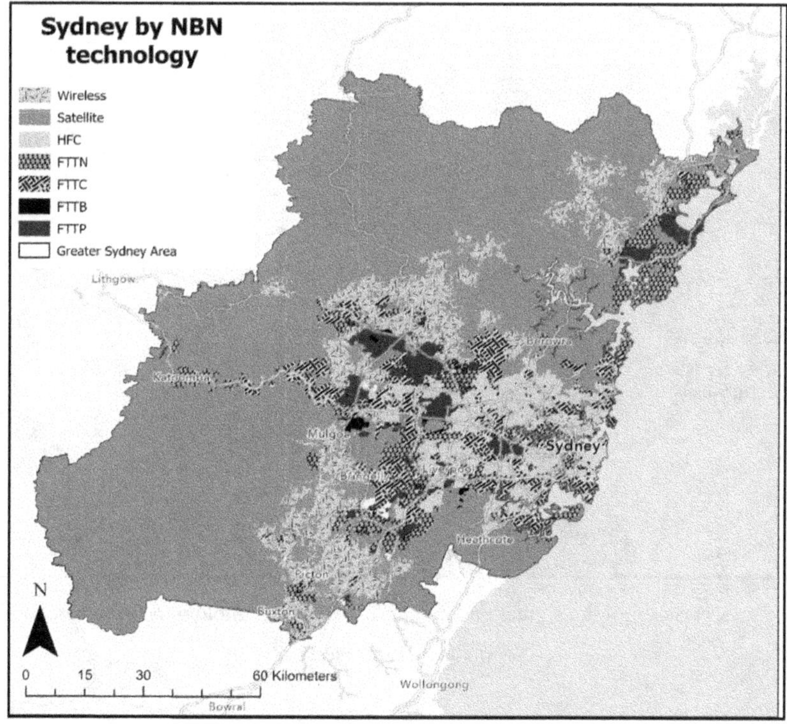

Figure 18.1: Spatial patterns of the mixed-technology NBN across the Sydney metropolitan region

Table 18.2: NBN tech coverage across the Sydney metropolitan region

NBN Tech	Average coverage per SA1 polygon (%)	Sydney areal coverage (sq km)	Sydney areal coverage (%)
WL	1.0%	1209	9.8%
Sat	2.5%	8443	68.4%
HFC	43.5%	677	5.4%
FTTN	17.4%	775	6.3%
FTTC	23.4%	776	6.3%
FTTB	2.5%	55	0.4%
FTTP	9.3%	415	3.4%

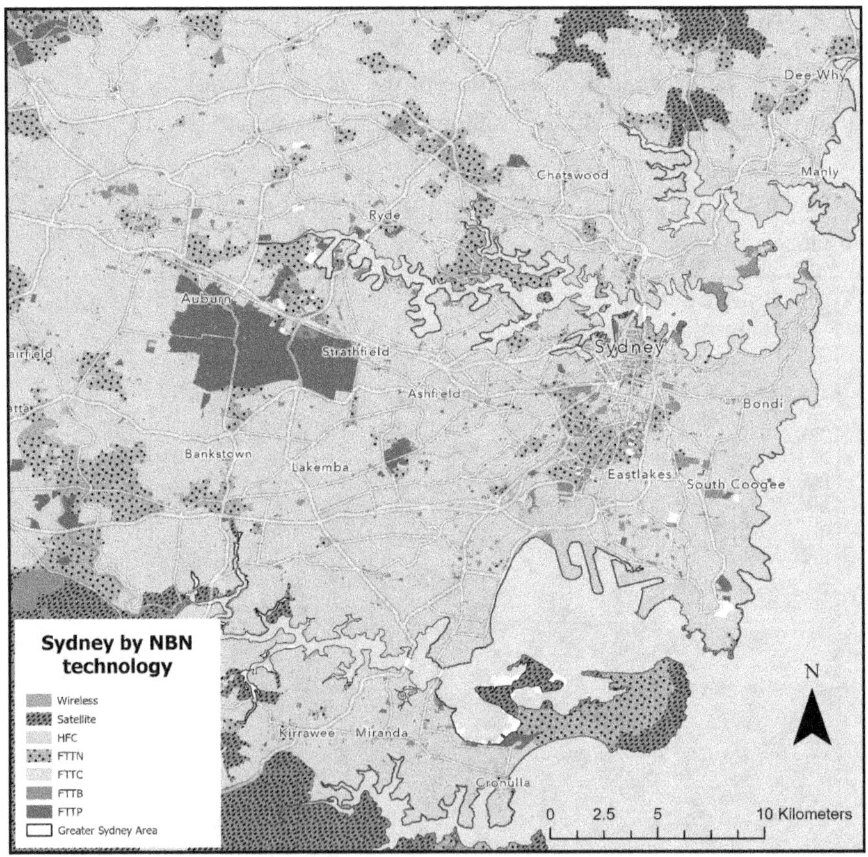

Figure 18.2: A close up of the spatial patterns of the mixed-technology NBN across the Sydney metropolitan region

As discussed earlier in the chapter, our analysis is mostly based on the average coverage at SA1 as it indicates the distribution patterns of the network across the population rather than across the land. In line with what has been seen earlier in Table 18.1, HFC is the most dominant broadband delivery platform for the Sydney metropolitan region. The second and third most common technologies in Sydney are FTTC and FTTN. As mentioned previously, FTTC was a late addition to the NBN, serving as a partial solution to the mounting complaints associated with the HFC network (Mason, 2017; Sas, 2018). If it was not for this late addition of FTTC, it is likely that HFC would have further dominated the NBN footprint in this metropolitan region.

The NBN footprint in the Sydney region suggests that 43.5% of the population in the metropolitan region are connected to the NBN using HFC. There is a strong presence of HFC across the entire metropolitan region, but especially in the eastern suburbs (e.g., Bondi), inner west (e.g., Marrickville and Ashfield), North and North-west Sydney (e.g. Chatswood, North Ryde), and western Sydney (e.g. Bankston). Multiple reports from the Australian media suggest that HFC is not the most reliable part of the mixed-technology NBN, highlighting the challenging experiences of the HFC customers over the years (Kiernan, 2017; Pearce, 2019; Rowland, 2021). Having said this, it is also important to acknowledge that the NBN's recent updates have mostly focused on the HFC platform (Australian Government, 2020a; NBN Co. Ltd., 2021a) adopting a few strategies including node splitting to reduce oversubscription on existing HFC nodes to allow greater bandwidth and better quality of service (Crozier, 2017).

Only 9.3% of the addresses connect to the mixed-technology NBN by fibre to the premises (FTTP), which was supposed to be used for 93% of all premises in the original NBN. A scattering of FTTP connections is identified in the metropolitan region, including portions of western Sydney (parts of Auburn and Strathfield), and its outer western suburbs (Blacktown and Liverpool). FTTN, which receives significant criticism in terms of service quality and reliability (ACCC, 2019a), accounts for 17.4% of the addresses in the region, and is present throughout the inner Sydney, including Newtown, Alexandria, and Erskineville, as well as western Sydney (e.g., Sydney Olympic Park and Wentworth Point). The presence of FTTN in these locations does not align with the emphasis put on these locales as development and employment priority areas in the strategic metropolitan plan for Sydney (GSC, 2018).

Final Words

Our findings shed light on a multilevel spatial divide in the NBN. First, they point out to a clear urban-regional divide in telecommunication infrastructure across the nation. The divide manifests in variations between technological platforms and their availabilities in different parts of Australia. Specifically, there is a bifurcated pattern of HFC versus FTTN in urban versus regional locales. Considering the last major rounds of the NBN upgrade mostly focused on the HFC platform (Australian Government, 2020a; NBN Co. Ltd., 2021a), there is a possibility to exacerbate the existing divide. In saying so, we welcome Labor's recent announcement (Labor, 2022) focused on the NBN upgrade in regional Australia (too early to comment, as details yet to be released). Second, the fine-grained analysis at the Sydney metropolitan region confirms that HFC dominates the largest metropolitan region in Australia. The mounting consumer complaints (ACMA, 2017) in recent years have pushed the NBN to admit the shortcomings of HFC as a technology and prioritise its upgrade (Karp, 2018). Nevertheless, the NBN Co. routinely fails to provide detailed information on where or when these updates were made (the released data is limited to the suburb). As a result, policy analysts remain in the dark as to the true scale and scope of these updates. More importantly, the spatial patterns of the NBN serve to open a discussion on how telecommunication infrastructure provision aligns (or not) with the strategic plans put forward to direct the growth and future development of our cities, suburbs, and regions, as well as the NBN. The ability to provide high-quality, reliable telecommunications infrastructure is critical to maintaining the urban fabric in an equitable way, while simultaneously enabling economic growth and opportunity for all residents.

It is important to note that the analyses offered in this paper are highly constrained by the data limitations around the NBN in Australia. As a result, the investigation of the equity implications of the national telecommunication project is by no means complete. Additional data including individual quality of service (QoS), final speed, pricing, and demand-side analysis are required to fully understand the extend of digital divide in our cities, suburbs, and region.

References

ACCC. (2019a). *Measuring broadband Australia*. Canberra: Australian Competition and Consumer Commission.

ACCC. (2019b). NBN affordability a growing issue. Retrieved from https://www.accc.gov.au/speech/nbn-affordability-a-growing-issue

ACCC. (2020). *Inquiries into NBN access pricing and wholesale service standards*. Canberra: Australian Competition and Consumer Commission.

ACMA. (2017). *Migrating to the National Broadband Network—the consumer experienceKey findings from analysis of industry information*. Canberra: Australian Communications and Media Authority.

Alizadeh, T. (2015). "The spatial justice implications of telecommunication infrastructure: the socio-economic status of early national broadband network rollout in Australia", *International Journal of Critical Infrastructures, 11*(3), 278-296.

Alizadeh, T., & Farid, R. (2017). "Political economy of telecommunication infrastructure: An investigation of the National Broadband Network early rollout and pork barrel politics in Australia". *Telecommunications Policy, 41*(4), 242–252.

Alizadeh, T., Grubesic, T., & Helderop, E. (2020). "Socio-spatial patterns of the National Broadband Network revealed: Lessons from Greater Sydney, Melbourne, and Brisbane", *Telecommunications Policy, 44*(5), DOI:10.1016/j.telpol.2020.101941.

Australian Government. (2020a). $4.5 billion NBN investment to bring ultra-fast broadband to millions of families and businesses and create 25,000 jobs. Retrieved from https://www.paulfletcher.com.au/media-releases/joint-media-release-45-billion-nbn-investment-to-bring-ultra-fast-broadband-to

Australian Government. (2020b). National Broadband Network: Connections by technology type – July 2020. Retrieved from https://data.gov.au/dataset/ds-dga-c79b2219-7e1f-46a9-961f-e87668122f02/details

Coalition. (2013). The Coalition's Plan for Fast Broadband and an Affordable NBN. Retrieved from https://www.malcolmturnbull.com.au/assets/Broadband.pdf

Crozier, R. (2017). NBN Co. pursues more physical HFC node splits. Retrieved from https://www.itnews.com.au/news/nbn-co-pursues-more-physical-hfc-node-splits-474845

Gregory, M. (2019). "How to Transition the National Broadband Network to Fibre To The Premises", *Journal of Telecommunications and the Digital Economy, 7*(1), 57-67.

Grubesic, T., & Mack, E. A. (2015). *Broadband Telecommunications and Regional Development*. London: Taylor & Francis Ltd.

GSC. (2018). *Greater Sydney region plan: A metropolis of three cities*. Sydney: Greater Sydney Commission.

Helderop, E., Grubesic, T., & Alizadeh, T. (2019). "Data deluge or data trickle? Difficulties in acquiring public data for telecommunications policy analysis", *The Information Society, 35*.

Karp, P. (2018). NBN's speed slowed by reliance on copper network, its CEO admits. Retrieved from https://www.theguardian.com/technology/2018/apr/27/nbns-speed-slowed-by-reliance-on-copper-network-its-ceo-admits?CMP=share_btn_tw

Kiernan, S. (2017). NBN to pause all HFC rollouts over customer experience issues. Retrieved from https://www.crn.com.au/news/nbn-to-pause-all-hfc-rollouts-over-customer-experience-issues-478514

Labor. (2022). Boost Fibre and Fast-Track the NBN Repair Job. Retrieved from https://www.pbo.gov.au/elections/2022-general-election/2022-election-commitment-costings/boost-fibre-and-fast-track-nbn-repair-job-ecr128

Mason, M. (2017). "NBN halts HFC rollout 'effective immediately' as issues mount", *Financial Review*, Retrieved from https://www.afr.com/technology/web/nbn/nbn-halts-hfc-rollout-effective-immediately-as-issues-mount-20171127-gztg2i

NBN Co. Ltd. (2020). National Broadband Network: Connections by technology type - July 2020. Retrieved from https://data.gov.au/data/dataset/c79b2219-7e1f-46a9-961f-e87668122f02

NBN Co. Ltd. (2021a). 300,000 more homes and businesses to become eligible for nbn fibre upgrade by ordering selected higher speed plans. Retrieved from https://www.nbnco.com.au/corporate-information/media-centre/media-statements/300000-more-homes-and-businesses-to-become-eligible-for-nbn-fibre-upgrade-by-ordering-selected-higher-speed-plans

NBN Co. Ltd. (2021b). The technology that connects your premises. Retrieved from https://www.nbnco.com.au/learn/network-technology

Pearce, R. (2019). NBN's HFC worst for outages, FTTP best: ACCC report. Retrieved from https://www.computerworld.com/article/3456332/nbn-s-hfc-worst-for-outages-fttp-best-accc-report.html

Rowland, C. (2021). HFC is shaping up as a nightmare for NBN and for customers alike. Retrieved from https://ausdroid.net/nbn/2021/01/28/hfc-is-shaping-up-as-a-nightmare-for-nbn-and-for-customers-alike/

Sas, N. (2018). "NBN launches fibre-to-the-curb technology, but existing customers won't benefit", *ABC News,* Retrieved from http://www.abc.net.au/news/2018-04-08/nbn-launches-fibre-to-the-curb-technology/9631262

Schram, A., Friel, S., Freeman, T., Fisher, M., Baum, F., & Harris, P. (2018). "Digital Infrastructure as a Determinant of Health Equity: An Australian Case Study of the Implementation of the National Broadband Network", *Australian Journal of Public Administration, 00*(0), 1–14

19

Case Studies in Retrofitting Suburbia: Urban Design Strategies for Urgent Challenges*

June Williamson and Ellen Dunham-Jones

Change is everywhere in the suburbs of northern America, the built landscapes where most residents of the United States and Canada live. Speculative visions of futuristic solar suburbs powering electric cars and e-bikes make headlines at the same time that mid-century-modern ranch house renovations are all the rage. Exurban "McMansions" fill with multigenerational families while new infill housing and backyard cottages are built to meet the needs of smaller households in inner suburban neighborhoods. Established suburbs largely built for young white families are more likely to be populated today by older white faces and younger faces of colour.

The shopping centres, office parks, garden apartment complexes, and highway strip corridors of the twentieth century are aging and changing too. Many are being retrofitted to meet new needs. In areas experiencing growth pressure, they're being redeveloped into more "urban" places—read: more mixed in use, walkable, and

---

* Following are excerpts from *Case Studies in Retrofitting Suburbia: Urban Design Strategies for Urgent Challenges*, a book published in 2021 as a companion volume to our award-winning book *Retrofitting Suburbia: Urban Design Solutions for Redesigning Suburbs*, first published in 2008 and updated in 2011. In the new book we argue that there are several urgent challenges with which the next generation of suburban retrofits must grapple both to raise the bar on the big project of retrofitting the least resilient and sustainable aspects of existing suburban form and to absorb new development that would otherwise produce further sprawl. It received the 2021 Great Places Book Award from the Environmental Design Research Association (EDRA). Copyright 2021, June Williamson and Ellen Dunham-Jones. Published by John Wiley & Sons, Hoboken, New Jersey. Some edits have been made for clarity.

dense in building area. In communities with little to no economic growth pressure, many of these failing properties are providing lower-cost space for entrepreneurs to start or expand small, local businesses.

The growing vacancies in weaker markets make visible longstanding discrimination and structural racism in the built environment and growing societal inequalities, expressed by a shrinking middle class and increased rates of poverty in suburban populations. As the gap between rich and poor places widens, so does the ability to cope with infrastructure maintenance, adaptations to prepare for the impacts of climate change, public health pandemics and epidemics of obesity and loneliness, as well as the economic shifts presented by online shopping and the automation of labour...

Readers will benefit from understanding the larger context for the book, starting with how we define "suburban." We've chosen not to engage ongoing debates over how to quantitatively define suburbs.[1] We focus on built form. A property with a building surrounded by surfaces that are lawn or paved for parking we define as suburban form. If the building fronts a sidewalk and places the parking either under or behind it, that's urban form. If the road infrastructure is dendritic – branching out like a tree – that's suburban form. If the streets are networked – interconnected and walkable, with frequent intersections – that's urban form. Most instances of suburban form are located in places we generically refer to as suburbs or suburbia. There are many cities, however, that have properties within them characterisable as suburban form that are good candidates for retrofitting. And there are many suburbs with districts of good urban form that should be preserved, if not extended.

Places built with suburban form have been highly resistant to change. Land-use policies, defended by NIMBYs (neighborhood activists who protest "Not in My Back Yard"), and highway investments have directed new growth to the places of least resistance, at the ever-expanding metropolitan periphery. These developments have often come at the expense of opportunities to densify already developed properties. A shift started with a handful of private-sector-led retrofits in the late 1980s and picked up steam by the mid-2000s with the growing popularity of new urbanism, smart growth, and the "return to the city" movement. In our first book we featured case studies on redeveloping "underperforming asphalt" (developer-speak for underused parking lots) into more sustainable, compact, walkable, mixed-use places.[2]

The Great Recession of 2008 hit suburbs hard and resistance to change began to fade as dead shopping centres and stalled subdivisions proliferated. An occupied or demolished building was better than a vacant one and the number of reinhabitation and regreening projects in our database of examples grew.[3] The Great Recession also prompted ambitious public planning efforts. [New] federal programs resulted in successful community revitalisations, demonstrating the benefits of integrating mixed travel modes, uses, and incomes – especially in suburbs.

The combination of an increasingly ambitious public sector willing to invest in public-private partnerships, ongoing vacancies due to the so-called "retail apocalypse," and a significant market shift in favor of walkable, urban lifestyles dramatically expanded the movement to retrofit suburban sprawl.[4] The market interest in walkability aligns remarkably well with the public sector's efforts to meet the challenges of improving public health, equitable and affordable access to opportunities, a society with more people living longer, and the pressing need to mitigate climate change impacts. Our database of retrofitting examples has exploded over the past decade from 80 to over 2,000 entries. Slightly more than half we classify as redevelopments, only 2% as regreenings, and the rest comprise incomplete tallies of the vast number of reinhabitations and adopted corridor retrofit plans. This book is inspired by how complex, diverse, and creative the newest retrofits are. If the previous generation of retrofits were mostly about reducing auto dependency, these projects continue that effort but also layer on aspects of solutions to multiple challenges. We are humbled by the tremendous imagination it took to envision such change and the dedication of the numerous public- and private-sector champions without whom these projects would not have been implemented...

Disrupt Automobile Dependence

Trying to cure traffic congestion by adding more capacity is like trying to cure obesity by loosening your belt.

If every place worth visiting had enough parking for all the people who wanted to visit, there would be no places left worth visiting.

Widely cited amongst traffic engineers, unknown sources

Suburban form has always been shaped predominantly by transportation. Early suburbs from the mid-nineteenth century centered on the railroad stations, while early twentieth-century streetcar suburbs were designed with row after row of narrow-lot blocks a short walk from the transit corridors. The rapid, widespread adoption of private cars enabled the emergence of late twentieth-century auto-oriented suburban sprawl, characterised by low-density urbanism, separated uses, and "leapfrog" development patterns wherein lower-cost agricultural or forested land further out on the periphery, accessible from a highway exit, was preferred for new construction over closer-in sites. Soon, many more households were in locations where private cars were the default mobility choice.

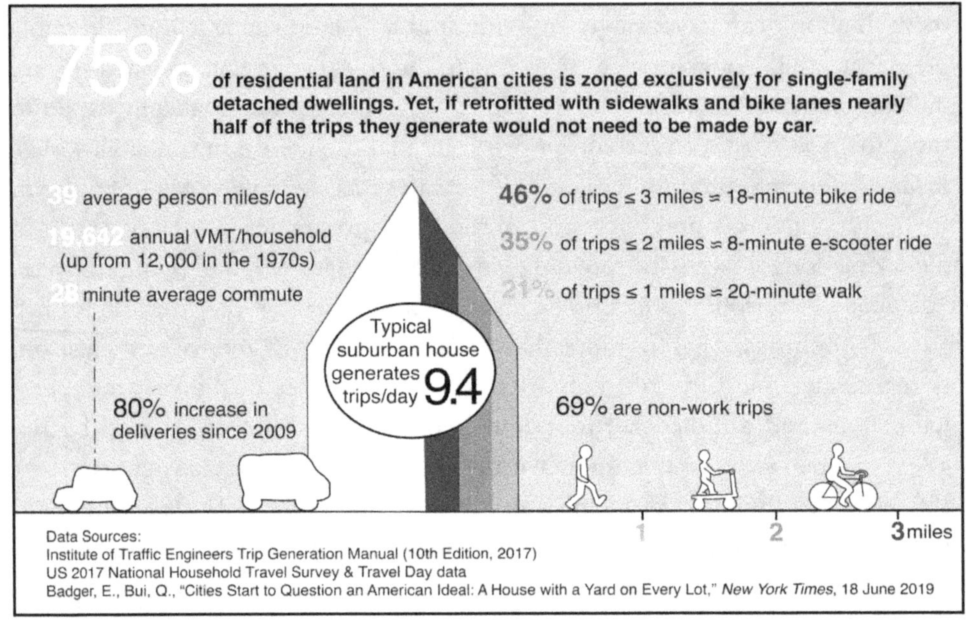

Figure 19.1: Nearly half of the trips in suburban areas dominated by single-family detached houses [in the US] are under three miles, yet over 90% of those are made by car. More sidewalks, bike lanes, and everyday uses could dramatically reduce auto dependency. Rezoning to allow denser housing types could even make transit feasible. (Source: Authors)

In 2016 there were 1.97 motor vehicles per US household.[5] No one knows just how many parking spaces there are nationwide, but there are some startling city-wide numbers. Des Moines, Iowa, has 19 parking spaces per household while Jackson, Wyoming, has 27. Seattle, Washington has 29 parking spaces per acre servicing a population density of 13 people per acre, while Los Angeles County has 200 square miles worth of parking spaces.[6] In the words of the US Supreme Court, car ownership is now a "virtual necessity."[7] This sense of "necessity," we believe, can be altered. We don't really require that much parking. And couldn't the land be put to better use?

Meanwhile, the growing global middle classes, in pursuit of lower-density living and the status and convenience of the private automobile, are at risk of becoming just as auto-dependent as northern Americans. That convenience comes at a staggering cost to public and environmental health, let alone the $25[USD] per day on average that

Americans pay to own a car.

Yet converging forces are increasingly disrupting conventional patterns of private car ownership and automobile dependency. These include:

- New forms of mobility such as carsharing, carhailing, electric vehicles, mobility-as-a-service models, autonomous shuttle buses, autonomous cars, and drones
- New forms of electric micromobility that help with the "first/last mile problem" such as e-bikes, e-scooters, and e-skateboards
- Increased traffic congestion in areas of growing population, reducing the convenience of travel by private car
- Increasing investments in public transit (although results in ridership are mixed)
- Apps with real-time information about transit schedules, weather, and traffic
- Online shopping and the transfer of consumer trips to delivery trips
- Increasingly crowded and crumbling highways and subways
- Younger generations' reduced interest in car ownership and increased preference for urban lifestyles and shared mobility

All of these disruptive factors are accelerating the trends to retrofit underperforming and vacant suburban commercial properties and excess "greyfield" parking lots that we identified in our first book, *Retrofitting Suburbia: Urban Design Solutions for Redesigning Suburbs*. Back in the 2000s, we were focused on projects that did *anything* to reduce automobile dependency. Since then, retrofits have become both more common and more ambitious at tackling the many challenges facing suburban landscapes.

Increasingly, the question isn't just "What are you doing to reduce dependence on the car?" – it's also "What are you doing for climate change, social equity, and the loneliness epidemic?" Many retrofits more directly address these social and environmental challenges by reinhabiting underperforming properties with more community-serving uses or by regreening them. However, the imperative to pursue a variety of steps to reduce automobile dependence remains fundamental because of the cascade of impacts. This isn't a war to get rid of the private car and the freedom associated with it, although the future impact of autonomous vehicles might lead in that direction. It is about expanding the freedom of transportation choices, reducing the number and length of car trips, and creating healthier and more prosperous communities at the same time...

Improve Public Health

Our bodies, our health and buildings are forever connected. The links between architecture and well-being are richer than merely affording safety from injury; buildings can be, should be, agents of health–physical, mental and social health. Good buildings and urban plans do precisely that Humanity faces powerful challenges, a "perfect storm" of colliding dangerous forces, namely accelerating climate change, resource depletion and population pressure, and staggering harm and costs from an inundation of chronic diseases like diabetes.[8]

Richard J. Jackson, MD MPH, FAAP

The potential of suburban retrofitting to transform people's lives begins at the most fundamental level: in their individual bodies. Exemplary suburban retrofits incorporate design elements that can improve people's physical health as well as their mental and social wellness and mitigate the aspects of conventional development that contribute to crisis levels of obesity and diabetes. Dr. Richard Jackson, public health professor [emeritus] at UCLA and former director of the US Centers for Disease Control's National Center for Environmental Health, reminds us of the crucial role played by designers and planners who can activate buildings and physical neighborhoods into agents of better physical, mental, and social human health.

There are many facets to the design and planning challenge of improving public health. Design changes in the built landscape can reduce the known risks to human health presented by conventional suburban built form in urbanised environments. Facets of the challenge are wide-ranging and include:

- Encouraging everyday physical activity, especially walking, stair climbing, and biking
- Incorporating tenets of biophilia, or contact with nature
- Reducing social isolation with communal gathering spaces
- Improving safety from the risks of car crashes, toxins exposure, fire, flood, and crime
- Mitigating and avoiding ill effects from polluted air, soil, and water
- Increasing access in all neighborhoods to healthy foods and routine preventative health care
- Reducing the stresses of income and resource inequality

This last facet is crucially linked to all the others.

Figure 19.2: Highland Greenway Park, on the left, is the first of three planned parks on former parking lots at the Highland Mall, in Austin, Texas. It features a community garden, picnic areas, and a fitness trail that will eventually loop the entire site and is here shown wrapping a new apartment building. On the right, the former Dillards department store's cladding has been removed as it gets transformed into Austin Community College classrooms and KLRU-TV office and production facilities. (Source: Photo by Phillip Jones, 2019)

Suburban retrofitting patterns that result in compact places, conducive to walking and biking, that are close to transit, retail, services, schools, workplaces, and other everyday amenities, are increasingly recognised as a key component to improving health. However, this recognition – and the recommendations to follow – is complicated by a paradox: Adding more compact urban patterns throughout urbanised metropolitan areas can mitigate the primary health risk factors associated with sprawling urbanisation – epidemic levels of chronic diseases like diabetes linked to obesity and lack of everyday exercise – but at the same time may exacerbate the human health risks associated with pollutants produced by urban congestion. The COVID-19 pandemic is revealing that individuals with these chronic conditions are more vulnerable to serious, life-threatening complications from coronaviruses.

Despite greater rates of chronic diseases compared to infectious diseases, the pandemic seems to have revivified distrust of compact urbanism. How then to best promote the generally more healthy compact patterns, while mitigating the associated risks? Many scholars, practitioners, and advocates believe this paradox can be addressed, indeed *must* be tackled, in the face of the "perfect storm" described by Dr. Jackson.

How? Through thoughtful, informed planning policies and design techniques. Many suburban areas were built around assumed use of private automobiles, which enable sedentary lives. Communities and designers can choose to pursue policies and adopt design strategies for introducing more compact patterns that promote physical activity at the regional and neighborhood scales. At the same time, they might introduce design elements at the neighborhood, block, and building scales to minimise human exposure to unhealthy pollutants and other health stressors.

Retrofitting the many unhealthful aspects of suburban form while avoiding introducing new ones is a worthy task, and a significant challenge for the twenty-first century...

Leverage Social Capital for Equity

America's history of racial exclusion repeats and deepens itself as low-income people of colour are displaced from newly chic neighborhoods, shut out of all but the lowest-wage jobs, and isolated in aging, disinvested communities—these days, in the suburbs.[9]

Angela Glover Blackwell, Founder of PolicyLink

Despite lingering depictions of outdated cultural stereotypes, recognition is finally gaining that suburbs are not physically homogenous, nor are suburbanites all the same in terms of socioeconomics, race, or ethnicity. However, built landscapes within metropolitan regions remain highly fragmented and segregated; they have been structured that way through codes and laws over decades of growth cycles, and supported by entrenched systems of racialised control and policing. The barriers to decreasing segregation and inequality stubbornly persist.

The task of confronting this challenge is vital at a time when poverty in suburbia has increased in many neighbourhoods while awareness of these changes and their causes is not yet widespread.[10] As leading US equity activist Angela Glover Blackwell informs us, people who are newly displaced from gentrifying urban areas may find themselves in suburban communities that have become disinvested in over time, as their former neighborhoods once were. There they may join the newest immigrants and longtime residents who find themselves in communities with struggling schools, a lack of gathering places, and access to fewer well-paying jobs. The number of suburban census tracts with high levels of poverty is growing; many governments are caught off-guard in a vicious spiral of reduced revenues, increased maintenance costs, and obsolete, discriminatory policies. Yet, while poor places get poorer, many rich places get richer, and the uneven playing field gets more inequitable.

Not only are suburbs not homogeneous, but there will be no singular fix to make them more equitable. Jason Schupbach, expert on the role of arts and design in making better communities, reminds us why mindful design matters, asserting, "Inequity will die from a thousand cuts, not a silver bullet."[11] It is imperative for designers to contribute to vanquishing inequity by leveraging social capital to promote urban and suburban justice, delivering one small but significant cut at a time...

Within the context of suburban retrofitting, we frame social capital as the introduction or enhancement of *social infrastructure* within a project. This is especially needed in suburbs that were designed to maximise privacy and centre social life primarily around schools, yet today have ageing populations, smaller households, and fewer children. A strengthened social infrastructure, often integrated with greater accessibility and environmental quality, builds urban resilience: the capacity to survive, adapt, and even grow in the face of both chronic and acute stresses and shocks, whether economic, climactic, political, or all three.

In the spirit of Peter Newman's, Timothy Beatley's, and Heather Boyer's inspirational volume *Resilient Cities*, we advocate for embrace of hope in the face of fear in responding to stresses and preparing for shocks to the suburban polis.[12] To paraphrase their *cri de coeur*, suburbs of fear make short-term, panicky decisions, driven primarily by divisive competition, while suburbs of hope plan for the long term, guided by visions for future change formed through consensus and cooperation. Suburbs of fear see threats, while suburbs of hope seize on periods of crisis as opportunities to seek continuous improvement.[13]

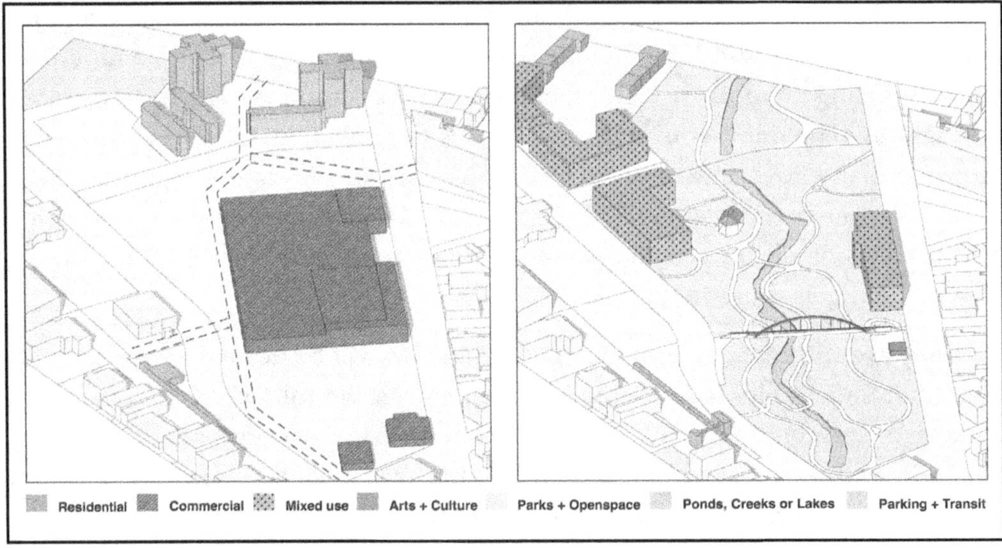

Figure 19.3: Before retrofitting, the urban renewal-era Meriden Hub mall in Meriden, Connecticut, sat squat in a parking lot, over a culverted brook (dashed lines in diagram). After retrofitting, the mall site is regraded into Meriden Green, with new housing, relocated subsidised housing, and a sophisticated piece of green infrastructure including a daylit brook and stormwater park. (Source: Authors)

How can retrofits address the challenges of leveraging social capital to promote equity and justice and of building social infrastructure that increases resilience? To summarise a few of the ways:

- Reinhabitation retrofits of commercial spaces in all suburbs including "ethnoburbs" (that is, places where recent immigrant populations have concentrated) can support the flourishing of locally owned businesses.

- Redevelopment retrofits can add and preserve jobs, housing affordability and choice.

- Regreening retrofits can provide equitable access to an enhanced civic realm of public and shared green spaces and help assert a "right to the suburb."

These strategies can and should be employed both in communities with high rates of poverty where needs are greatest, but also in more prosperous places with greater access to opportunity. The scale of operations for leveraging suburban social capital is varied, from the very local, at the level of a neighborhood or even a single block; to the larger metropolitan region in which suburban jurisdictions and areas of suburban form are embedded. Each scale of engagement depends on defining and locating the target community or communities that stand to benefit...

Compete for Jobs

So, rather than decentralising the American labour pool, the rise of the internet and digital technologies had the opposite effect: It accelerated its concentration.[14]

Daniel Oberhaus, staff writer at *Wired*

The success of suburbia has long been predicated on providing good jobs with the kind of security and stability that built the middle class and enabled workers to build wealth, invest in their children's education, and support their communities. Today, many suburbs are confronting a double whammy: the shrinking middle class upon which their job base and tax revenue has historically depended and, as Daniel Oberhaus observes, a technologically enhanced generational shift away from "job sprawl" toward agglomeration, toward the advantages of urbanism.

The US middle class has been consistently shrinking from 61% of the population in 1971 to 50% in 2015.[15] Some of this is caused by new technologies that have replaced many middle-skilled routine jobs with new high- and low-skilled jobs. However, most of the blame is attributed to stagnant wages unable to support the rising cost of living.[16] ... It isn't only the US whose middle class is shrinking. So are those of the 42 member countries of the Organisation for Economic Cooperation and Development (OECD)...

Figure 19.4: A business incubator in a suburban strip mall? Developer Monte Anderson and the City of DeSoto, Texas, converted a former hardware store into Grow DeSoto Market, regreened a swath of the parking lot into a twinkle-lit networking space with food trucks and

plan to build 20 loft apartments on the side. (Source: Photo by Phillip Jones, 2019)

Lower-income suburbs, many of them former manufacturing hubs that lost their job base to offshoring in the 1970s and 1980s, still haven't recovered and are seeing increases in poverty. Higher-income suburbs that grew up around suburban office parks and corporate campuses are now seeing job losses as those properties start emptying out. Their TAMI tenants (technology, advertising, media, and information) are increasingly moving to "innovation districts" with "creative office" lofts in both downtowns and urbanised suburban retrofits that provide live-work-walk environments and transit access. *Urbanism* – a desirable mix of uses, walkable urban form, and lively streetscapes rather than remote megastructures set in lush verdant landscapes accessible only by car – is the new amenity companies are increasingly looking for to attract the next generation of skilled employees. Suburban retrofits in suburbs of all kinds are helping communities compete in new ways to attract and retain a diverse array of jobs...

Add Water and Energy Resilience

As the unparalleled costs associated with the hurricanes of the past decade demonstrate, we suppress or deny the interdependence of constructed systems, as well as their combined reliance on natural systems, at our peril What if the services provided by power plants, sewage treatment plants, and other elements of infrastructure were based on an ecological model of interdependency, instead of an industrial model of segregation?[17]

Hillary Brown, FAIA

Suburbia was not designed with climate change, sustainability, or resilience in mind. Rather, its infrastructure reflects what Hillary Brown, professor [emerita] of architecture and sustainability at the City College of New York and Fellow of the Post-Carbon Institute, describes as an industrialised worldview of convenience, efficiency, and bureaucratic control. Instead of the "three-legged stool" concept used to describe sustainability, wherein environmental, economic, and social equity systems are understood as overlapping and interdependent, twentieth-century suburban development is more often described in terms of discrete "silos." In planning for new communities, engineers devised and followed standards for transportation, water, and energy systems, each optimised for a single variable.

To facilitate development on greenfield land, meandering creeks and headwaters were routinely cut off from the ecosystems they had supported and rerouted into open-air concrete drainage channels or buried in underground pipes.[18] The pipes and power lines stretching from centralised water treatment, sewer, and power plants across large metros dramatically altered local ecology and suffer from transmission loss and leakage. To pay for it all, utilities established to deliver water and power encouraged the creation of an auto-dependent, culverted landscape of detached, air-conditioned buildings surrounded by lawns, septic tanks, and parking lots.[19]

Planners similarly enacted zoning and land-use ordinances to separate uses and segregate income levels. Financing practices evolved to deliver standardised real estate products with little consideration of local climate, geography, or culture. As a consequence, suburban form has high per capita water and power consumption.

Together our habits have substantially altered our climate, polluted our air and surface waters, drained groundwater aquifers enabling saltwater intrusion, and led to soaring maintenance costs of ageing infrastructure.[20] There is now far greater recognition of the damage such systems have wrought on the environment – and of how climate change is increasing flooding, droughts, sea level rise, wildfires and urban heat island impacts.

Retrofitting enables integrated approaches to these challenges:

-   Designers increasingly view stormwater as a resource, not a nuisance, and locally produced energy as a smart investment.

-   Regreening strategies reduce flooding and sewer overflows and provide wildfire buffers, while more compact redevelopment reduces per capita demand for water and energy and reduces loss from leaks.

-   Integration of green infrastructure and water harvesting on the one hand and district energy plants and district energy plants and distributed renewable energy generation on the other reduce strains on existing centralised water and power systems and increase capacity for more resilient local solutions.

Such efficiency is particularly impactful given "the water-energy nexus." Most of us assume that our homes' water and power arrive through entirely separate systems. In fact, the production of all forms of energy requires a great deal of water and the distribution and treatment of water requires a great deal of energy. While percentages vary significantly across systems, approximately 40% of freshwater withdrawals in the US go to cooling thermoelectric power plants.[21] At the same time, in some municipalities up to half of the energy bill is consumed by water and wastewater utilities.[22] This interdependency compounds the risks when severe weather events occur...

Figure 19.5: Revitalising a suburban corridor into the Fiesta District in Mesa, Arizona, involved a road diet with widened sidewalks and stormwater swales that irrigate new trees. Urban heat island effects are further mitigated by paseo pocket parks offering cooling, seating, and night lighting as shown here, with the mid-block shade and fountain at the entrance to a big box store renovated into high rent office space. (Source: Photo by Ellen Dunham-Jones, 2015)

The good news is that wealthy and less affluent communities alike are increasingly pursuing net-zero energy and water-neutral targets. However, most of the US has deferred maintenance on municipal water and power infrastructure, leading to a vicious cycle of dependence on continued high consumption and higher rates to cover repairs.[23] US federal regulations continue to encourage centralised systems while local utility programs primarily encourage individuals to reduce usage...

[New] solar suburbs and community-scale net-zero energy and water strategies around the world have begun to demonstrate dramatic improvements through integrating infrastructure ecologies.[24] But upgrading the performance of *existing* suburban water and energy systems is harder and tends to be piecemeal. This is precisely where retrofits are playing a critical role delivering water and energy more efficiently and substantially improving resilience and environmental quality.

The process often starts by breaking down larger problems into individual components whose solutions can be appropriately layered. [There are many] physical changes that suburban retrofits are employing to address water quality, too much and too little water, as well as shifts to renewable energy and district-scale combined cooling, heating, and power systems.

Endnotes

1   Despite suburbs being where the majority of US citizens live, neither the US Census Bureau or the Office of Management and Budget provide a systematic definition of the term. They distinguish and report on urban and rural, metropolitan and micropolitan (small towns). By default, the suburbs are simply those parts of a metropolitan urban area that aren't the core cities. This has prompted numerous attempts to better distinguish types of suburbs through history and in the present. A few of many sources include Ann Forsyth, "Defining Suburbs," *Journal of Planning Literature*, 5 June 2012; June Williamson, *Designing Suburban Futures: New Models From Build a Better Burb* (Washington, DC: Island Press, 2013); RCLCO, ULI Terwilliger Center, "The New Geography of Urban America: An Interactive Map for Classifying Urban Neighborhoods," 19 June 2018; Whitney Airgood-Obrycki and Shannon Rieger, "Defining Suburbs: How Definitions Shape the Suburban Landscape," Working Paper, Joint Center for Housing Studies of Harvard University, 20 February 2019, https://www.jchs.harvard.edu/research-areas/working-papers/defining-suburbs-how-definitions-shape-suburban-landscape.

2   We only track examples that, one way or another, are improving sustainability. We do not track examples where new retail replaces old retail.

3   See the foreword to the updated edition of Ellen Dunham-Jones and June Williamson, *Retrofitting Suburbia: Urban Design Solutions for Redesigning Suburbs* (Hoboken, NJ: Wiley, 2011).

4   The significance of changing demographics driving new market preferences should be understood as communities plan for tomorrow's residents. The majority of households in the US today are one- to two-person and the proportion is expected to rise. While each local condition varies, the majority of households in suburbs overall are either empty-nester Baby Boomers or Millennials (in 2020, they aged 56-74 or 24-39 respectively). Despite their different motivations, both generations' interests have converged to drive the market to retrofit the suburbs for more urban lifestyles, contributing to the 75% rent premium that walkability now adds to real estate values. See Tracy Hadden Loh, Christopher B. Leinberger, and Jordan Chafetz, *Foot Traffic Ahead* (George Washington University School of Business & Smart Growth America, 2019). See also Arthur C. Nelson, *The Reshaping of Metropolitan America* (Washington DC: Island Press, 2013).

5   Michael Sivak, "Has Motorization in the US Peaked? Part 9: Vehicle Ownership and Distance Driven, 1984–2015," University of Michigan Sustainable Worldwide Transportation, Report No. SWT-2017-4, February 2017.

6   Eric Scharnhorst, "Quantified Parking: Comprehensive Parking Inventories for Five U.S. Cities," Research Institute for Housing America and Mortgage Bankers Association, May 2018. See also David Z. Morris, "L.A.'s Massive 'Crater" Shows Why Parking is the Biggest Fight in Urban Planning," *Fortune*, 14 January 2016.

7   Gregory H. Shill, "Americans Shouldn't Have to Drive, but the Law Insists on It," *The Atlantic*, 9 July 2019.

8   American Institute of Architects, *Local Leaders: Healthier Communities Through Design* (December 2012).

9   Angela Glover Blackwell, "The Case for All-In Cities," in Toni Griffin, Ariella Cohen, David Maddox, eds., *The Just City Essays* (Philadelphia: Next City, 2015), 154.

10 Michelle Chen, "Why Are America's Suburbs Becoming Poorer?" *The Nation*, 22 June 2017.

11 Jason Schupbach, "Why Design Matters," *The Just City Essays*, 226.

12 Peter Newman, Timothy Beatley, and Heather Boyer, "Urban Resilience: Cities of Fear and Hope," *Resilient Cities, Second Edition: Overcoming Fossil Fuel Dependence* (Washington, DC: Island Press, 2017), 1–14.

13 Ibid., 6.

14 Daniel Oberhaus, "How Smaller Cities Are Trying to Plug the Brain Drain," *Wired*, 12 August 2019.

15 Pew Research Center, "The American Middle Class is Losing Ground," *Social & Demographic Trends*, 9 December 2015: https://www.pewsocialtrends.org/2015/12/09/the-american-middle-class-is-losing-ground/.

16 See Drew Desilver, "For Most US Workers, Real Wages Have Barely Budged in Decades," Fact Tank, 7 August 2018, Pew Research: https://www.pewresearch.org/fact-tank/2018/08/07/for-most-us-workers-real-wages-have-barely-budged-for-decades/.

17 Hillary Brown, *Next Generation Infrastructure: Principles for Post-Industrial Public Works* (Washington DC: Island Press, 2014).

18 Jake J. Beaulieu, Helen E. Golden, Christopher D. Knightes, et al., "Urban Stream Burial Increases Watershed-Scale Nitrate Export," PLoS ONE 10(7): e0132256, 17 July 2015: https://doi.org/10.1371/journal.pone.0132256.

19 Adam Rome documents the electric utilities' success at marketing "electric homes" over "solar homes" in the 1930s and '40s, as well as the growing concerns over the loss of "open space" due to suburbanisation in the 1950s and '60s in *The Bulldozer in the Countryside* (Cambridge, UK: Cambridge University Press, 2001).

20 See Patricia Buckley, Lester Gunnion, and Will Sarni, "The Aging Water Infrastructure: Out of Sight, Out of Mind?" *Issues by the Numbers*, March 2016, Deloitte Insights: https://www2.deloitte.com/insights/us/en/economy/issues-by-the-numbers/us-aging-water-infrastructure-investment-opportunities.html.

21 J.F. Kenney, N.L. Barber, S.S. Hutson, K.S. Linsey, J.K. Lovelace, and M.A. Maupin, *Estimated Use of Water in the United States in 2005* (Reston, VA: US Geological Survey, 2009).

22 International Energy Agency, *Water Energy Nexus*, Excerpt from the 2016 World Energy Outlook (Paris), 34.

23 Danielle Ivory, Ben Protess, and Griff Palmer, "In American Towns, Private Profits from Public Works," *New York Times*, 24 December 2016; Daniel Herriges, "$3.2 Billion to Fix Tampa's Aging Pipes? From Where?" Strong Towns, 30 August 2019: https://www.strongtowns.org/journal/2019/8/30/32-billion-to-fix-tampas-aging-pipes-from-where.

24 Arka Pandit, et al., "Infrastructure Ecology: An Evolving Paradigm for Sustainable Urban Development," *Journal of Cleaner Production* (1 October 2017): S19–S27.

20

Trends Shaping the Future of Australian (Sub)Urbanisation

Jason Byrne

Introduction

"urban sustainability objectives cannot be advanced in Australia if suburban environments are demonised, their populations patronised and homogenised, or new challenges understood as independent of historical legacies."[1]

Australia is an urban nation, but many commentators argue it is more so a suburban nation, and has been almost since European invasion, colonisation and dispossession.[2,3]Australian suburbanisation has been closely tied to global trends in trade and economic development, technology (including transportation, sanitation, and telecommunications), urban planning, building design and even aesthetics, urban design, and garden fashions. Suburbs are the product not only of physical forms, but also of ideas beliefs and values about gender, division of labour, social reproduction, and what makes the "good life".[4] The history of Australian suburbanisation is covered in Chapter 1 [also see: Endnote 5].

When looking to the future, we can take cues from how past trends have affected the suburbs.[5] Twentieth century patterns of suburbanisation were shaped first by horses, trains, and trams, and then by buses, but foremost by the private automobile.[6] Originally, the 19th century tightly compact suburban terraces and workers cottages found in the inner core were located within walking distance of workplaces (shops, factories, and warehouses). In the early 20th century, modest single-family houses were located further away from the CBD, as suburbanites sought to escape pollution, congestion, noise, and poor sanitation. Houses were initially built on smaller blocks near railway stations and tram stops. But urban expansion post-Second World War saw more substantial houses built on larger blocks, near shopping malls, office parks, and industrial estates.

These development patterns were upended in the late 20th century and early 21st century. Inner city landscapes, once characterised by industrial areas mixed with working class housing, were redeveloped for high end, high-rise apartment buildings.[7] This was supported by Commonwealth and State Government policies and strategies, such as the Building Better Cities Program in the 1990s.[8] Currently we are seeing outlying dormitory suburbs or commuter belts of the 20th century increasingly diversifying into mixed-use, mixed-density neighbourhoods.[9] Affordable housing is now located on the far outskirts of Australia's cities, away from services and reliable public transportation. And more than two decades of urban consolidation have increased densities in the inner and middle suburbs, but at the expense of vegetation cover across almost every Australian capital city, substantially changing the character of our suburbs.[10]

This chapter anticipates what the future might hold for Australian suburbs. Signposts point to major challenges and opportunities that lie ahead. These include climate change, rapidly ageing populations, healthcare and infrastructure provision, housing, and changing employment.

Environmental Impacts and Climate Change

Australian patterns of suburbanisation have largely resulted from access to cheap fossil fuels. The making of housing, production and consumption of goods and services, provision of transport networks, and infrastructure provision are all energy intensive activities and generate carbon pollution. Suburban development is not environmentally benign, and has resulted in large-scale land clearing, local species extinctions, air and water pollution, and changes to the water cycle.[11] Arguably the single biggest driver of future environmental change affecting Australian suburbs is climate change. The Intergovernmental Panel on Climate Change (IPCC) has reached a grim conclusion - anthropogenic climate change is accelerating in scale and intensity; we are on track to breach planetary thresholds this century.[12] The future will be characterised by more extreme heatwaves, drought, flooding, severe storm events, and coastal erosion, among other problems. Urgent action is required to hasten mitigation and adaptation.

Mitigation is already occurring via the large-scale electrification of nearly everything (transport, garden care equipment, cooking, heating etc.). The ongoing uptake of rooftop solar electricity generation, among the highest in the world, offers some hope for lowering emissions.[13] A switch to electricity and hydrogen to power transport, especially freight, and for energy storage, also holds promise for emission reduction. Peer to peer systems of energy exchange and microgrids may further reduce emissions. But older, poorly designed inner suburban housing with low energy efficiency and newer suburban development characterised by black roofs, large houses, small blocks and little private greenspace (see Figure 20.1), means large-scale retrofitting will be essential in the decades ahead.[14]

Figure 20.1: New suburban housing in Kingborough, Tasmania on Hobart's outskirts

Adapting to climate change will be an essential activity in the future. Because retrofitting can reduce emissions and improve household cost of living expenses, as well as improving thermal comfort, we can expect to see more neighbourhood scale battery storage, micro wind turbines, biogas digesters, better roof insulation and double glazing, among other adaptation responses. A growing realisation that many suburbs have been developed in risky places is beginning to shape climate change adaptation responses. Devastating bushfires and flooding have ravaged suburbs across Australia in recent years. Coastal erosion is increasing too, with billions of dollars of housing and infrastructure at risk of flooding and erosion.[15] And outer suburban development on the fringes of Sydney, Melbourne, Brisbane, and Perth, is prone to extreme heat events. Already Western Sydney is at risk of becoming unliveable, with temperatures nudging $50°C$, at the limits of human tolerance. Older people (65 years+) and young children (0-4 years) are especially vulnerable. Unsurprisingly, insurance premiums are also rising quickly; some places are now uninsurable.[16]

Adaptation responses in the decade ahead will likely see coordinated and decentralised action, crossing scales from individual households to entire metropolitan areas. Adaptation will require both defending in place and relocation. Large-scale urban greening will be essential to reduce extreme heat hazards. Increasingly, we are seeing public pressure for buy-backs of flood prone property and there have been similar calls for bushfire prone land. In the decades ahead we will likely see retreat away from places deemed too hazardous for settlement and the large-scale deployment of regenerative practices. Parts of some suburbs may be repurposed for wetlands and forests. Water sensitive urban design (sponge cities) and urban silviculture can help stem biodiversity loss, act as carbon sinks, reduce temperatures, and maintain human health and wellbeing. We are also likely to see innovations in urban metabolism and the circular economy for reducing waste, a point we return to shortly.

Demographic Trends

A second global driver affecting Australian suburbs in the future is rapidly ageing populations. While cities in Africa and some parts of Asia are still growing through natural increase, Australia's fertility rate is below replacement.[17] Without immigration, the population of Australia's suburbs will decrease over time. This will be partly offset by increases in lifespan as older people live longer. We are likely to see continued immigration as well as internal migration. But planners will potentially need to grapple with demographic transitions that will affect schools, religious institutions, healthcare facilities, social services and the like.

The COVID-19 pandemic has seen remarkable population shifts away from large capital cities to regional centres, and especially to sunbelt suburbs in Queensland, showing how large changes can occur in short timeframes. In the future, we can also expect increasing migration away from places too hot for human health and wellbeing, especially for older people. As some suburbs experience severe water shortages, food insecurity and increased heatwaves, quality of life will decline. Planners will need to be careful that such changes do not entrench and amplify socio-economic inequality and disadvantage. Social polarisation is already a problem across suburban Australia.[18]

Household composition is also changing in response to global trends. While many older people have a strong desire to age in place, they are seeking opportunities to downsize and move into units, townhouses, and apartments.[19] Multigenerational households are also on the rise, partly in response to reduced housing affordability and partly due to shifting lifestyle and cultural factors. And new family structures of unrelated adults are also becoming more common. LGBTQIA+ communities are increasingly suburban, and many suburbs are becoming more ethno-racially diverse.[20]

In the future we can expect to see these emergent trends continue and Australian suburbs will become more heterogeneous. Shared houses will likely become more common as will retrofitting single-family housing for multi-generational living. And changing transport technologies (e.g., autonomous vehicles and transit on demand), growing secularisation, and smaller numbers of children will produce further changes. We may see garages repurposed for studio housing, churches repurposed for community facilities, and some schools repurposed for affordable housing.[21]

Healthcare

The changing social and demographic composition of suburbs will have healthcare implications. The COVID-19 pandemic has shown that infectious diseases can bring cities to a standstill. Lockdowns have foregrounded the importance of local parks, greenspaces and gathering places for residents' health and wellbeing. Future outbreaks of infectious diseases are almost certain, pointing to the need to revisit lessons learned during prior outbreaks, such as the tuberculous outbreaks of the 20th century.[22] The need for sufficient ventilation in dwellings and offices, access to natural light and greenspaces, and the ability to source goods, services, and healthcare close to home are key lessons. But so-called preventable diseases such as obesity, diabetes, and coronary heart disease, associated with sedentary lifestyles, are also on the rise. They have become the focus of design interventions to improve walking, cycling, and active transport.[23] Diseases related to older age (dementia, diabetes, arthritis, heart disease) are also increasing as our population grows older; they will become increasingly common in the future. Poor mental health is also emerging as a critical concern.

Australian suburbs are often portrayed as salubrious places - with generous, verdant backyards, fresh air, sunshine, and access to fresh food.[24] But environmental quality across suburbs is not uniform. Idealised representations belie the lived experience of many suburbanites. The field of environmental (in)justice, which began in the United States in the late 1970s as a social movement and field of scholarly endeavour, shows how health and wellbeing are spatially and socially differentiated.[25] In other words, where you live can predict how healthy you are and how long you will live. Socio-economic characteristics of populations such as race, class, gender, age, and nationality are predictors of access to environmental benefits and exposure to environmental harms. People of colour and low-income earners, for instance, are more likely to live in housing that lacks adequate heating and cooling, near polluting highways and factories, with more fast-food restaurants and fewer supermarkets with quality fresh food, having limited access to safe and reliable public transport.

The future health and wellbeing of people living in Australia's suburbs will require implementing strategic and evidence-based policy and planning actions to overcome the above-described problems. For example, minimum standards for energy efficiency and thermal comfort will be essential to ensure new suburban housing does not expose residents to heatwave risks. Access to quality greenspaces within a short walk of where people live will be vitally important for mental and physical health. Food security will continue to be a concern, and residents will need access to heathy food options close to home. Different forms of urban agriculture, from verge gardens to urban farms, will assume growing importance. Access to quality healthcare services close to home will be vitally important as populations continue to age. New insights into dementia-care research suggest that in the future Australian suburbs will need better footpaths and benches for improved mobility, higher quality greenspaces for mental restoration, and even better landmarks to help wayfinding and place-memory.[26] And because housing markets can shape health outcomes, we must ensure that lower income earners are not relegated to hot and flood-prone suburbs with associated health impacts (exposure to mould, heatstroke, vector borne disease).

Infrastructure and Service Provision

Infrastructure – from roads and freeways to drains, sewers, powerlines and even parks and schools – has been a critical ingredient to the success of Australia's suburbs. However, it was not until the mid-20th century that many suburban developments had infrastructure that we now take for granted (e.g., sewerage). Many older suburbs have infrastructure that requires extensive investment to keep it operational. And rapid changes in electricity generation, water management, waste management and telecommunications suggest that the future of infrastructure is likely to become more decentralised, increasingly shared between private owners, community groups and governments, and may even feature more peer to peer provision.[27]

In the mid-1980s, scholar Aharon Kellerman presciently observed that the future of metropolitan forms would be strongly influenced by telecommunications infrastructure.[28] He pointed to a lag-effect between the development of new technologies and their uptake and integration within built environments. At the time, Kellerman contemplated the potential for new computing technologies to enable telecommuting and even remote manufacturing through increased automation. Some four decades later, many of these changes are manifesting – confirming Kellerman's capabilities as a futurist and his astute observations about inertia or path dependence hardwired, as it were, into (sub)urban form.

In coming decades, we are likely to see infrastructure integrated into regenerative futures, such as via increased use of district level waste management and heating.[29] Materials loops will be closed as much as possible. Sewage, green waste, food waste and other organics will increasingly be diverted to neighbourhood biogas digesters, where they are converted into methane for cooking and heating. Residual waste compost could be used for growing food locally. Synergies between residential, commercial, and industrial land uses will likely increase, as will recycling and cradle-to-cradle design.

Similarly, we are likely to see the adaptive retrofitting of drainage systems to provide better flood management and improved habitat for non-human species, as well as opportunities for recreation. Water sensitive urban design will entail not only local stormwater capture, but even treatment for potable uses. Changing patterns of private automobile ownership associated with driverless vehicles will likely lead to decreased private car ownership and increases in quasi-public transport use. The trend for younger people giving up cars in favour of transit on demand services is expected to continue. Micro-mobility (walking, cycling, scooters) and carshare/rideshare/bus-share will combine to improve suburban mobility. Freeway removal is likely to occur in some places and surplus road space could be repurposed for housing, greenspace, and growing food.[30]

Service provision will likely be disrupted through peer-to-peer models, new delivery modes, and even local scale manufacturing. Many outer suburbs currently lack essential services or so-called soft infrastructure, such as libraries, recreation facilities, local shopping and employment, schools, healthcare, and community gardens. Suburban co-working spaces could evolve into multi-functional hubs, with a degree of informality and even spontaneity. Services such as library facilities, child-care, schooling, aged-care, medical facilities, and recreation centres may co-locate with parks, marketplaces, light manufacturing (e.g., 3D printing), revitalised cottage industry-style artisan spaces, and local scale production (e.g., scaled-up repair cafes). And community-owned energy generation and storage will become more common.

Housing

Single family housing has been the mainstay of Australian suburban development for more than half a century. Mostly brick veneer and single story in construction, the form of suburban housing has changed little since the Second World War. From the 1980s onwards though, Australian houses have increased in size, becoming among the largest in the world. And two-storey houses have become common. While land use planning has sought to consolidate development within existing footprints, and to reduce lot sizes, houses have not downsized. This has led to a substantial loss of private greenspace across the suburbs.

In the coming decades we are likely to see a downscaling of suburban house size due to rising construction costs and materials shortages associated with the COVID-19 pandemic and ongoing disruption to supply chains as well as with rising inflation due to increasing climate change costs. We will likely see an increase in medium density housing, the so-called "missing middle", such as townhouses, terraces and 3-5 storey apartment buildings (see Figure 20.2) in the suburbs. Some likely social trends have already been mentioned above – increased multi-family and multigenerational households, increased shared housing, the rise of housing cooperatives, and the conversion of garages into apartments and studios as driverless vehicles disrupt car-ownership.[31]

New technologies will likely disrupt traditional modes of housing construction. The 3D printing of housing is already emerging in some European and Asian counties and will likely grow in popularity in Australia. So too will the modularisation and pre-fabrication of housing, especially using carbon positive construction material and techniques. These include hemp, wood composites, and recycled materials. The adaptive reuse of existing housing stock will also increase – especially in the retrofitting of climate change adaptation responses (insulation, energy efficient appliances, water efficiency, and increased reflectivity of roofs). Greywater reuse will increase, as will stormwater capture, onsite energy generation, passive cooling and heating, natural ventilation, and the inclusion of greenery (e.g., green walls and green roofs). And we will likely see a blurring between public and private space in share farming, verge gardening, and common-use facilities such as kitchens and laundries.

Figure 20.2: New suburban housing in Glenorchy, Tasmania, in metropolitan Hobart

Changing Patterns of Employment

Finally, suburban futures will likely see increasing changes in land use. Mixed use developments are already becoming more common in suburban renewal projects. So too is telework / working from home, especially in response to the COVID-19 pandemic. Changes to older suburbs such as Glenorchy in Tasmania point to what lies ahead. In older suburbs we can see strip malls that have diverse tenancies, especially in immigrant owned small businesses. And we can find light manufacturing that has tenaciously persisted beside old rail freight lines, in affordable warehouse and old factory spaces. We will likely see increasing flexibility in working spaces, hours, and styles.

In the past, the production of goods has been seen as incompatible with suburban lifestyles due to noise and light pollution and traffic and has been actively discouraged through zoning. But we are already seeing a trend for food production in the city, through hydroponics and aquaculture and this will likely intensify into the suburbs in the future. So too, different types of retail, warehousing, and distribution (e.g., automation and drone delivery), and peer-to-peer exchange will become more visible. Doughnut economics and regenerative practices associated with climate change mitigation and adaptation will drive new ways of living.[32]

In the future we are likely to see increasing manufacturing and goods handling in the suburbs as new, cleaner technologies allow the production and distribution of goods at smaller scales. This will also be true for the recycling of materials and for waste management. And as noted earlier, multipurpose, and collocated services are also likely to become more common. These changes will likely result in an increase of employment opportunities in the suburbs and a reduction of travel between suburbs and urban core. It may lead to the rise of truly networked neighbourhoods.

Conclusion

In the past, the suburbs have been maligned by many scholars and practitioners as bland, banal, and even environmentally destructive.[33] Yet, as Fiske, Hodge and Turner so cogently observed in their book on Australian popular culture, much of the meaning and sense-making about the Australian identity derives from the suburbs.[34] Past popular cultural portrayals of the suburbs such as *Kingswood Country* are cringeworthy for their overt racism and sexism.[35] But they do highlight the radical changes that have occurred in many Australian suburbs since the 1970s, as suburbs have become more ethno-racially diverse and socially inclusive. Many challenges remain. People with a disability and the LGBTQIA+ community still face discrimination. While we are seeing greater recognition of Aboriginal Australians, and the fact that our cities and suburbs are built on stolen land, much work remains in reconciliation.[36] Many new suburban developments are still not child-friendly, with a high reliance on private automobile use making roads unsafe for kids. And rapidly ageing populations means that future suburbs will need to be more age-friendly for older people (e.g., ramps). Predicting the future is risky and prone to error. What is clear though, is the suburbs, in many ways, will shape our collective future.

Endnotes

1   Davison, A., "Stuck in a cul-de-sac? Suburban history and urban sustainability in Australia", *Urban Policy and Research*, 2006. 24(2): p. 201-216.

2   Davison, G., *The past and future of the Australian suburb*, in *Urban Research Program Working Paper*. 1993, Australian National University: Canberra, ACT. p. 1-20.

3   Maginn, P.J. and K. Anacker, eds. *Suburbia in the 21st Century: From Dreamscape to Nightmare?* 2022, Routledge: Milton Park, Abingdon, UK. 310.

4   Podmore, J.A. and A.L. Bain, "No queers out there"? Metronormativity and the queer suburban", *Geography Compass*, 2020. 14(9): p. e12505.

5   Frost, L. and S. O'Hanlon, "Urban history and the future of Australian cities", *Australian Economic History Review*, 2009. 49(1): p. 1-18.

6   McCarty, J.W. and C.B. Schedvin, *Australian Capital Cities: Historical Essays*, 1978, Sydney: Sydney University Press.

7   Randolph, B., "Dimensions of urban segregation at the end of the Australian dream", in *Handbook of Urban Segregation*, S. Musterd, Editor. 2020, Edward Elgar: Cheltenham, UK, p. 76-100.

8   Troy, L., et al., *Vertical sprawl in the Australian city: Sydney's high-rise residential development boom.* Urban Policy and Research, 2020. 38(1): p. 18-36.

9   Maginn, P.J., P. Burton, and C. Legacy, *Disruptive urbanism? Implications of the 'sharing economy'for cities, regions, and urban policy*, Urban Policy and Research, 2018. 36(4): p. 393-398.

10 Hall, T., "Goodbye to the backyard? - the minimisation of private open space in the Australian outer-suburban estate", *Urban Policy and Research*, 2010. 28(4): p. 411-433.

11 Byrne, J., N. Sipe, and J. Dodson, eds. *Australian Environmental Planning: Challenges and Future Prospects*. 2014, Routledge: London.

12 Ferretto, A., et al., "Planetary boundaries and the doughnut frameworks: A review of their local operability", *Anthropocene*, 2022: p. 100347.

13 Jones, K. and D. Ginley, "Materials for electrification of everything: Moving toward sustainability", *MRS Bulletin*, 2022: p. 1-9.

14 Newton, P.W., et al., "The global greyfields transition: Why urban redevelopment in low-density, car-based middle suburbs needs a new model", in *Greening the Greyfields*, 2022, Palgrave Mamillan: Singapore, p. 1-48.

15 Dedekorkut-Howes, A., E. Torabi, and M. Howes, "Planning for a different kind of sea change: lessons from Australia for sea level rise and coastal flooding", *Climate Policy*, 2021. 21(2): p. 152-170.

16 de Vet, E., et al., "An unmitigated disaster: Shifting from response and recovery to mitigation for an insurable future", *International Journal of Disaster Risk Science*, 2019. 10(2): p. 179-192.

17 Ofori-Asenso, R., et al., "Measures of population ageing in Australia from 1950 to 2050", *Journal of Population Ageing*, 2018. 11(4): p. 367-385.

18 Randolph et al., 2020

19 Baldwin, C., T. Matthews, and J. Byrne, "Planning for older people in a rapidly warming and ageing world: the role of urban greening", *Urban Policy and Research*, 2020. 38(3): p. 199-212.

20 Podmore et al., 2020; Stratton, J., "Pizza and Housos: neoliberalism, the discursive construction of the underclass and its representation", in *Multiculturalism, Whiteness and Otherness in Australia*, 2020, Springer/Palgrave Macmillan: Cham. p. 231-259.

21 Lynch, N., "Remaking the obsolete: Critical geographies of contemporary adaptive reuse", *Geography Compass*, 2022. 16(1): p. e12605.

22 Connolly, C., R. Keil, and S.H. Ali, "Extended urbanisation and the spatialities of infectious disease: Demographic change, infrastructure and governance", *Urban Studies*, 2021. 58(2): p. 245-263.

23 Lowe, M., et al., "Liveability aspirations and realities: Implementation of urban policies designed to create healthy cities in Australia", *Social Science & Medicine*, 2020. 245: p. 112713.

24 Gaynor, A., *Harvest of the Suburbs: An Environmental History of Growing Food in Australian Cities*. 2006, Perth: University of Western Australia Press.

25 Byrne, J., *Urbanisation: Towns and cities as sites of environmental (in) justice*, in *Environmental Justice: Key Issues*, B. Coolsaet, Editor. 2021, Routledge: Milton Park, Abingdon, UK. p. 193-206.

26 Astell-Burt, T. and X. Feng, "Greener neighbourhoods, better memory? A longitudinal study", *Health & Place*, 2020. 65: p. 102393.

27 Hall, 2010; Newton et al., 2022

28 Kellerman, A., "Telecommunications and the geography of metropolitan areas", *Progress in Human Geography*, 1984. 8(2): p. 222-246

29 Warden, J., *Regenerative Futures: From Sustaining to Thriving Together*, 2021, London: Royal Society for the Arts. 1-41.

30 Byrne, J., "From freeways to greenways", in *Planning After Petroleum: Preparing Cities for the Age Beyond Oil*, J. Dodson, N. Sipe, and A. Nelson, Editors. 2016: Milton Park, Abingdon, UK, p. 157-166.

31 Newton et al. (2022)

32 Ferretto et al. (2022)

33 Davison (2006)

34 Fiske, J., B. Hodge, and G. Turner, *Myths of Oz: Reading Australian Popular Culture*, 2016, Sydney: Allen and Unwin.

35 Stratton et al. (2020)

36 Jackson, S., L. Porter, and L.C. Johnson, *Planning in Indigenous Australia: from Imperial Foundations to Postcolonial Futures*, 2018, New York: Routledge.

List of Contributors

A/Prof Tooran Alizadeh

 Tooran Alizadeh is an ARC Future Fellow, investigating the socio-spatial implications of smart city development in India. She is also the co-convener of Smart Urbanism (Research) Lab at the University of Sydney, the lead investigator on the Infrastructure Governance Incubator funded by the Henry Halloran Trust, and the Associate Editor of Telematics and Informatics - an interdisciplinary high impact journal (IF: 9.140) on the social impacts of new technologies. A/Prof. Alizadeh served as the program director for the Master of Urban Design (2017-2020) and the Urban Studies Major (2020-2021); and was a recipient of the prestigious Research Accelerator Fellowship (SOAR) at the University of Sydney (2019 and 2020).

She has investigated the socio-spatial patterns of telecommunication infrastructure deployment in Australia and beyond; if and how the advanced infrastructure is accounted for in the strategic plans for the future of our cities; and finally, the extent to which smart city initiatives respond to the strategic challenges of each city and its citizens. Her work has resulted in over 85 refereed publications; and made meaningful contributions to the public discourse around the urban and equity implications of the National Broadband Network in Australia - evidenced by numerous prime time TV and radio interviews, and hundreds of quotations in the print media.

A/Prof. Alizadeh joined academia after a decade of working as a professional urban designer, planner, project manager, and adviser. This professional background has given her a solid ground in private consultancy structure, public policy, and public-private dynamics in urban processes.

Prof Alan M. Berger

Alan M. Berger is Professor of Landscape Architecture and Urban Design at Massachusetts Institute of Technology where he teaches courses open to the entire student body. He is founding director of MIT's P-REX lab, a research lab focused on environmental problems caused by urbanisation, including the design, remediation, and reuse of waste landscapes worldwide.

All of his research, teaching, and practice emphasise the links between urbanisation and the loss of natural resources and growth of waste, to help us better understand how to proceed with redesigning intelligent outcomes. Alan's research spans a wide interdisciplinary range, including: sustainable cities and suburban forms, urban planning for autonomous mobility, resilient urbanism, growth boundary landscapes, reclamation of ecological systems, and stormwater wetland design. Unlike conventional practice, there are no scalar limits in his outlook or pedagogy: Projects are defined by the extent of the urban and environmental problems being addressed. He coined the term "Systemic Design" to describe the reintegration of disvalued landscapes into our urbanised territories and regional ecologies.

His most recent book is entitled *A Blueprint for Coastal Adaptation: Uniting Design, Economics, and Policy* (co-authors Carolyn Kousky, William Fleming), published in early 2021 by Island Press. Berger's award-winning anthology *Infinite Suburbia* (with Joel Kotkin, Celina Balderas Guzman) presents the global suburban expansion through the research of its 74 authors, and the co-editors' own perspectives and work. Previous award-winning books include *Drosscape: Wasting Land in Urban America,* and *Reclaiming the American West*, his other books include *Designing the Reclaimed Landscape, The Infrastructural Monument and Scaling Infrastructure* (with Alexander D'Hooghe), *Nansha Coastal City: Landscape and Urbanism in the Pearl River Delta* (with Margaret Crawford), *Systemic Design Can Change the World,* and *Landscape + Urbanism Around the Bay of Mumbai* (with Rahul Mehrotra), and LCAU's 2013 Report on the State of Health + Urbanism (with Andrew Scott).

He was Director of the MIT Norman B. Leventhal Center for Advanced Urbanism (LCAU) from 2015-2020, and LCAU Research Director from 2010-2015. Prior to MIT Berger was Associate Professor of Landscape Architecture at Harvard-GSD, 2002-2008. He is a Prince Charitable Trusts Fellow of The American Academy in Rome. He is a Visiting Honorary Professor at Oslo School of Architecture (AHO).

Prof Paul Burton

Paul Burton trained as a planner at the Polytechnic of the South Bank in London, graduating in 1979 with a Bachelor of Town Planning with Honours. He then worked as a planning officer in the development control section of the London Borough of Richmond upon Thames before joining the School for Advanced Urban Studies at the University of Bristol to carry out research for his PhD on the redevelopment of London's Docklands, under the supervision of Professors Murray Stewart and Robin Hambleton. He remained at the University of Bristol, working on a variety of projects, including the implementation of equal opportunities policies in the Youth Training Scheme, the evaluation of UK urban policies and programs and leading a major comparative study of living conditions and then youth homelessness in European cities. In 2007 he moved to Australia to take up a Chair in Urban Planning and Management at Griffith University, working closely with the City of Gold Coast. He became Deputy Director of Griffith's Urban Research Program and inaugural Director of the Cities Research Centre and then the Cities Research Institute in 2017. He remains a member of the Cities Research Institute and is currently researching the growing popularity of tiny houses and the opportunities for better inter-professional working among built environment professionals.

Prof Jason Byrne

Jason Byrne is a Professor of Human Geography and Planning at the University of Tasmania. He undertakes research on three related topics: urban political ecologies of green-space; climate change adaptation; and environmental justice - with a focus on urban heat. Jason has over 100 scholarly publications, including a multi-award-winning co-edited book - *Australian Environmental Planning: Challenges and Future Prospects* (Routledge). Jason is on the editorial board for *Australian Planner*, *Local Environment* and *Journal of Political Ecology* and is an Associate Editor with *Landscape and Urban Planning*.

A Fellow of the Planning Institute of Australia, Jason has previously been awarded the Planning Institute's national award for cutting edge research and teaching and has twice been awarded the PIA Queensland award in that category - as well as their overall award for planning excellence. Before becoming an academic, Jason worked as a planning officer, environmental officer, and policy writer with the Western Australian government. He now provides research services to state and local government and makes regular radio and television appearances.

Wendell Cox

Wendell Cox is a leading proponent of adopting land use and transport policies based on their effectiveness in improving the standard of living and alleviating poverty. He is principal of Demographia (Wendell Cox Consultancy) in the St. Louis metropolitan area. He specialises in urban policy, transport and demographics and is author of *Demographia World Urban Areas* and co-author of *Demographia International Housing Affordability Survey*. He is also author of *Toward More Prosperous Cities*, a framing essay on urban areas, urban planning, urban transport and sustainability.

He has consulted for public authorities and private companies in the United States, Canada, Europe, Asia, Australia and New Zealand and for public policy organisations and lectured widely. He has served as visiting professor at the Conservatoire National des Arts et Metiers (a national university) in Paris, in transport and demographics.

Wendell Cox is contributing editor of new.geography.com, for which he writes a regular column. This includes *The Evolving Urban Form* series, which analyses demographic trends in world urban areas.

Prof Ellen Dunham-Jones

Ellen Dunham-Jones is a professor of architecture and directs the MS in Urban Design at the Georgia Institute of Technology in Atlanta. She hosts the Redesigning Cities podcast series and was recognised in 2017 and 2023 by Planetizen as one of the 100 most influential urbanists. She is co-author with June Williamson of a pair of pioneering and award winning books on retrofitting suburbia, maintains their unique retrofits database, and researches how communities should plan for autonomous vehicles. She is a Fellow of the Congress for the New Urbanism as well as the Brook Byers Institute of Sustainable Systems, and was an AFS high school exchange student to Darwin, Australia in 1976.

Ross Elliott

Ross Elliott has held leadership roles as CEO and Senior Executive of a number of businesses and organisations during his extensive career in the property industry.

With impeccable industry and political networks, he is widely recognised for his expertise in urban development and brings a multi-disciplinary background covering wide range of industry professions and advisory roles from construction to design to project management to engineers to economists to development. He commenced his career in research and market analysis and has maintained an active and ongoing Interest in researching urban development, demography and market trends since.

Ross' interests and reputation saw him Invited by the Brisbane Lord Mayor in 2019 to Chair the newly formed Better Suburbs Initiative, which has led to substantial changes to Industrial and mixed-use opportunities across Brisbane. He has written extensively on industry Issues and delivered several keynote addresses on urban development within Australian and the United States.

Ross is a Director of Suburban Futures.

Dr Richard Ferrers

Richard Ferrers is a Data Consultant at Australian Research Data Commons (ARDC). His specialties include: innovation and consumer value analysis; understanding consumer value meanings and practices - value management; and applying innovation value theory to national innovation policy.

Prof Robert Freestone

Robert Freestone has diverse research interests in urban studies and planning education, being highly regarded internationally for expertise in the development of urban planning. He is a Professor in the School of Built Environment at the University of New South Wales. He joined UNSW in 1991 after six years with a Sydney planning, research and heritage consultant firm as well as working for the NSW State Government. Over the course of his career, he has authored over 400 publications. His research has been credited with making "an unparalleled contribution to urban planning and planning history research" by leading academics in the field. He has been awarded several Planning Institute of Australia Prizes for Planning Excellence for his published work. His teaching encompasses research design and urban history. He has played a key strategic role in School, Faculty and University Governance, notably through terms as Head of the City Planning program and Associate Dean Research for Built Environment. Amongst a range of external engagement duties, he sits on the editorial boards of leading journals such as *Cities, Town Planning Review, Progress in Planning* and *Australian Planner*. He also chairs the international editorial board for *Planning Perspectives*.

Guy Gibson

Guy Gibson is an experienced manager and non-executive Board member with a long career in town planning and urban development, including 25 years with Lendlease. When he retired from Lendlease in October 2021, he was the Head of Development in Queensland. During his career at Lendlease, he worked on over thirty new community projects, covering all aspects from site identification and acquisition, conversion, planning and design, delivery, marketing, and sales. Prior to joining Lendlease in 1996, Guy was Director of Town Planning at Brisbane City Council from 1993 to 1996 and Project Manager of the Council's Urban Renewal Program from 1991 to 1993. Before joining BCC in 1987, he worked for the National Capital Development Commission in Canberra. He is a Life Member and past President of the Property Council of Australia (Queensland), and is a previous National Director of the Property Council of Australia. Guy is a Director of Suburban Futures.

Prof Robin Goodman

Robin Goodman is Emeritus Professor in the Centre for Urban Research at RMIT University.

Robin is an urban planner with broad interests in many aspects of planning, housing, transport and public policy. She was Dean of the School of Global, Urban and Social Studies 2017-2020 and prior to that she led the team of Sustainability and Urban Planning academics as the Deputy Dean from 2013. Robin was the Director of RMIT's Australian Housing and Urban Research Institute (AHURI) for four years and the inaugural Director of the Centre for Urban Research.

Robin is a Fellow of the Planning Institute of Australia and serves on its National Education Committee. She is also a graduate of the Australian Institute of Company Directors and is active in a range of other community and professional roles.

Prof Peter Gordon

Peter Gordon is Professor Emeritus in the University of Southern California's Sol Price School of Public Policy.

Gordon's research interests are in applied urban economics. He has recently written on how cities evolve and grow as well as the problems of the "sprawl" debate.

Gordon is also interested in cities and institutions. He is co-editor (with David Beito and Alexander Tabarrok) of *The Voluntary City* (The University of Michigan Press, 2002).

Gordon and his colleagues have developed various economic impact models which they apply to the study of the effects of infrastructure investments or disruptions from natural events or terrorist attacks.

Recent work involves the modelling and study of economic impacts. Some of this is reproduced in *The Economic Impacts of Terrorist Attacks* (Edward Elgar 2005, co-edited with Harry W. Richardson and James E. Moore II) and *The Economic Costs and Consequences of Economic Terrorism* (Edward Elgar, 2007, co-edited with Harry W. Richardson and James E. Moore II).

Peter Gordon has published in most of the major urban planning, urban transportation and urban economics journals. His recent papers are at http://www.petergordon.us/. He has consulted for local, state and federal agencies, the World Bank, the United Nations and many private groups. Peter received the Ph.D. from the University of Pennsylvania in 1971.

Prof Tony Grubesic

Tony Grubesic is Professor and Associate Dean for Research in the School of Information at the University of Texas at Austin, where he also serves as the director for the Geoinformatics & Policy Analytics Lab (GPAL). His research expertise is GIScience, telecommunications policy, regional science, spatial analysis and vulnerability.

Ray Haeren

Ray Haeren is an Urban and Regional Planner with more than 30 years' experience in the government and private sectors in both Perth and regional WA. Ray has been a Director at Urbis for 15 years and most recently was the National Planning Director with over 300 planners in WA, NSW, Victoria and Queensland.

A former President and current Board member of the Planning Institute of Australia, Ray has a keen interest in Australian Cities and their ability to respond to the ever changing environmental, social and economic challenges. Ray also is the Presiding member of the Perth Local Development Assessment panel and has managed the local reactions to social housing and supported accommodation projects.

Ray has been a vocal advocate for informed decision making through quality research and the delivery of dynamic environments which respond to the changing needs of communities and society. This has included leading research for the Federal Government on the impacts of planning requirements on housing and residential land delivery in all jurisdictions to inform potential planning reform.

Dr Edward Helderop

Edward Helderop is a systems analyst and associate director of the Center for Geospatial

Sciences at the University of California, Riverside. His main interests include GIScience, big data, and network analytics (particularly as applied to urban infrastructure systems). His previous research explored turnover and resiliency in plant-pollinator networks and urban disaster evacuation modelling. Eddie received his M.S. in Geography from Oregon State University and his Ph.D. in Geography from Arizona State University.

Joel Kotkin

Described by the New York Times as "America's uber-geographer," Joel Kotkin is an internationally-recognised authority on global, economic, political and social trends. His latest book, *The Coming of Neo-Feudalism: A Warning to the Global Middle Class* is now available at Amazon. He authored *The Human City: Urbanism for the Rest of Us* (Agate Press) in 2016 and co-edited, with MIT's Alan Berger, the 2018 collection *Infinite Suburbia* (Princeton University Press). Mr. Kotkin is the Roger Hobbs Presidential Fellow in Urban Futures at Chapman University in Orange, California and Executive Director of the Houston-based Urban Reform Institute - formerly Center for Opportunity Urbanism (UrbanReformInstitute.org). He is Senior Advisor to the Kem C. Gardner Policy Institute. He is Executive Editor of the widely read website www.newgeography.com and a regular contributor to the *City Journal, Daily Beast, Quillette, American Affairs* and *Real Clear Politics.*

Dr Laurel Johnson

Laurel Johnson is an urban and social planner with over 25 years of experience as a practitioner and an educator/researcher. As well as being a full-time academic in the UQ urban planning program, Laurel manages her own planning consultancy service with Government and non-Government clients throughout Australia. Her practice, research and educator roles are complementary. Her research interests include resident activism in urban planning and transport disadvantage and social disadvantage. Laurel's social infrastructure analysis in many communities in Victoria, Western Australia and south east Queensland has delivered infrastructure and services for community building in those locations.

Dr Annette Kroen

Annette Kroen is a Research Fellow in the Centre for Urban Research.

Annette is an urban and regional planner with expertise in outer suburban development, integrated land use and transport planning, community engagement, urban governance, and policy analysis. She has worked on projects investigating integration of planning and transport in greenfield development; social connectedness in communities on the urban fringe; and housing policy, settlement planning, and disaster prevention, preparedness and response.

Prior to joining RMIT University, Annette was a Research Fellow at the University of Applied Sciences and Arts in Dortmund, Germany. She has also worked in transport and planning with the Victorian State Government, and in private practice as a facilitator and consultant on a range of planning related projects.

Dr Michele Lobo

Michele Lobo is a social and cultural geographer and Honorary Fellow in the School of Humanities and Social Sciences (SHSS), Deakin University, Narrm Melbourne. Michele is Editor, *Social & Cultural Geography*, Reviews Editor, *Postcolonial Studies* and Council Member, *Institute of Australian Geographers*. She has published more than sixty scholarly outputs including three books supported by prestigious Australian Research Council national grants.

Michele's research focuses on climate change, encounter and belonging in the Anthropocene and draws on southern, Indigenous and Black traditions of thought. She has engaged in research with Indigenous peoples, ethnic/ ethno-religious minority migrants, refugees, asylum seekers and international students in Darwin, Melbourne, Sydney, Detroit, Paris, and Mumbai.

Michele has previously held lecturing/prestigious research positions at the Alfred Deakin Institute for Citizenship and Globalisation/School of Humanities Social Sciences, Deakin University, School of Geography and Environmental Science, Monash University, Faculty of Architecture, Building and Planning, the University of Melbourne and School of Geography, Loreto College, Calcutta University, India.

Antony Lorius

Antony Lorius is an economist and land use planner with over 20 years of professional consulting experience. Antony is best known for his strategic advisory work in the public sector, including growth management and land needs assessment, economic development and investment attraction, site selection and evaluation, and long-range planning policy. Antony is part of the team that leads the Community Strategies group at Dillon Consulting Ltd., based in Toronto, Canada. He is an experienced public speaker, Registered Professional Planner (RPP), Professional Land Economist (PLE) and member of Lambda Alpha International and the Royal Institution of Chartered Surveyors (MRICS).

Mike Quirk

Mike Quirk has qualifications in Geography from Macquarie University and Town and Country Planning from Sydney University.

Following graduation he joined National Capital Development Commission initially in the Urban Economics Branch before moving to the Metropolitan Planning Section of the Town Planning Division. He was part of the team that prepared the 1984 Metropolitan Policy and Development Plan. In 1988 he joined the Building Industry Efficiency Branch in the Commonwealth Department of Industry, Technology and Commerce where he was primarily involved in the Joint Venture for More Affordable Housing which promoted the adoption of cost-effective land development techniques. He joined the Portfolio Analysis Unit of the Department of Health, Housing and Community Development where he contributed to an analysis of the impact of ageing on Commonwealth and State social outlays.

He began a 27 year career in the ACT government when he joined the Land Development Branch in 1990. In his time in the ACT administration, he managed several sections including Land Release, Land Sales and Planning Policy. A highlight was the preparation of the 2003 Spatial Plan. He had several articles published in Australian Planner between 2006 and 2011 on the challenges of demographic change in Canberra; effective centres; responses to increases in house prices; and transport, land use, the built environment and greenhouse emissions. In 2008 his article on Responses to Retailing Change in Canberra was published in *Urban Policy and Research*.

He retired in 2017 and recently began contributing to *Canberra City News* on planning, demographic and transport issues.

Emma Riley

Emma Riley is a highly experienced city and regional planner with a successful professional background supporting a range of public, private and not-for-profit organisations. She currently sits as a board Director and National Vice President of the Planning Institute of Australia, and is the founder and Director of ERA Planning and Environment.

Emma has more than 23 years' technical experience and continues to practise as a planner. She has been involved in leading major regulatory reform projects, including time as the Chair of the Tasmanian Planning Reform Taskforce and supports clients in advocating for planning outcomes, presenting to high level boards and committees. Through ERA, Emma has developed a reputation for successfully taking on some of Tasmania's most challenging, sensitive and high-profile planning, engagement and environmental projects. She has a thorough understanding of community issues in the context of Tasmania and regularly appears as an expert witness before the Resource Management and Planning Appeal Tribunal and the Tasmanian Planning Commission.

Dr Sebastian D. Rossi

Sebastian Rossi is a researcher at the Argentine National Research Council, Instituto Argentino de Investigaciones de Zonas Arides (IADIZA), CCT-CONICET, Mendoza, Argentina, Ceplades-Turismo, Universidad Nacional del Comahue, Neuquen, Argentina, and an Adjunct Researcher at the University of Tasmania. His research includes protected areas planning and management, outdoor recreation and nature–society interactions including environmental justice and environmental psychology. His research touches on emerging issues in the cultural politics of nature and the environmental humanities. Sebastian completed his PhD in Human Geography in 2015 at Griffith University. He has also teaching experience in Geographic Information Systems, Reserve System Planning, Wilderness Management and Professional Research Methods at Griffith University and the University of Tasmania. Previously Sebastian was as park Ranger in Argentina and a Research Officer in the Department of Environment and Science in Queensland, Australia.

Peter Seamer

Peter Seamer was the CEO of the Victorian Planning Authority for ten years, the CEO of Federation Square during its building phase and first few years, and has been the CEO of several cities, including Sydney. He recently authored *Breaking Point: The Future of Australian Cities.*

Dr Gary Shiels, AM

Gary Shiels is a distinguished town planner, having received an AM for his services to town planning, and working with the community, on Australia Day 2023. Gary has a PhD with the research topic, Planning for Successful Ageing in an Age-Friendly Built Environment and three master's degrees in planning, urban design, and traffic engineering. His research studied the behaviours of persons between the ages of 80 and 106 who were ageing successfully. The research also involved interviews with health professionals specialising in different parts of the human anatomy who worked with older persons and studying the lifestyle habits of the longest lived persons on this planet.

Gary started his professional career in the late 1960s as an engineering assistant at the Department of Motor Transport, designing intersections and traffic signals. In the 1970s he was employed as an engineering assistant/planner by Kuring gai Council. Subsequently, he held the position of planner, then Deputy Town Planner Woollahra Council.

In 1984 he was appointed Director Planning and Community Development at Leichhardt Council where he was responsible for 120 staff. His role was to manage Town Planning, Social Planning, Long Day Care, Family Day Care, and Seniors Care. During his time at Leichhardt, he gained an appreciation of the importance of planning for ageing.

In late 1988 Gary left council and he and his wife Vicki established The Town and Traffic Planning company, Gary Shiels and Associates P/L (GSA Planning) where Gary was the Managing Director and Vicki was a Director.

In 1990, he established a planning office in Tweed Heads and undertook a number of master planning projects, involving different forms of residential development, with the Cobaki Lakes DCP winning a National Award for Planning Excellence.

After stepping down as Managing Director, of GSA Planning after 33 years, Gary retained the company name of Gary Shiels and Associates and worked as a consultant to the company. Gary then served as and Acting Commissioner in the Land and Environment Court.

He currently serves as alternate chair and expert member on a five Local Planning Panels. He is renowned for his professional judgement and ethical approach to planning.

Malcolm Smith

Malcolm Smith studied under the Birmingham City Council's town planning training scheme which was combined with six years part-time study for a diploma in town and country planning at the Birmingham School of Art. By the end of Malcolm's study, the diploma course had been absorbed into a degree course at the University of Aston. Prior to his town planning study Malcolm had completed a one-year Diploma in Public Administration. After working at the City of Birmingham town planning department, and at Dudley Borough Council, he applied for and was successful in winning a position at the National Capital Development Commission (NCDC) in Canberra.

In 1975 Malcolm was promoted to establish and head a new section in NCDC's Planning Division, the Development Implementation Group. In 1982 Malcolm was appointed to head the Tuggeranong Planning Section at a time when development of Canberra's largest new town was beginning to accelerate again after all growth had been frozen in the Fraser Government years (1977-82). In 1983 he was selected to manage the multi-disciplinary Tuggeranong Town Centre Task Force, responsible for the planning, design, development and delivery of Tuggeranong Town Centre. The Tuggeranong Town Centre project received a National Award for Planning Excellence in 1992 from the then Royal Australian Planning Institute. In 1987 Malcolm was promoted to the SES level and appointed Director of Policy Planning. He stayed with NCDC until it folded in 1989 when he took up the position of first Chief Planner of the National Capital Planning Authority. While at NCA Malcolm took up a temporary secondment to lead a multi disciplinary working group charged with preparing an urban development concept for the Multi Function Polis (MFP), a joint initiative of the Australian and Japanese Governments for a new city of the future.

He held this position until 1993 when, with a former NCDC colleague, set up a planning and design consultancy, Smith Kostyrko International. The company took on two other ex-NCDC senior professionals as Directors, the company eventually changing its name to Capital Planners. In 2006 the company merged with an international consultancy Parsons Brinckerhoff (PB). Malcolm left PB in 2008 to take up the position as Director of Planning with the Molonglo Group, a highly regarded and award winning Canberra based development company. He retired in March 2012 but still undertakes small scale consultancy work on projects of interest to him.

John Stimson

John Stimson has 30 years' experience in the town planning and development arena with successful projects and studies completed across Australia and South East Asia for the private sector, Local, State and National Governments.

John is currently the President of the Urban Development Institute of Australia (South Australian Division) and is on the National UDIA Executive Committee. He is the Treasurer of the Australian Council for New Urbanism as well as being a member of the Australian Institute of Company Directors, the Planning Institute of Australia and the Congress for New Urbanism. John has recently been appointed to the Development Policy Advisory Committee by the Minister of Planning.

A/Prof Laura Taylor

Laura Taylor is an Associate Professor and coordinator of the planning program in the Faculty of Environmental & Urban Change, York University, Toronto. She studies the urban-rural fringe and exurbia where planning, development, and conservation are incredibly uneven. She is co-editor of two books, *A Comparative Political Ecology of Exurbia and Landscape: Planning, Environmental Management and Landscape Change* (2016) and *Landscape and the Ideology of Nature: Green Sprawl* (2013). Her most recent work connects land-use planning—policy, practice, and the profession itself – and climate action.

She earned her PhD in geography from the University of Toronto and has been a registered professional planner with the Ontario Professional Planners Institute since 1996. She was a member of Ontario's Greenbelt Council from 2010–2020. She is a member of Lambda Alpha International and the Urban Land Institute's Women's Leadership Team. She maintains a small but active consulting practice in the greater Toronto area.

Dr Peter Walters

Peter Walters is an urban sociologist at The University of Queensland. His research focuses on how we live in cities and the way our social lives influence how cities look, feel and work. He has investigated the ways new communities form in master planned outer suburban estates, in collaboration with one of Australia's largest property developers. He has researched inner-city neighbourhoods in Brisbane to understand the way that gentrification influences culture and community in these places. He has investigated the ways that urban community responds to disasters to better understand the relative importance of local community, government institutions and strangers respond and work to recover from disaster. His research has also taken him to Bangladesh, Indonesia, India and the Pacific where he has led research in collaboration with local universities, to investigate how the urban poor understand themselves as citizens and contribute to the economic and social fabric of cities in the Global South.

Prof June Williamson

June Williamson is professor and director of graduate architecture programs at the Spitzer School of Architecture at The City College of New York/CUNY, where she teaches design studio and urban site analysis. An urban designer and registered architect, she worked across the USA, in Boston, Salt Lake City, Atlanta, and Los Angeles, before arriving in New York City in 2003. She is author of *Designing Suburban Futures: New Models from Build a Better Burb* (Island Press, 2013) and co-author with Ellen Dunham-Jones of *Case Studies in Retrofitting Suburbia* (Wiley, 2021) and *Retrofitting Suburbia: Urban Design Solutions for Redesigning Suburbs* (John Wiley & Sons, 2009, updated 2011).

Dr George Wilkinson III

George Wilkinson III is an Adjunct Lecturer at the Australian Urban Design Research Centre, University of Western Australia. His research interests include institutional economics and urban growth dynamics, in particular the scarcity of large non-capital cities in Australia. In 2023 George received his PhD from the University of Western Australia, focused upon regional development and economic geography.

David Wright

David Wright read sociology at the University of Bath, graduating with honours in 1968. An early secondment with the Welwyn Garden City Development Corporation fired his growing interest in town planning. David later studied town planning at the University of Sydney where he won the Royal Town Planning Institute Prize. After working with Jim Colman for almost 4 years, David took up a position at the National Capital Development Commission (NCDC) in Canberra working variously in social planning, metropolitan planning, development planning and as the resident town planner for the new town of Tuggeranong.

Following the abolition of NCDC, David worked for the then National Capital Planning Authority from its establishment in 1989 until he retired in 2006 as the Authority's Director of Planning and Urban Design. During that time he managed the challenges of the divestment of Commonwealth properties - the key strategic tool in managing the metropolitan distribution of employment - of diplomatic leasing and of the privatisation of Canberra Airport.

Following his retirement from the now National Capital Authority, David established his own consultancy which he operated for four years, primarily advising the ACT Government on a variety of planning policy issues but in particular on the impact of competition policy on the size, location and distribution of supermarkets in the ACT.

During his career, David was an adviser to two Commonwealth Parliamentary Committees, the latest when the Parliamentary Joint Standing Committee on the National Capital and External Territories conducted an inquiry into the National Capital Authority in 2008 - two years after his retirement. David's contribution to the Committee's findings which was made over a period of several weeks, provided on a pro bono basis, had a significant influence on the Committee's final report - *The Way Forward*. David died in December 2023.

Stephanie Wyeth

Stephanie Wyeth is a Professional Planner in Residence / Senior Lecturer in urban planning at the University of Queensland (appointed in January 2019). As a practising urban and social planner, her interest is in ensuring city-makers and community builders (government, industry and community) have the knowledge and capabilities to plan and design a better future for our cities, towns and communities. Stephanie has significant industry and leadership experience. Prior to joining The University of Queensland, she held a senior position with a national multidisciplinary property, planning and design firm responsible for the social planning and engagement offer in Queensland.